THE PRIMARY TRIANGLE

THE PRIMARY TRIANGLE

A Developmental Systems View of Mothers, Fathers, and Infants

ELISABETH FIVAZ-DEPEURSINGE
ANTOINETTE CORBOZ-WARNERY

BASIC
BOOKS

A Member of the Perseus Books Group

Mi'Qwood

Published by Basic Books, A Member of the Perseus Books Group

A CIP catalog record for this book is available from the Library of Congress.
ISBN 0-465-09582-8

99 00 01 02 03 ❖/RRD 10 9 8 7 6 5 4 3 2

2/23/01

To Roland, Mathieu, and Juliette
To Jean-Paul, Mathias, and Jérôme

Contents

Foreword

I believe that this book will become a classic for both clinicians and researchers. The history of our understanding of the family is curious. Until now, very few researchers have given detailed, rigorous attention to the earliest origins of the primary triangle—that is, the family. Traditional psychoanalytic approaches largely had the primary triangle enter the developmental scene when the child began the oedipal phase at around three to four years of age. Effectively, the serious history of the family triangle as a central issue began only at that time.

In systemic and family theory and practice, the family hardly has an origin at all. In this approach, the initial impetus to understand families emerged when the schizophrenic adolescent and his family came under clinical focus. This provided the original paradigm in family systems theory. Since this beginning, families with younger children have been studied and to great advantage. But again, as with psychodynamic theory, the earliest history of the family was never placed at center stage of the inquiry.

The result of this particular history is that we have evolved extremely important theories about families and powerful therapeutic methods to treat them, but there is a gap concerning the early beginning of the primary triangle. We have a field without a well-understood developmental origin.

It is exactly here that this book fills in the missing pieces of the whole picture. It provides a clinical perspective founded on extremely rigorous research focused on the development of the primary triangle from the earliest months of the baby's life. It addresses this question at many levels of organization, from a minute, behavorial microanalysis to global clinical patterns. In so doing it shows the behavioral and narrative structures that underlie the larger clinical patterns. And the patterns that emerge have clear, clinical utility. It is in this sense that the authors have opened up a new field.

When an insufficiently studied domain finally gets properly addressed, it is invaluable, in fact necessary, to create a new method to reveal fundamental properties of the phenomena under study. Attachment theory and research provides a good example. When Mary Ainsworth and colleagues hit upon the "strange situation" to study attachment, they created a procedure that enabled the field of attachment to take wing, rapidly pushing foward theory elaboration, research, and clinical exploration. The Lausanne triadic play (LTP) situation is just such a tool for studying the early family. It, too, like the "strange situation," is based on clinically and ethologically important, naturally occurring events that take place daily within a young family, but these events are standardized so that they are maximally useful for research and can be widely used by others. In a similar vein, I think that the different types of family "alliances" that Fivaz-Depeursinge and Corboz-Warnery describe may prove to have the same predictive clinical power as the attachment patterns.

When a new or insufficiently studied field is opened, the pioneers who first go there in depth are in the ideal position to mark the territory and create the maps that those who follow will work with and against. And when the pioneers are sophisticated theoreticians, experienced clinicians, and rigorous researchers, as are Elisabeth Fivaz-Depeursinge and Antoinette Corboz-Warnery, the result of their exploration is a classic.

Daniel N. Stern

Preface

Imagine a mother and her baby daughter on a Sunday morning in the kitchen. The child has been fed and contentedly engages the mother in a round of dialogue play under the benevolent eye of her father. She looks at him invitingly and it is now his turn. Deeply moved by their complicity, the mother watches them in pure delight. Then the three of them join in the dialogue. There are moments of utter joy when they all laugh together and then tenderness and sympathy when the baby is tired and fussy. She eventually withdraws and the parents enthusiastically comment on her beauty and excellence. The baby becomes interested in watching the conversation.

This scene has a dramatic progression beginning with mother and baby together, and father in the periphery; it gains impetus with father and baby under mother's eye and reaches a high point when the three of them join together in sharing joy; then it recedes. Perhaps it will become one of those stories told in families: "On Sunday mornings when you were a baby the three of us would hold hands and swing our arms. You would laugh and get so excited that we would have to stop so that you could quiet down . . . and then you would look at us as if you were understanding what we were saying about you."

Dialogue and trilogue play are simply and purely for fun, just like a party with friends. They are for establishing affective communion, sharing pleasure, tying and retying bonds, for better or for worse. The art of affective communion is at the core of our intimate relationships. Since the basic unit in which we develop these relationships is most often the primary triangle, constituted by father, mother, and infant, it is surprising that we scarcely know how a new family develops its intimate relationships as a threesome.

True, we know much about their one-on-one relationships, mother and infant, father and infant, husband and wife. Yet how these relationships merge into a threesome is uncharted territory. Perhaps we have not yet provided ourselves with the opportunity to see that it was nature's design to preadapt us to dealing with more than one relationship. After all, we are born from two human beings.

We felt that reconstructing the family from its dyadic components was not sufficient, so we developed the Lausanne triadic play (LTP). We needed to capture the family as a unit. We decided on a scenario after much brainstorming among our team and with colleagues who had new babies. Its four parts follow the narrative line sketched above with its four successive scenes (see photos 1 through 4): (1) a two-plus-one configuration, perhaps mother and baby playing together, and father in the periphery; (2) a switch to the other two plus one, that is, father and baby playing together, and mother in the periphery; (3) the three together, that is, father, mother, and baby playing; and (4) receding to the two plus one, with baby in the periphery and father and mother talking together. Not only does this situation include the four scenes but also the moments of transition between them. We know that negotiating transitions requires close coordination. Finally, it cannot be overstated that beyond its partition into four parts and transitions, the LTP constitutes a whole, that is, a family trilogue play.

Although we had imagined various daily chores such as feeding or diapering as the context for this scenario, we preferred trilogue play because it is the purest form of affective communication unmediated by objects. More practical, yet of considerable importance for observational research, we needed a continuing record of the three partners, in frontal view, to enable us to fully and systematically describe their interactions. How to set this up for video-recording was mind-boggling. It is clear that parents and babies tend to mingle together when they play, and cameras were liable to mainly capture hair and a bunch of hands, heads, and toes. We also wanted the parents to have an "equal" position with respect to their child—having either parent holding the baby would have introduced a bias. We finally placed the baby in an infant seat, which was set on a table facing the parents so that the three of them would make an equilateral triangle. Observing that the parents tended to turn the seat in order to be in full view, we fitted the table so that they could orient it toward either one of them or in the middle, according to their wishes. Thus, we were able to record a full view of the infant, by means of a camera hanging from the ceiling, as well as a quasifrontal view

Family with three-month-old in the four scenes of the LTP: 1. Two plus one with father and baby playing together and mother in the periphery. 2. Two plus one with mother and baby playing together and father in the periphery. 3. Three together. 4. Father and mother together, baby watching in mother's direction.

means of a camera hanging from the ceiling, as well as a quasifrontal view of the parents, by means of a camera placed above the head of the baby.

Observing and recording also meant that, by necessity, the family would enact the scenario "on stage," which was in itself an important feature of the situation and it necessitated a plan of action to provide the family with feedback on their performance that would repay them for their service to research and hopefully would be as growth-enhancing for them as it was for us. Therefore, the observation session was led by an experienced clinican-researcher who would review the tapes with the families and give them appropriate feedback.

Acknowledgments

We cannot begin to mention all the people and institutions who molded this book. It would not have been possible without the help of Professors Christian Müller, Henri Dufour, François Ferrero, Patrice Guex, and François Borgeat, heads of the Adult Psychiatry Department of the Lausanne University, which supported the Center for Family Studies and thus helped to cross boundaries that separated infancy and adulthood. The Swiss National Foundation for Research has our gratitude for their long-term funding of a not quite conventional program of research since 1977 (current subsidies: 32–052508).

The Primary Triangle grew out of a long companionship between the two authors and our research collaborators who came and went over the years: Barbara Cornut-Zimmer, Pascale Forni, Joëlle Guillemin, Monique Borcard-Sacco, Christine Gertsch-Bettens, Nicolas Favez, Yves de Roten, Jean-Claude Métraux, Daniel Jean Stern, Joëlle Darwish, France Frascarolo, Rosine Lob, Véronique Wasem, Vincent Besse, Claudio Carneiro, Florence Donzé, and Anne-Charlotte Plancherel. We thank our colleague, Nicolas Duruz, codirector of the Center, for his patience with our studies, and Elisabeth Gros and Linda Serero for their unfailing secretarial support.

We are most indebted to the families who agreed to collaborate with us. They gave us their time, their attention, and their understanding. They led us into their family life and have taught us what we know about primary triangles.

Then there were these colleagues/friends with whom we shared conversations and debates about big and small issues: Luc Kaufmann, who also created the Center; Roland Fivaz; John Gottman; Robert Emde; Starkey Duncan; Hanus and Mechthild Papousek; Edward Tronick; David Reiss; members of the Interfaces study group: Dieter Bürgin, John Byng-Hall, Martine Lamour, and Serge Lebovici; members of the Trilogie network: Alyson Fearnley, Monica Hedenbro, Annette Lidén, Louise Arve, Heidi Simoni, Marie-Louise Hervé, and Michèle Maury. Much will be said about their contributions in the opening and closing chapters. Likewise, we owe much to exchanges with colleagues working closely with our Center: Monique Bidlowski, Pierre Bovet, Amilcar Ciola, Joseph Duss von Werdt, Mony Elkaïm, Nahum Frenk, Edmond Gilliéron, François Grasset, Elvira Pancheri, Blaise Pierrehumbert, Christiane Robert-Tissot, Sandra Serpa-Rusconi, Gérard Salem, Fernand Seywert, Carlos Sluzki, and Rose-Marie Welter-Enderlin.

Daniel N. Stern has inspired much of this work. He read earlier drafts of this book and provided many useful suggestions. We are especially grateful to him.

At last, we are able to express our gratitude to our executive editor, Jo Ann Miller, who agreed to consider a manuscript from overseas. Mary Dorian was a manuscript editor with much patience and imagination.

It will come as no surprise that we dedicate this book to our partners in our own primary triangles.

Introduction:
How to Approach the Family

The primary triangle is as much ignored as it is acclaimed in the clinical and research domains on family process and development. Even though psychodynamic and family process triangles are congenial to clinical minds, the research has been lacking with respect to how this crucial triangle works and develops. In spite of the importance of life cycle developmental processes, research on family process during infancy is weak. Even if developmental researchers view the primary triangle as the ecological niche for development, the mainstream research in this domain remains the study of one-on-one relationships, mainly the mother–infant dyad.

As we set out to study the primary triangle in the early 1980s, we made six major choices influenced by our psychoanalytic and family therapy practices, by the developmental and family process theories with which we were working, and by the ethological/microanalytic methods of research with which we were familiar. Most of all, the following objectives were aimed at bridging the domains of child development and family process:

1. To explore the stable functional/clinical patterns of family alliances that developed from the very beginning in the primary triangle in order to assess a family's resources and vulnerabilities
2. To study the family as a unit from its inception, in contrast with the family as a set of dyads

3. To study the family as a "practicing" group in interaction, rather than the family as represented in the minds of its members; this decision logically implied that the research situation would be growth-enhancing and that the possibility of preventive or therapeutic interventions would be built in
4. To parallel the family process view of problematic triangulation with normative triangulation
5. To trace the development of triangulation between the infant and parents
6. To begin with a microdescription of the family's interactions in order to make out its specific patterns

Not only did these choices correspond to our own preferences but we were convinced they were the first steps in facing the primary triangle outright, even if they would not suffice to fully describe it. We have stuck to these choices while we are keenly aware of the necessity to open up from here to other avenues.

FAMILY ALLIANCES

We assumed that observing the family patterns that exist from the very beginning of the primary triangle would have important clinical implications, widespread theoretical interest, and intense research value. The term *family alliance* best captured the essence of our interests. The question we asked was: Does this family work together as a team and do the partners, namely the parents and the infant, help each other? In comparison with the working alliance in groups or the therapeutic alliance in psychotherapy, the family alliance was the systems property that emerged from the interactions between the three partners and constituted their identity as a group.

Like other groups that function to enhance human development, the father–mother–infant unit was composed of two main subunits: the *framing* subunit (coparenting party) and the *developing* subunit (infant). The framing subunit's function was to facilitate and guide the infant's development, whereas the developing subunit's function was to grow, to enhance its autonomy and thus drive the framing subunit. Yet it was only through cooperation that the two parties would constitute the alliance, which would in turn enable them to implement these functions. The strengths and weaknesses of the two parties would combine into original patterns that, under various environmental conditions, would give rise to different types of alliances, from the most functional to the most problematic ones. Thus, the family alliance had two faces: the father–mother–infant unit and the contributions of the parties (Fivaz-Depeursinge, 1991).

Our work involved three study areas: clinical practice, observational research, and systems theory models.

CLINICAL PRACTICE

Both of us were doing therapeutic work with families in which the mother or the father had suffered a psychotic or depressive breakdown after the birth of a child. The mother, or sometimes both parents, were hospitalized with their infant in order to directly work on their relationships.

There were several difficult clinical issues in these situations. The mother's relationship with her child was obviously at risk and so was her relationship with her own family of origin, in particular her mother. Not only was her "motherhood constellation" in shambles (Stern, 1995) but her psychiatric patient status often played into the father's need to prove his parental competence at a time when he also found himself in a crisis in his family of origin. For instance, in some cases the father's own mother had suffered a breakdown when he was born, so the birth of his own child reactivated the crisis. Or, his marriage with the mother of his child was not accepted by his own family, so he was caught in a loyalty conflict between his nuclear and origin families. As a consequence, the coparenting party in the new family was dysfunctional from the very beginning. The infant suffered and in some cases developed functional disturbances on his or her own. Therefore, assessing the family patterns that developed from the beginning and devising therapeutic interventions were crucial (Corboz-Warnery, 1985; Corboz-Warnery, 1986).

OBSERVATIONAL RESEARCH

One of us had previously conducted an observational study of dialogue play in these families. One of the most intriguing findings was that not only the mothers, as index patients, but also the fathers tended to establish an ambiguous form of interaction with their babies (Fivaz-Depeursinge, 1987; Fivaz-Depeursinge, Cornut-Zimmer, and Martin, 1984).

The parents solicited dialogue from their babies while persistently inviting disengagement. This paradoxical engagement was in contrast with the normative engagement pattern these same babies would establish with the consultant; thus, the babies' contribution to the paradoxical pattern with their parents was not in question. However, in some families, one of the parents—and not always the father—established a more straightforward dialogue interaction with the infant.

With respect to the eventual alliance of the family unit, these results were challenging. What would become of these dyadic interactions when the family would be united? Would the dyads support or aggravate each other? These results clearly pointed to the necessity of directly observing the family.

SYSTEMS THEORY MODELS

We were greatly helped in this conceptualization by the interdisciplinary research in systems theory that one of us conducted with Roland Fivaz, a physicist, and Luc Kaufmann, a psychiatrist. We studied the processes of change, stabilization, and deadlock in complex systems, such as family or therapeutic groups. The physicist was the provider of models, and he, the psychiatrist, and the psychologist applied these models to therapeutic or developmental research data. This is not the place to account for this complex, multifaceted work (for details, see Fivaz, 1989, 1996; Fivaz-Depeursinge, Fivaz, and Kaufmann, 1982, 1983), but it should be acknowledged that much of the present study was theoretically inspired and supported by reflections on the behavior of complex systems. One of the foremost issues was: Under which conditions is a developmental system likely to make a transition from a state that it has already acquired to a new, more complex state? This question, for instance, was applicable to the following: Under which family conditions is an infant more likely to make the transition from the social to the intersubjective stage of communication with both her parents in an optimal way? This subject is discussed in Chapter 5. In fact, this question is relevant to all framing–developmental interactions, in particular in therapy.

Another related issue was: How does a complex system move between states it has already integrated in its repertoire? For instance, under which conditions is the infant's moving between dialogue with father and dialogue with mother most facilitated? Again, this was to be a crucial issue in the family. Or, how can we best characterize the difference between the interaction of a conflictual versus a disordered family system and the social environment? The implications of this difference would considerably influence how to approach these families in therapy. Pertinent answers were also found in physical systems modeling.

THE FAMILY AS THE UNIT OF RESEARCH

Our second objective was to study the family as a whole and from its inception, in contrast with studying the family's constituent parts such as the dyads. However, there has been an ongoing controversy concerning the appropriate research unit (Hinde and Stevenson-Hinde, 1988). On one hand, proponents of the effects of relationships on relationships prefer to work with two-person exchanges, namely relationships. Note that in this context relationships exclude exchanges involving more than two people.[1]

On the other hand, family systems proponents are not satisfied with less than the "whole" family. "Since that is the realistic context of development and/or relationships within the family . . . it must eventually be studied in its own terms" (Minuchin, 1988, p. 17).

Several lines of research in child development have been converging on this perspective (see McHale, 1995, 1997). Using the systems approach, researchers studying the transition to parenthood have been alerted to the necessity to integrate the different perspectives of the family—sociological, developmental, clinical—sometimes reluctantly in view of the abstraction of systems concepts.[2]

It was inevitable that researchers studying father–infant relationships (Clarke-Stewart, 1978; Pedersen, 1985; Yogman, 1982) would be attentive to the family unit. Indeed, exploring the father's role in traditional research required its comparison with the mother's role; consequently, it also drew attention to the importance of the spouses' relationship and eventually to the effects of dyadic interactions on other dyadic interactions. A number of landmark studies were published that shed light on these multiple influences (Parke, 1988).[3]

There is a growing consensus that models that limit the examination of the effects of interactive patterns in the family to the dyads are insufficient (Minuchin, 1985; Parke, 1990). The few researchers (including ourselves in our first attempts) who have explored the father–mother–baby triad with the goal of capturing the unit of the family somehow did not attain it. It is our contention that this shortcoming has been due to the choice of researchers to infer the property of the triad from its dyadic components rather than taking a leap to the triadic gestalt.

As early as 1979, Parke, Power, and Gottman had elaborated a sophisticated model for conceptualizing and quantifying influential patterns within the family triad. Their model recognized the influence of the three partners, the child included; it provided for direct influences (acting on the other) as well as indirect ones (influencing through the mediation of another) and described their different paths. Finally, it included interaction in the absence as well as in the presence of the partners. However, the authors themselves recognized the model's emphasis on pairs of dyads, and thus its inability to fit the perception of the triad as a whole (Parke, Power, and Gottman, 1979).[4]

The first thorough and sophisticated attempt in infancy research to capture the family was a Pennsylvania study by Jay Belsky and collaborators (Belsky, Gilstrap, and Rovine, 1984). Recruiting couples during the last trimester of pregnancy, the authors carefully mapped the developmental course of mother, father, and infant at several levels: individual, dyadic–marital, father–infant, and mother–infant. In their attempt to arrive at the family level, they proposed a typology of families by analyzing the various combinations of the three dyads in each family.[5]

This remarkable study illuminated many of the internal workings of the family and generated hypotheses about family types. Again, the method selected does not reach the level of the family unit because the attempt is to extrapolate it from the dyads.[6]

Besides our study (Fivaz-Depeursinge, 1987), we know of only one originating in the family process field and focusing on infancy. *The Birth of the Family* investigation (Lewis, 1989) was conducted in the context of a larger longitudinal study of family competence (Beavers, 1977) that approached the family as a unified whole. A major merit of this study is that it included the "incorporation" of the first child in the family with the goal of approaching the triad as a system. Yet again, the parental triadic competence variable was actually a dyadic one rated in the context of the triad. Nevertheless, the investigation underscores the necessity for the family process field to move into early family interaction and to put to empirical test the main systems assumptions.

In our view, R. Parke's prescription succeeds in resolving the "whole-relationships" controversy: We must begin to study each level in its own right and then examine the connections (Parke, 1988). Indeed, he argues, individuals, dyads, and families may follow disparate developmental pathways.

Whereas it is important to acknowledge the interplay between them, each constitutes a systems entity in its own right. For instance, it may be that a father–son relation develops a specific complicity that only emerges when they are alone together, whereas they may entertain a different relationship when they are with mother. Or, the marital relationship may be in crisis, yet the parental alliance remains immune to this particular conflict when the parents are with the child. Hence the necessity to study the triad and its constituent dyads separately.

To summarize Parke's notion of separate but connected developmental pathways is theoretically and methodologically sound: It provides the necessary basis for the testing of the whole versus relationships assumptions. It is with this perspective that we propose the primary triangle as an appropriate research unit in its own right.

THE PRACTICING FAMILY IN A CONTEXT OF CHANGE

Following logically from the focus on the family as a unit, we decided to study the primary triangle in action, or as a "practicing group," in David Reiss's terms (Reiss, 1989), which was in contrast with the dominant trend to study the family one imagined, or the "represented family." The action took place in a clinical research setting that was growth-enhancing; it also included the possibility of preventive or therapeutic interventions targeted at interactions and allowed us to closely relate the findings to our clinical practice.

The two perspectives, the represented versus the practicing family, agree that family relationships markedly shape our development because they are stable and coherent. But they differ on where the stability and coherence of these influences primarily reside. D. Reiss suggested that the argument has at its core the "memorial" function of relationships (Reiss, 1989). For the proponents of the represented family, the memorial function for family relationships mainly resides in the working models that the partners individually construct mentally (Bowlby, 1980). Children progressively absorb and internalize the relationships they establish with their parents, especially their mother, modeling these relations in their minds.

Obviously, individuals have brains that permit them to exhibit continuity by means of representations. In contrast, dyads, triads, or larger groups do not. The proponents of the practicing family locate the memorial function foremost in the family's shared, coordinated practices. The emphasis is on the interactive patterns themselves. Prime examples of coordinated practices are family rituals such as mealtimes, reunions after school or work, games, bedtimes, as well as larger-scale rituals such as birthdays and holidays. Closer to our concern, patterned interactions are one form of repetition or ritualized behavior, thus qualifying as coordinated practices. "The interaction of the group—above and beyond the memories of its individuals—conserves relationships and regulates and perpetuates many aspects of ongoing family life" (Reiss, 1989, p. 193). Hence, rituals are regularly enacted precisely because they fulfill these functions.[7]

It is to be noted that highlighting practices does not deny the influence of individual representations. But the core idea is that family-coordinated practices serve to "align the individuals' representations with group practice" (Reiss, 1989, p. 193). It is not our purpose to discuss at length the issue of interaction versus representation, but we can briefly state our position. We are well aware of the importance of representations as the other face of the interactional phenomena we observe. Nevertheless we are convinced that interaction patterns are the obligatory entry into representations. They are, as D. Stern stated, "the arena in which the parents' representations are played out . . . similarly it is the arena for the enactment of the infant's representations, which once enacted directly influence the parents" (Stern, 1995, p. 71). Therefore, we consider the patterns of interaction we observe in Lausanne triadic play (LTP) as coordinated practices. Moreover, in following the families over the first year, we examine how they ritualize the LTP procedure and how the parents initiate their baby into participating in this practice.

We are not overlooking the necessity of also exploring the subjective experience of the partners and their representations. We see describing triangular interactions only as the necessary first step in a multifaceted inquiry and discuss promising pathways to interface interaction with representation and intergenerational issues in Chapter 8.

Adopting the perspective of the practicing family has important implications with respect to how research is conducted. As D. Reiss puts it, "Students of the Practicing Family are inclined to action" (Reiss, 1989, p. 199). Therefore, the core focus of this research is not etiology—the origin of the observed patterns—but the potential for development. To the extent that the observation is challenging—if only because it takes place "on stage" and, as in the LTP, is semistandardized—it frames the family's interactions in a new way; it constitutes a context for change, a sort of problem-solving task that challenges the adaptation skills and creativity of the family members. The core question is: What are the resources and what is the potential for developmental change in the patterns we observe? The way a family travels this course is particularly significant. In very problematic families the task may overflow their resources rather than being growth-enhancing. Then it may be productive to directly intervene to provoke a change and thus make the experience helpful. We describe such interventions in Chapters 6 and 7. Observation as intervention is gaining recognition.[8] It is also implicitly or explicitly inherent in many research paradigms.[9]

Our goal in adopting the practicing family perspective was to trace the earliest processes of coordinated practices as well as to conduct the research hand-in-hand with preventive or therapeutic intervention.

TRIANGULATION AS A NORMATIVE PROCESS

Triangulation is the first clinical notion that comes to mind when thinking of the primary triangle. Interestingly, it is used in psychodynamic and family systems theories. In the former, this term captures the oedipal child's subjective experience of exclusion from the parents' relationship. In the latter, it refers to a problematic process in which a child is drawn into his or her parents' conflictual relationship in order to deflect its tension.

Family therapy literature is replete with case descriptions of family "coalitions" (Caplow, 1968) and "alignments and splits" (Wynne, Ryckoff, Day, and Hirsch, 1958; Singer, Wynne and Toohey, 1978), "perverse triangles" (Haley, 1971), and "rigid triangles" (Minuchin, Baker, Roseman, Milman, and Todd, 1975; Minuchin, Rosman, and Baker, 1978) that covertly and enduringly divert the child's resources into the service of regulating the marital conflict. The process may take different forms: The child is drawn into a parental dispute, covertly encouraged to take sides and collude with one parent against the other, ending up in a position of generational inversion— namely "parentification" (Boszormenyi-Nagy and Sparks, 1973). Or, the child may be led to assume the outsider position, as a scapegoat (Vogel and Bell, 1960) or as a sick or otherwise vulnerable person, again with the aim or benefit of detouring the marital conflict (for a review, see Broderick, 1993). Perhaps triangulation at its worst is seen in the famous double-bind relationship, in its (amended) tripartite version between father, mother, and child (Bowen, 1972; Weakland, 1960). Here the parents collude in producing the paradoxical injunctions and/or in "forbidding" the metacommunication.

In both psychodynamic and family process triangulation, it is the poignant quality of the conflict that makes it a foremost clinical issue: Triangles are inherently dynamic. In Bowen's terms, "The emotional forces within a triangle are in constant motion, from minute to minute and hour to hour, in a series of chain reaction moves as automatic as emotional reflexes" (Bowen, 1972, p. 115). Bowen sees triangulation as the main issue in developing an autonomous self: even in times of stress, maintaining emotional contact with both parties in a triangle without being drawn into their conflict.

Likewise, the oedipal child learns to cope with the subjective feeling of exclusion and is prepared to do so by his or her experience with triangles, which are precursors of the oedipal drama. Indeed, we may look further back into development, as R. Emde suggested (Emde, 1994a), by construing this process along a developmental line with different levels of competition: exclusion from an attentional space in infancy, from a control space in toddlerhood, and from sexual intimacy in childhood. Psychodynamic theoreticians have also envisaged the precursors of oedipal triangulation in early infancy (Golse, 1990).

However salient the subjective experience of exclusion, it must have its counterpart in inclusion. Not only does the child's experience potentially involve the "two against one" or "two minus one" (exclusion) but also the "two for one" (she is the focus of parental attention), the "two plus one" (she is included but in the periphery), and, above all, the "three together" (she experiences threesomeness). Likewise, however salient the problematic triangulation may appear in family interaction, we need other triangles, clinical and functional, to fully account for triangular process and for therapeutic interventions. In particular, instead of making a coalition against the child, we need triangles in which the parents ally for him or her in a two-for-one process, establishing a parental collaborative leadership. The interest of this coparenting alliance also lies in its normative perspective on family structure. The assumption is a family structure that works entails a strong marital–parental alliance, whereas a family structure that does not work entails stronger, even if covert, cross-generational coalitions (McHale, Kuersten and Lauretti, 1996; Sroufe, 1989; Christensen and Margolin, 1988). These notions are central in both Haley's strategic and Minuchin's structural models of family therapy. We later make the same case for the other two-plus-one triangles and for the three-together one. Thus, we propose to redefine family triangulation within a larger framework that encompasses normative triangular process (Bürgin and von Klitzing, 1995).

TRIANGULATION DEVELOPMENT
BETWEEN INFANT AND PARENTS

We chose to retrace the infant's triangulation development and examine the parents' adjustments to this development. If the clinical notions of triangulation lack a developmental, normative foundation, what does developmental theory have to offer?

Developmentalists also accord great importance to triadic interactions, but it relates to the infant's accession to referential communication and intersubjectivity as studied mostly in controlled situations. Indeed, under the label of *triadic interactions,* they specifically describe the interaction between the infant and mother about an object or an event (Klinnert, Campos, Sorce, Emde, and Svejda, 1983). These triadic interactions appear in development only at seven to nine months, "combining communication about action on objects with direct dyadic interaction" (Trevarthen and Hubley, 1978, p. 335). Indeed, at that age, the baby goes through a major developmental leap. As D. Stern explains, the infant comes to realize that her parents, and she, herself, have "things in mind," such as a focus of attention or an intention or an inner feeling. These states of mind can be similar or different, shared or not shared, brought in line or not (Crossley, 1996; Stern, 1985). Triadic interactions manifest this new possibility even though it is still expressed nonverbally.

Indicative of this new competence is coordinated attention (Bakeman and Adamson, 1984); a nine-month-old might coordinate her attention with that of her mother by following her mother's line of vision or her mother's pointing toward an object; or, she might try to align her mother's attention with hers by insistent gazing or pointing toward the object. These behaviors show that she understands the referent of her mother's attention.

Most importantly, this new competence also involves the sharing of inner feeling states by means of affect sharing, social referencing, and affect signaling. In affect sharing (Kasari, Sigman, Mundy, and Yirmya, 1990), the infant will briefly look up at her mother, smiling, in a bid to sharing her joy in currently playing with a toy; the fact that she then will return to the game indicates the change in orientation was actually reflecting this intention to include her mother in her inner experience. In social referencing, on being presented with an uncertain stimulus, such as a scary or strange toy, the infant will look up at her mother with a quizzical or fearful look, seeking affective cues from her mother in order to appraise the event; the fact that she will then guide her behavior according to her mother's positive or negative cues indicates that this looking is actually intended to assess the purpose of the referent toy (Hagekull, Stenberg, and Bohlin, 1993; Hirschberg and Svejda, 1990a, 1990b; Klinnert et al., 1983; Walker-Andrews, 1988).

In affect signaling (Stern, 1985) the infant will deliberately look up at her mother with a cry or an angry face, or with a "hand-to-me" gesture, thus intending to influence her mother's conduct.[10] Or, on seeing that her mother is getting angry, she will deliberately look up at her with a winning smile in order to "bribe" her. Here the affect signal is used more for manipulation than for information purposes; indeed, once an infant can distinguish between inner experience and behavioral signals, she will be able to dissociate them and use behavioral signals to reach a goal—that is, to manipulate more than to inform.[11] It is important to note the intricacy of cognitive and emotional processes in these strategies (Campos, 1983; Klinnert et al., 1983).

The intersubjective shift in the infant corresponds with a change in the caregiver's responses: Affect attunement takes over imitation. Because the central issue is by now the alignment of inner affective states, the mother, instead of accurately matching the overt behavior of her baby, will align to this inner state by a "communing attunement" (Stern, 1985). "While imitation maintains the focus of attention upon external behavior, attunement behaviors are needed to shift the focus of attention to the inside, to the quality of the feeling that is shared" (Stern, 1984a, p. 6). The mother "recasts" her baby's overt behavior and translates it to reflect the properties of inner experience. For instance, to respond to her baby's enthusiasm expressed by joy in her facial expression, the mother would reciprocate in the form of a vocalization or a gesture while keeping the temporal and intensity contours of the baby's expression. Affect attunement, then, is "the performance of behaviors that express the quality of feeling of a shared affect state without imitating the exact behavioral expression of the inner state" (Stern, 1985, p. 142).[12]

Given the paramount importance of affective communion at the beginning of the intersubjective stage (Stern, 1985), it is surprising that developmentalists have not explored the same processes in triangular interactions, namely between three people; for instance, the infant and her mother communicating about another person (and why not father?). Indeed, why would the discovery that her internal, private mental world is invisible to others but that she can share it (or not) with them be restricted to communication about objects? Actually, there are a few experimental studies of social referencing verging on this issue, in that the uncertain stimulus is not the arrival of a scary toy but of an unfamiliar person, the "stranger." The results coincide with those obtained with objects.[13]

However, one may want to pursue the issue further and examine what happens in a more natural interaction in the primary triangle, for instance, asking about the infant's referencing her mother about the actions of the father (or vice versa); or the infant's affect sharing with her mother in referring to the joyful experience she is having with her father; or the infant's affect signaling to her mother about a negative experience with her father. In this way, following the same line that J. Dunn adopted for toddlers, we could begin to grasp how the infant works at understanding the "family politics" well before she can reflect on it (Dunn, 1988).

Likewise, regarding the parent's responses to an infant's affect signal about the other parent: How does a father comment or commune with his baby about the latter's negative or positive affective experience with her mother? And vice versa. And how do the parents comment or commune with their baby together? Do they "co-attune"? Are their comments congruent or incongruent? These issues are what bring us to the core of family process.

As we set out to observe the infant with both her parents, the infant's triangular competence earlier than the intersubjective stage—that is, from the beginning of her development—is another issue of concern. Up to now, the infant has been considered to be preadapted for dyadic interactions. The question of her triangular competence has not been raised. We will return to the three-month-old—the infant at the social stage—and will challenge this notion. Meanwhile, let us simply stress that preadapted dyadic interaction may prove to be an artifact of the classical dyadic settings for observing the young infant's interactions rather than an instrinsic limitation of the infant herself. It may be the story of science more than the story of the infant.

EXPLORATION OF FAMILY MICROPATTERNS

A necessary consequence of the forgoing decisions was that we would explore and describe in detail the triangular interactions of the family unit in order to make out their patterns. The studies conducted in the tradition of developmental human ethology and early interaction research have taught us that microanalysis of interactions provides a productive entry into uncharted territories, such as trilogue play. It allows us to generate hypotheses for experimental testing.

If we are going to take seriously the fact that "each level of social complexity has properties not relevant to that below" (Hinde and Stevenson-Hinde, 1988, p. 366), then methodologically we should not extrapolate from a level to another by using measures that pertain to one level in characterizing another—that is, drawing conclusions about individuals from studies of relationships or families, or describing relationships or families from studies of individuals.[14]

In a way, dyads have been misleading to researchers: It is within the grasp of our minds to represent the interrelations between two people, therefore overlooking the difference between the dyad as a relationship and the dyad as a unit. It is significantly more difficult to represent interrelations between three people.

In our view, the main reason why researchers have failed to design triangular-level variables pertains to the complexity of nonverbal interactions—a reason that, curiously, is overlooked or only briefly mentioned (Barrett and Hinde, 1988), even though infancy researchers are aware of the incredibly multifaceted nature of nonverbal interactions, particularly triangular ones. The sequential ordering of expressions is important; to follow the path of two simultaneous sequences and study their relationships is hard enough. There are as yet no established methods to accommodate more than two sequences simultaneously, though new methods are promising (Duncan and Farley, 1990; Magnusson, 1988).

Moreover, and unlike verbal communication in which speakers take successive turns in talking, nonverbal communication forces us to deal with simultaneous expressions, such as in music (Fentress, 1989). Partners in nonverbal play simultaneously express many affective dispositions, at different levels: turning the body to a face-to-face position, looking at the partner, smiling, and so on. In the best cases, these dispositions are congruent and may be globally captured in one category, such as "positive engagement." Yet they may not be congruent, especially in problematic interactions, which we shall illustrate at length.

The final consideration is that an individual in a triad can direct his or her behavior to both the other participants. In discussing their attempt at studying triadic interactions, Barrett and Hinde (1988) cite the observation by the animal ethologist Kummer: "A female in the harem of a hamadryas baboon male may simultaneously try to drive off another female, present to the male, and position herself in such a manner that if the threatened female reciprocates, her threat will be interpreted by the male as directed to him" (p. 189).

The baboon example neatly demonstrates why even the most careful description of the three dyads in this exchange would not capture how they specifically connect to generate the event in question. Clearly, we have to adopt methods that are able to catch these actions, notwithstanding the partners' concurrent and subsequent actions.

However, for all the methodological difficulties we mentioned, once convinced of the interest of describing the triangular level, we see that the pioneers in the field actually envisioned original ways of dealing with the issue, namely A. Scheflen and A. Kendon. In a way, the "trick" is merely to mimic in our coding procedures the way in which we actually perceive interactions in groups—that is, to rely on gestalt perception to make the leap to the whole.[15]

DATA

Since we started, in the early 1980s, we have observed and recorded about a hundred families in the LTP situation. The clinical families were mostly addressed by the Adult Psychiatry Department of Lausanne University, where one parent, generally the mother, was hospitalized with her baby for serious postpartum breakdown (psychotic or depressive). A few families were addressed by their pediatrician for functional problems manifested by the infant. The nonclinical families were volunteer.

We selected two samples for intensive analysis. In both samples, the infants were full-term and normal. Sample one included eighteen families observed once; nine clinical families were paired with nine nonclinical ones for the infant's age (two to nine months) and sex, and the parents' level of education. Sample two included twelve nonclinical families. They volunteered for collaboration by answering a letter sent to them based on birth announcement ads. We selected them on the following criteria: There was no previous professional help; the child was the firstborn; there was an equal number of girls and boys; the socioeconomic status was as balanced as possible. The infants were delivered without complications and there were no significant pediatric problems.

The parents were informed that we did a study on how children develop in the nuclear family. They got copies of their infant's videos and were paid for expenses. We observed them longitudinally five times over the first twelve months (eight, twelve, twenty-four, thirty-seven, and fifty-two weeks) and followed them up at four years. The data of sessions two (twelve weeks), three (twenty-four weeks), and four (thirty-seven weeks) were assessed for the type of family alliance. In this way, the first session counted as a familiarization with the studio and the LTP procedure. The parents who were to play first were designated in order to have half mothers and half fathers. It is from this sample that we obtained the elements to make up the four prototypes of family interactions that illustrate the typology of family alliances. It is also from the data of this sample that quantitative results are presented (see Appendix A for details). Note that identifying characteristics of the families and their members have been eliminated or disguised.

CONCLUSIONS

Studying the primary triangle involves the following steps:

1. Exploring the systems property that emerges from the family's interactions, namely the family alliance
2. Considering the family as a unit in its own right
3. Observing the practicing family in a context that facilitates development or therapeutic change
4. Backing up the clinical notion of problematic triangulation with the normative triangular process
5. Retracing the infant's development in the context of the primary triangle
6. Designing methods to study the family as a whole and minutely describe interactive patterns

This is not to say that these are the last steps to be taken. In our opinion, they are the steps required to begin. And indeed they open wide the windows onto the other crucial aspects of the primary triangle: its constituent dyads and monads, its representations, and the many clinical implications thereof.

These choices have led us to propose a model of family interactions in the LTP. More precisely, as we developed a sense for how families enact the LTP procedure, we learned to read their interactions in real time as well as in microanalytic time. Thus, four readings form the backbone of the model and hence organize this book.

In the *functional/clinical* reading (Chapter 2), we work in the tradition of clinical case stories. Constructing a narrative account of the entire course of the LTP, we follow through the interaction and continuously ask whether the group is working together and how the parties help each other. This reading leads up to defining the family alliance, from the most functional to the most problematic, from the most coordinated and effective to the least in attaining the goal of trilogue play: the cooperative, the stressed, the collusive, and the disordered family alliances. The next three readings are microanalytic. They uncover the underpinnings of the family alliances typology.

In the *structural* reading (Chapter 3), we work in the tradition of ethological/structural research. It is a fact that a family working together imposes the observer's perception of the representation of a structure. Authors have used various metaphors to convey this notion: music, dance, theater, architecture, as well as structures observed in nature. This serves particularly to convey that a structure imperatively implies an order, consisting of the hierarchical layering of various actions into a framework, as well as definable directions of influences between these layers.

By microanalyzing the interactions we observe in the LTP, we derived a model of the triangular frameworks that work in attaining the goal of trilogue play versus those that do not work. We can precisely detect where in the structure an eventual problem originates, thus providing a blueprint for assessing interactions. Practically, we map a family's interactions against this model and we ask: Does the framework they have constructed advance playful, positive affect sharing or does it more likely impede it? And, if so, where precisely in the structure does the problem originate?

In the *process* reading (Chapter 4), we attempt to reach the dynamics that sustain the triangular framework, that is, how the partners coregulate it. In the tradition of process research, we have found that there are brief sequences that offer us a detailed view of the processes: the transitions between the parts of the LTP. The reason is that these moments require particularly tight coordination; accordingly, they shed light on precisely how the partners work together—or fail to. Also, it is at these moments that they are most liable to make "false steps" or "miscoordinations" and then to have to "repair" them. We know that these processes are natural enough— not only inevitable but profitable. Yet repair is an all-or-nothing operation; either it may reestablish the course of action or amplify the problem. Much depends on the affective tonality of the interaction at this point. Practically, we ask: How do the partners coordinate their actions during the transitions and how do they repair eventual miscoordinations?

In the *developmental* reading (Chapter 5), we work in the tradition of the developmentalists and their appraisal of the first-year leap from social to intersubjective, socioaffective communication. However, since it is with two partners rather than one that the infant interacts, it is his or her handling of triangular interactions that we assess. Practically, we scrutinize representative events and ask: Does the infant handle the four configurations that constitute a three-party relationship, and how? How do the parents deal with their child's handling of triangles? Do they facilitate this differentiation of triangular relationships and do they validate their infant's bids for threesome communion?

Finally, the four readings also apply, in a summary version, to the categorization of the working alliance between observers and family, whether in the context of preventive (Chapter 6) or therapeutic (Chapter 7) interventions. It is our view that each of the readings is necessary to fully understand the interactions of a family in the LTP in a clinically, theoretically, and methodologically sound way.

We begin with an overview of the model. Then, based on the prototypes of the four family alliances, we illustrate and discuss each of these readings in separate chapters. We describe in detail the framing of volunteer families in the research context as well as the direct therapeutic interventions that we practice within the LTP setting. Finally, we discuss the implications of this model for bridging infant development and family process, particularly with respect to understanding interactions in later life stages.

NOTES

1. R. Emde went so far as to contend that family therapists are actually working at this level as well:

> The major working area of all forms of family therapy involves the effects of relationships on relationships. . . . It will be argued that the proposition simply cannot be true because there is another emergent level of family phenomena in which the whole is greater than the sum of the parts. . . . Still, I maintain this proposition remains to be proven wrong with empirical research. (Emde, 1988, p. 361)

2. J. Belsky commented on the contribution of systems theory to research:

> When stripped of much of its rhetoric . . . the notion of a system . . . does seem to have at least one important lesson to teach those interested in the developing family. . . . The family must be conceived in terms of multiple levels of analysis,

consisting of elements that together constitute subsystems, and that like the elements are reciprocally interrelated, comprising an entity that is not reducible to the sum of its parts. (Belsky, Rovine, and Fish, 1989, p. 121)

3. For instance, authors in the domain of father–infant interactions have shown that parents behave differently when alone as opposed to when together with their infant. In particular, they support each other's attention to their child and as a consequence are more affectionate with their baby in the presence of the other parent. Moreover, parents influence their infants indirectly as well as directly—that is, through the mediation of the other parent; they also influence the other parent through the mediation of the child (Parke, 1988). F. Frascarolo showed that when the father was involved in day care the entire family system was different: Involved fathers had more sociable infants and their wives as mothers were less controlling (Frascarolo, Chillier, and Robert-Tissot, 1996; Lecamus, Labrell, and Zaouche-Gaudron, 1977). Finally, the impact of the husband–wife relationship on the parent–infant one is well documented (Belsky and Isabella, 1985; Cowan and Cowan, 1990; Emery, 1982; Pedersen, Anderson, and Cain, 1980): Studies show that marital conflict influences children's social and emotional development both directly (Cummings and Davies, 1994) and indirectly through parent–child dyadic interactions (Erel and Burman, 1995).

4. Although the triad was not their primary goal, researchers of father–infant interactions were inevitably drawn to observing this dyad in the context of the triad. On the one hand, their procedures consisting of comparing dyads and perhaps in analyzing the effects of dyads on other dyads were legitimate. On the other hand, these procedures were in contradiction with the idea they were acquiring of the triad as a system. For instance, consider M. Yogman's notion of the triad as a cybernetic system:

The larger triadic system provides some overall stability while the feedback system within any one of the dyads can be transiently disrupted. This carries with it the opportunity for differentiation, separation and individuation within a dyad while a stable matrix for developmental organization is maintained in the larger system. (Yogman, 1982, p. 262). However, the empirical work does not show that the triad provides this stability.

5. Toward the end of this study, the authors eloquently stated their opinion:

Although it is apparent . . . that our investigation was systematic, focusing on elements of the family system (individuals), subsystems comprised of interacting elements (relationships) and the interrelation of relationships subsystems, we remain ambivalent about the extent to which this research is truly systemic in nature. Systems theorists are inclined to define systems in terms of very general principles such as self-stabilization, self-organization, and hierarchical organization. . . . It remains unclear to us at the present time that any of these basic characteristics of a system or of the family system have been revealed by our investigation. The basic reason for this is that it has never been clear to us

... how such conceptualizations are to be operationalized in the research process. (Belsky et al., 1989, p. 160)

6. As P. Minuchin states in her discussion of developmental research in the light of systems theory: "It seems difficult for researchers to take on the family as a natural unit, with multiple members and with organized patterns that involve more than two people and sequences of more than two steps" (Minuchin, 1988, p. 17).

7. D. Reiss and his colleagues have gathered substantial evidence on the importance of the dynamics of family rituals, particularly in the intergenerational transmission of alcoholism (Bennett, Wolin, Reiss, and Teitelbaum, 1987).

8. In 1984, Stern (1984b) mentioned that the therapeutic effect of the research observation was beginning to be discussed in the literature. Observation has been documented in various types of early interventions (Cramer and Palacio-Espasa, 1993; Lamour and Lebovici, 1991; Lebovici, 1983, 1992; Stoleru and Moralès-Huet, 1989; for a review, see Stern, 1995). It has also been formally built into several forms of early intervention; for instance, in therapy sessions interactional guidance begins with a videotaped play session that is replayed to identify the behaviors that become the subjects of therapeutic work (McDonough, 1993).

9. D. Reiss's Card Sorting Test is a classification task in which the subjects may ask for information from the researchers. After an individual round, the members of the family repeat the procedure together and have to arrive at a consensus on the classification criteria. Beyond the research interest of comparing the individual and family performance, this test shows the family their differences in individual and group functioning (Reiss, 1981). J. Gottman also conceived his Couple Conflict Discussion task to be growth-enhancing (Gottman, 1994). Having separately asked the husband and the wife to indicate the areas of continuing conflict they have in their relationship, the facilitator selects with the couple the area of conflict they both agree is an issue and asks them to work toward a resolution. Afterward, the spouses review the video-recordings from different perspectives, coding their subjective experience as they interacted or discussing key moments with the facilitator.

Other well-known observational paradigms include the Ainsworth strange situation, where the parent and the child have the opportunity to experience a gradation of separation/reunion episodes (Ainsworth, Belhar, Waters, and Wall, 1978), or narratives where the child and the parents complete stories on conflictual themes (Emde, 1994b; Oppenheim, Emde, and Warren, 1997).

10. It has been shown that infants start to use crying as a communicative signal for controlling parents at around seven months (Papousek and Papousek, 1993; Wolff, 1969).

11. The infant learns very early to evaluate the degree of authenticity/manipulation of her parents' displays (Stern, Barnett, and Spieker, 1983).

12. It may be presumed that affect attunement originates in the repertoire of intuitive parenting behaviors described by the Papouseks (Papousek and Papousek, 1978, 1987) that form the dialectic counterpart to the infant's preadapted competence.

13. In designs controlling for the mother's positive versus negative response to the infant's referential look regarding the stranger, the infant guides her behavior according to the mother's cue. Interestingly, in observing naturally occurring infant and maternal behaviors in this same uncertain situation, Hagekull, Stenberg, and Bohlin discovered new elements: Not only did the ten-month-olds whose mothers had spontaneously responded positively to their referencing show more positive responses to the stranger (Hagekull et al., 1993) but a minority of infants did not reference at all to their mothers. These babies had experienced less sensitive mothering and showed more irritability at an earlier stage. In another study, Dickstein and Parke showed that infants referred to their fathers as frequently as to their mothers when confronted by a stranger. Interestingly, the marital satisfaction of the fathers predicted the frequency of infants referencing to their fathers (not to their mothers) (Dickstein and Parke, 1988). In the same vein, Hirschberg and Svejda (1990a, 1990b) compared the infant's referencing of father and mother in the presence of both parents. They observed no preference to either parent.

Klinnert and coauthors also confronted one-year-old infants with a novel toy in the presence of two adults: An experimenter familiar to the infants posed either happy or fearful expressions, whereas the mother remained at a distance and neutral. Interestingly, the infants interrelated with both adults, but they guided their behavior according to the most expressive one, namely the experimenter (Klinnert, Emde, Butterfield, and Campos, 1986).

Finally, in another perspective, H. Tremblay-Leveau and J. Nadel (1995) studied the triadic interactions of toddlers with a peer and an adult. They have shown that at eleven months, toddlers are able to address both their partners simultaneously by means of "double-oriented" behaviors when they bid for having themselves included in the peer–adult dyadic interaction (Tremblay-Leveau and Nadel, 1995).

14. It is common practice in research to "reconstruct" a couple's past interaction on the basis of the spouses' separate reports of marital satisfaction. If they are a legitimate measure of each individual's recollection of the marital relationship, they may not substitute for a measure of conjoint recollections—for instance, by merely averaging the individual scores—because, in the context of their interaction, the spouses will reconstruct their story in a different way. Conversely, the conjoint recollection would be no substitute for the spouses' separate perceptions. In their study on the transition to parenthood, J. Lewis and colleagues separately evaluated the individuals and the couples. They measured the psychological health of the husband and the wife and interviewed each of them on their perception of their origin family. They concurrently also observed the partners together in interactive tasks, such as negotiating a divergence. The researchers found that they were unable to predict the quality of the couple's interaction on the basis of the individual measures (Lewis, 1988). One of the major challenges of systems research is to document the unique properties that characterize systems.

In the field of early dyadic interaction, the methods developed by Tronick and colleagues are exemplary. On the one hand, they measure separately the degrees of engagement of the infant and mother (monadic phases), thus analyzing their contributions to the interaction. On the other hand, they measure their combined engagement (dyadic phases), but then leave aside the consideration of individual contributions (Cohn and Tronick, 1987). The first type of measure is a monadic-level variable, whereas the second type is a dyadic-level variable. Studies that do not make this distinction miss the dyadic level.

15. A. Scheflen and A. Kendon notably suggested "F-formations" (F stands for "face") to describe group interactions (Kendon, 1977). An F-formation refers to a geometrical arrangement (i.e., "body formation") of participants; for instance, the spatial arrangement between the locations of people while in standing conversation. A "gaze formation" could be obtained by drawing the patterns of the preferred gaze orientations within the context of the body formation. Formations literally draw shapes in space. The main point is that these shapes are dynamically sustained by the group—for instance, suppose one partner withdraws; then you will probably observe another one compensating for this move, trying to reinclude the former. Or, one member leaves, and the circle is reconstituted. In other words, and for the sake of brevity (because we will come back at length to these notions), body formations have systems properties.

If we are going to capture the methodological pathway to take to the triad, we need to make the leap to the gestalt of the group—as illustrated by the notion of body formation. There is no way we can reconstruct a circle or an L-shaped formation by looking at the locations of the partners two by two and then correlating them.

REFERENCES

Ainsworth, M. D. S., Belhar, M. C., Waters, E., and Wall, S. (1978). *Patterns of Attachment: A Psychological Study of the Strange Situation*. Hillsdale, NJ: Lawrence Erlbaum.

Bakeman, R., and Adamson, L. B. (1984). Coordinating attention to people and objects in mother–infant and peer–infant interaction. *Child Development, 55,* 1278–1289.

Barrett, J., and Hinde, R. A. (1988). Triadic interactions: Mother-first-born-secondborn. In R. A. Hinde and J. Stevenson-Hinde (eds.), *Relationships Within Families. Mutual Influences* (pp. 181–190). Oxford: Clarendon Press.

Beavers, W. R. (1977). *Psychotherapy and Growth: A Family Systems Perspective*. New York: Bruner/Mazel.

Belsky, J., Gilstrap, B., and Rovine, M. (1984). The Pennsylvania infant and family development project: I. Stability and change in a family setting at one, three and nine months. *Child Development, 55,* 692–705.

Belsky, J., and Isabella, R. (1985). Marital and parent–child relationships in family of origin and marital change following the birth of a baby: A retrospective analysis. *Child Development, 56,* 342–349.

Belsky, J., Rovine, M., and Fish, M. (1989). The developing family system. In M. R. Gunnar and E. Thelen (eds.), *Systems and Development* (Vol. 22, pp. 110–165). Hillsdale, NJ: Lawrence Erlbaum.

Bennett, L. A., Wolin, S. J., Reiss, D., and Teitelbaum, M. A. (1987). Couples at risk for transmission of alcoholism: Protective influences. *Family Process, 26,* 111–129.

Boszormenyi-Nagy, I., and Sparks, G. (1973). *Invisible Loyalties.* New York: Harper and Row.

Bowen, M. (1972). Toward the differentiation of self in one's own family. In J. L. Framo (ed.), *Family Interaction: A Dialogue Between Family Researchers and Family Therapists* (pp. 11–173). New York: Springer Verlag.

Bowlby, J. (1980). *Attachment and Loss: Vol. 3. Loss: Sadness and Depression.* New York: Basic Books.

Broderick, C. B. (1993). *Understanding Family Process.* Newbury Park, CA: Sage Publications.

Bürgin, D., and von Klitzing, K. (1995). Prenatal representations and postnatal interactions of a threesome (mother, father and baby). In J. Bitzer and M. Stauber (eds.), *Psychosomatic Obstetrics and Gynaecology* (pp. 185–192). Bologna: Monduzzi.

Campos, J. J. (1983). The importance of affective communication in social referencing: A commentary on Feinman. *Merril–Palmer Quarterly, 29*(1), 83–87.

Caplow, T. (1968). *Two Against One: Coalition in Triads.* Englewood Cliffs, NJ: Prentice-Hall.

Christensen, A., and Margolin, G. (1988). Conflict and alliance in distressed and nondistressed families. In R. A. Hinde and J. Stevenson-Hinde (eds.), *Relationships Within Families* (pp. 263–282). Oxford: Oxford Science Publications.

Clarke-Stewart; K. A. (1978). And daddy makes three: The father's impact on mother and young child. *Child Development, 49,* 466–478.

Cohn, J. F., and Tronick, E. Z. (1987). Mother–infant face-to-face interaction: The sequence of dyadic states at 3, 6 and 9 months. *Developmental Psychology, 23,* 1–10.

Corboz-Warnery, A. (1985). Crises familiales au post-partum: Le père dans la perspective systémigue. Unpublished doctoral thesis in medicine, Université de Lausanne.

Corboz-Warnery, A. (1986). Echange du père avec la dyade mère-bébé dans une famille décompensée au post-partum. In G. Garrone, A. Jablensky, and J. Manzano (eds.), *Jeunes parents psychotigues et leurs enfants* (pp. 141–146). Genève: SIMEP.

Cowan, P. A., and Cowan, C. P. (1990). Becoming a family: Research and intervention. In I. E. Sigel and G. H. Brody (eds.), *Methods of Family Research: Biographies of Research Projects, Vol. I: Normal Families* (pp. 1–51). Hillsdale, NJ: Lawrence Erlbaum Associates.

Cramer, B., and Palacio-Espasa, F. (1993). *La pratique des psychothérapies mères-bébés: Etudes clinique et technique.* Paris: Presses Universitaires de France.

Crossley, N. (1996). *Intersubjectivity. The Fabric of Social Becoming.* London: Sage Publications.

Cummings, E. M., and Davies, P. (1994). *Children and Marital Conflict. The Impact of Family Dispute and Resolution.* New York: The Guilford Press.

Dickstein, S., and Parke, R. D. (1988). Social referencing in infancy: A glance at fathers and marriage. *Child Development, 59,* 506–511.

Duncan, S., Jr., and Farley, A. M. (1990). Achieving parent–child coordination through convention: Fixed- and variable-sequence conventions. *Child Development, 61,* 742–753.

Dunn, J. (1988). *The Beginnings of Social Understanding.* Cambridge, MA: Harvard University Press.

Emde, R. N. (1988). The effects of relationships on relationships: A developmental approach to clinical intervention. In R. A. Hinde and J. Stevenson-Hinde (eds.), *Relationships Within Families* (pp. 354–364). Oxford: Clarendon Press.

Emde, R. N. (1994a). Commentary: Triadification experiences and a bold new direction for infant mental health. *Infant Mental Health Journal, 15*(1), 90–95.

Emde, R. N. (1994b). Early moral development, emotions, and the imaginative self: Implications for research, caregiving and mental health. *Conférence donnée à 1'hôpital psychiatrique de cery, 1. 11. 94.*

Emery, R. E. (1982). Interparental conflict and the children of discord and divorce. *Psychological Bulletin, 92* (2), 310–330.

Erel, O., and Burman, B. (1995). Interrelatedness of marital relations and parent–child relations: A meta-analytic review. *Psychological Bulletin 118,* 108–132.

Fentress, J. C. (1989). Developmental roots of behavioral order: Systemic approaches to the examination of core developmental issues. In M. R. Gunnar and E. Thelen (eds.), *Systems and Development* (pp. 35–76). Hillsdale, NJ: Lawrence Erlbaum Associates.

Fivaz, R. (1989). *L'Ordre et la Volupté.* Lausanne: Presses Polytechniques Romandes.

Fivaz, R. (1996). Ergodic theory of communication. *Systems Research, 13* (2), 127–144.

Fivaz-Depeursinge, E. (1987). *Alliances et mésalliances dans le dialogue entre adulte et bébé. La communication précoce dans la famille.* Neuchâtel et Paris: Delachaux & Niestlé.

Fivaz-Depeursinge, E. (1991). Documenting a time-bound, circular view of hierarchies: A microanalysis of parent–infant dyadic interaction. *Family Process, 30* (1), 101–120.

Fivaz-Depeursinge, E., Cornut-Zimmer, B., and Martin, D. (1984). Holding interactions in a clinical family. In J. Call, E. Galenson, and R. L. Tyson (eds.), *Frontiers of Infant Psychiatry* (Vol. 2, pp. 502–521). New York: Basic Books.

Fivaz-Depeursinge, E., Fivaz, R., and Kaufmann, L. (1982). Encadrement du développement, le point de vue systémique. Fonctions pédagogique, parentale, thérapeutique. *Cahiers Critiques de Thérapie Familiale et de Pratiques de Réseaux, 4–5,* 63–74.

Fivaz-Depeursinge, E., Fivaz, R., and Kaufmann, L. (1983). Agreement, conflict, symptom: An evolutionary paradigm. In J. Duss von Werdt and R.-M. Welter-Enderlin (eds.), *Zusammenthänge.* Zürich: Institut für Ehe unde Familie.

Frascarolo, F., Chillier, L., and Robert-Tissot, C. (1996). Relations entre l'engagement paternel quotidien, les représentations des rôles parentaux et l'identité sexuelle. *Archives de Psychologie, 64,* 159–177.

Golse, B. (1990). *Insister-Exister. De L'être à la personne.* Paris: Presses Universitaires de France.

Gottman, J.M. (1994). *What Predicts Divorce? The Relationship Between Marital Processes and Marital Outcomes.* Hillsdale, NJ: Lawrence Erlbaum.

Hagekull, B., Stenberg, G., and Bohlin, G. (1993). Infant–mother social referencing interactions: Description and antecedents in maternal sensitivity and infant irritability. *Early Development and Parenting, 2* (3), 183–191.

Haley, J. (1971). Toward a theory of pathological systems. In G. Zuk and I. Boszormenyi-Nagy (eds.), *Family Theory and Disturbed Families.* Palo Alto, CA: Science and Behavior Books.

Hinde, R. A., and Stevenson-Hinde, J. (eds.). (1988). *Relationships Within Families.* Oxford: Oxford Science Publications.

Hirschberg, L., and Svejda, M. (1990a). When infants look to their parents: II. Twelve-month-olds' response to conflicting parental emotional signals. *Child Development, 61,* 1187–1191.

Hirschberg, L. M., and Svejda, M. (1990b). When infants look to their parents: I. Infants' social referencing of mothers compared to fathers. *Child Development, 61* (66), 1175–1186.

Kasari, C., Sigman, M., Mundy, P., and Yirmya, N. (1990). Affective sharing in the context of joint attention. Interactions of normal, autistic, and mentally retarded children. *Journal of Autism and Developmental Disorders, 20* (1), 87–100.

Kendon, A. (1977). Spatial organization in social encounters: The F-formation system. In A. Kendon (ed.), *Studies in the Behavior of Social Interaction* (pp. 179–208). Lisse, IN: Peter DeRidder Press.

Klinnert, M. D., Campos, J. J., Sorce, J. F., Emde, R. N., and Svejda, M. (1983). Emotions as behavior regulators: Social referencing in infancy. In R. Plutchik and H. Kellerman (eds.), *Emotion. Theory, Research and Experience* (pp. 57–86). New York: Academic Press.

Klinnert, M. D., Emde, R. N., Butterfield, P., and Campos, J. J. (1986). Social referencing: The infant's use of emotional signals from a friendly adult with mother present. *Developmental Psychology, 22* (4), 427–432.

Lamour, M., and Lebovici, S. (1991). Les interactions du nourisson avec ses partenaires: évaluation et modes d'abord préventifs et thérapeutiques. *Psychiatrie de l'enfant, 34* (1), 171–275.

Lebovici, S. (1983). *Le nourrisson, la mère et le psychanalyste. Les interactions précoces.* Paris: Le Centurion.

Lebovici, S. (1992). A propos de la transmission intergénérationnelle: de la filiation à l'affiliation. *Presidential Address, 5th World Congress of the World Association of Infant Psychiatry, Chicago, 9–13 Sept 1992.*

Lecamus, J., Labrell, F., and Zaouche-Gaudron, C. (1977). *Le rôle du Père dans le Développement du Jeune Enfant.* Paris: Nathan.

Lewis, J. M. (1988). The transition to parenthood: I. The rating of prenatal marital competence. *Family Process, 27,* 149–165.

Lewis, J. M. (1989). *The Birth of the Family. An Empirical Inguiry.* New York: Brunner/Mazel.

Lewis, J. M., Owen, M. T., and Cox, M. J. (1988). The transition to parenthood: III. Incorporation of the child into the family. *Family Process, 27,* 411–421.

Magnusson, M. S. (1988). Le temps et les patterns syntaxiques du comportement humain: modèle, méthode et le programme "THEME." *Revue des conditions de travail* (pp. 284–314). Marseille: Octaves.

McDonough, S. C. (1993). Interaction guidance: Understanding and treating early infant–caregiver relationship disorders. In C. Zeanah (ed.), *Handbook of Infant Mental Health* (pp. 414–426). New York: Guilford Press.

McHale, J. P. (1995). Coparenting and triadic interactions during infancy: The roles of marital distress and child gender. *Developmental Psychology, 31* (6), 985–996.

McHale, J. P. (1997). Overt and covert coparenting processes in the family. *Family Process, 36,* 183–201.

McHale, J., Kuersten, R., and Lauretti, A. (1996). New directions in the study of family-level dynamics during infancy and early childhood. In J. McHale and P. Cowan (eds.), *Understanding How Family-Level Dynamics Affect Children's Development: Studies of Two-Parent Families* (Vol. 74, pp. 6–44). San Francisco: Jossey-Bass.

Meltzoff, A. N., and Moore, M. K. (1995). A theory of the role of imitation in the emergence of self. In P. Rochat (ed.), *The Self in Infancy: Theory and Research* (pp. 73–93). Amsterdam: Elsevier.

Minuchin, P. (1985). Families and individual development: Provocations from the field of family therapy. *Child Development, 56,* 289–302.

Minuchin, P. (1988). Relationships within the family: A systems perspective on development. In R. A. Hinde and J. Stevenson-Hinde (eds.), *Relationships Within families. Mutual Influences* (pp. 7–26). Oxford: Clarendon Press.

Minuchin, S., Baker, L., Roseman, B. L., Milman, L., and Todd, T. C. (1975). A conceptual model of psychosomatic illness in children. *Archives of General Psychiatry, 32,* 1031–1038.

Minuchin, S., Rosman, B., and Baker, L. (1978). *Psychosomatic Families.* Cambridge, MA: Harvard University Press.

Oppenheim, D., Emde, R., and Warren, S. (1997). Children's narrative representations of mothers: Their development and associations with child and mother adaptation. *Child Development, 68*(1), 127–138.

Pape-Cowan, P. C., and Cowan, P. A. (1992). *When Partners Become Parents.* New York: Basic Books.

Papousek, H., and Papousek, M. (1978). Interdisciplinary parallels in studies of early human behavior: From physical to cognitive needs, from attachment to dyadic education. *International Journal of Behavioral Development, 1,* 37–49.

Papousek, H., and Papousek, M. (1987). Intuitive parenting: A dialectic counterpart to the infant's integrative competence. In J. D. Osofsky (ed.), *Handbook of Infant Development,* 2nd ed. (pp. 669–720). New York: Wiley.

Papousek, H., and Papousek, M. (1993). Early interactional signalling: The role of facial movements. In A. A. Kalverboer, B. Hopkins, and R. H. Geuze (eds.), *Longitu-*

dinal Approach to the Study of Motor Development in Early and Later Childhood (pp. 136–152). Cambridge, UK: Cambridge University Press.

Parke, R. D. (1988). Families in life-span perspective: A multilevel developmental approach. In M. E. Hetherington, R. M. Lerner, and M. Perlmutter (eds.), *Child Development in Life-Span Perspective* (pp. 159–190). Hillsdale, NJ: Lawrence Erlbaum Associates.

Parke, R. D. (1990). In search of fathers: A narrative of an empirical journey. In I. E. Sigel and G. H. Brody (eds.), *Methods of Family Research: Biographies of Research Projects* (pp. 153–189). Hillsdale, NJ: Lawrence Erlbaum Associates.

Parke, R. D., Power, T. G., and Gottman, J. M. (1979). Conceptualizing and quantifying influence patterns in the family triad. In M. E. Lamb, S. J. Suomi, and G. R. Stephenson (eds.), *Social Interaction Analysis: Methodological Issues* (pp. 207–230). Madison: University of Wisconsin Press.

Pedersen, F. A. (1985). Research and the father: Where do we go from there? In S. Hanson and F. Bozett (eds.), *Dimensions of Fatherhood* (pp. 437–450). Beverly Hills: Sage Publications.

Pedersen, F., Anderson, B., and Cain, R. (1980). Parent–infant and husband–wife interactions observed at age 5 months. In F. A. Pedersen (ed.), *The Father–Infant Relationship. Observational Studies in the Family Setting* (pp. 44–70). New York: Praeger.

Reiss, D. (1981). *The Family's Construction of Reality.* Cambridge, MA: Harvard University Press.

Reiss, D. (1989). The represented and practicing family: Contrasting visions of family continuity. In A. J. Sameroff and R. N. Emde (eds.), *Relationship Disturbances in Early Childhood* (pp. 191–220). New York: Basic Books.

Singer, M. T., Wynne, L. C., and Toohey, M. L. (1978). Communication disorders and the families of schizophrenics. In L. C. Wynne (ed.), *The Nature of Schizophrenia. New Approaches to Research and Treatment* (pp. 499–511). New York: Wiley.

Sroufe, L. A. (1989). Relationships and relationship disturbances. In A. J. Sameroff and R. N. Emde (eds.), *Relationship Disturbances in Early Childhood* (pp. 97–124). New York: Basic Books.

Stern, D. N. (1984a). Affect attunement. In J. D. Call, E. Galenson, and R. L. Tyson (eds.), *Frontiers of Infant Psychiatry* (Vol. 2, pp. 3–14). New York: Basic Books.

Stern, D. N. (1984b). The investigator–subject relationship in infancy research. *Infant Behavior and Development, 7,* 106.

Stern, D. N. (1985). *The Interpersonal World of the Infant.* New York: Basic Books.

Stern, D. N. (1995). *The Motherhood Constellation.* New York: Basic Books.

Stern, D. N., Barnett, R. K., and Spieker, S. (1983). Early transmission of affect: Some research issues. In J. D. Call, E. Galenson, and R. L. Tyson (eds.), *Frontiers of Infant Psychiatry* (Vol. 2, pp. 74–85). New York: Basic Books.

Stoleru, S., and Moralès-Huet, M. (1989). *Psychothérapies mère-nourrisson dans les familles à problèmes multiples.* Paris: Presses Universitaires de France.

Tremblay-Leveau, H., and Nadel, J. (1995). Young children's communication skills in triads. *International Journal of Behavioral Development, 18* (2), 227–242.

Trevarthen, C., and Hubley, P. (1978). Secondary intersubjectivity: Confidence, confiding and acts of meaning in the first year. In A. Lock (ed.), *Action, Gesture and Symbol. The Emergence of Language* (pp. 183–229). New York: Academic Press.

Vogel, E. F., and Bell, N. W. (1960). The emotionally disturbed child as the family scapegoat. In N. W. Bell and E. F. Vogel (eds.), *A Modern Introduction to the Family* (pp. 382–397). New York: Free Press.

Walker-Andrews, A. S. (1988). Infant's perception of the affordances of expressive behaviors. In C. Rovee-Collier and L. P. Lipsitt (eds.), *Advances in Infancy Research* (Vol. 5, pp. 173–221). Norwood, NJ: Ablex Publishing Corporation.

Weakland, J. H. (1960). The "double bind" hypothesis of schizophrenia and three-party interaction. In J. D. Jackson (ed.), *The Etiology of Schizophrenia* (pp. 373–388). New York: Basic Books.

Wolff, P. H. (1969). The natural history of crying and other vocalizations in early infancy. In B. M. Foss (ed.), *Determinants of Infant Behavior* (Vol. 2, pp. 113–139). London: Methuen.

Wynne, L. S., Ryckoff, I. M., Day, J., and Hirsch, S. I. (1958). Pseudo-mutuality in the family relationships of schizophrenics. *Psychiatry, 21* (2), 205–220.

Yogman, M. W. (1982). Development of the father–infant relationship. In H. E. Fitzgerald, B. M. Lester, and M. W. Yogman (eds.), *Theory and Research in Behavioral Pediatrics* (Vol. 1, pp. 222–279). New York: Plenum Press.

CHAPTER 1

The Lausanne Family Model: An Overview

In this chapter we provide an overview of the entire model. Figure 1.1 shows its makeup. The central organizing perspective of the model is the functional/clinical reading of the family alliances. The three microanalytic readings respectively lay the structural, dynamical, and developmental foundations of the typology. Finally, the reading of the observer/consultant–family interactions opens up the prospects for interventions.

THE FUNCTIONAL/CLINICAL READING OF TRILOGUE PLAY AND THE TYPOLOGY OF FAMILY ALLIANCES

Recall that we are after a functional/clinical typology of family alliances. In observing the family in real time and using our common sense, intuition, clinical experience, and knowledge of the LTP task, we assess whether the family is working together and helping each other. Therefore, our first order is to understand as fully as possible what is involved in this task (Corboz-Warnery, Fivaz-Depeursinge, Gertsch-Bettens, and Favez, 1993).

As stated in the Prologue, the task consists of family play. Its goal is to playfully enjoy each other as a threesome (Stern, 1974), within the confines of the Lausanne triadic play (LTP) and "on stage." The scenario is in four configurations linked by transitions. Each configuration and each transition

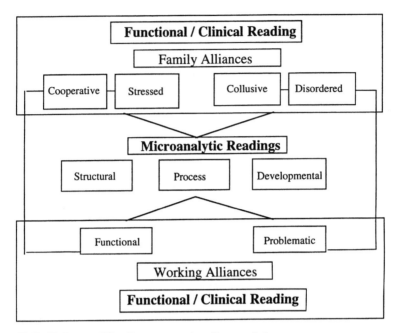

FIGURE 1.1   The Lausanne family model

provides a different vantage point on the same family's interactions. In addition, the play does not evolve in a vacuum but in a clinical research context. Therefore, the task not only includes family interaction per se but family interaction under observation. But let us leave out what is involved in working "on stage" for a separate reading, later in this chapter, and analyze the LTP task.

THE LAUSANNE TRIADIC PLAY SCENARIO

There are four facets to a triangle: three "two plus ones," when two are together and the third one is on the periphery, and a single "three together," when the three are coacting. As described above, we have arranged these four facets along a natural line to provide a scenario for a narrative-like trilogue play.

We can begin by placing four blocks corresponding to the four configurations (see Fig. 1.2). These facets imply many things: a positional arrangement of the three partners, an episode in time, some kind of triangular intentionality shared by the parents and the researchers. But these facets are also ordered according to a given succession, with either father or mother coming first as the active parent. Thus, we refer to them as *configurations* when wishing to underscore these properties and *parts* when it is this order that is more important for the description.

Imagine you are the parents and you have been introduced to the setting. In particular, you have been shown how to adjust the infant's seat inclination and how to turn the table. Your eight-week-old baby has been placed in the baby seat on the table and you are seated roughly facing her. You have received the Lausanne triadic play (LTP) instructions (see Appendix B) and memorized the succession of the four playing configurations: (1) one of you with baby, the other one on the periphery; (2) switching roles; (3) the three of you together; (4) the two of you together and baby on the periphery. Finally, you know it is up to you to decide how to orient the seat, when to change parts and terminate the play, and which one of you will play first with your child.

First, you are going to make practical decisions: who is starting and whether and how to turn the table. Perhaps as father, you might prefer mother to begin—to delay exposing yourself until after you have seen how mother, the "pro," handles the situation. Or perhaps you prefer to get it over with. Or you are eager to show how great you are at playing with your daughter. In any case, you have to move quickly, because you know that your baby's attention span is limited. The manner of these decisions reveals much about the coordination between the parents. The natural hesitation may be quickly resolved, perhaps dealt with humorously; or it may be the first subtle cue of some tension between the parents.

Part 1: Mother–Baby Plus Father

Let us say mother begins. She and your baby quickly become so entranced in their play that you forget about the cameras too and let yourself get caught up in the dance, taking care not to make your affective participation too conspicuous so that you do not distract the baby. At some points, the three of you laugh or sigh together. During a pause, your baby turns to you, smiling, and you are tempted to move in. Yet, playing by the rules, you turn engagingly to mother in order to redirect the baby's attention to her. Mother gratefully acknowledges your move with a comment to baby: "Oh, wouldn't you love to play with Dad? . . . His turn will come!"

One way to define the task of the third-party parent is to be a participant observer. Clinicians are familiar with the demands of participant observa-

4

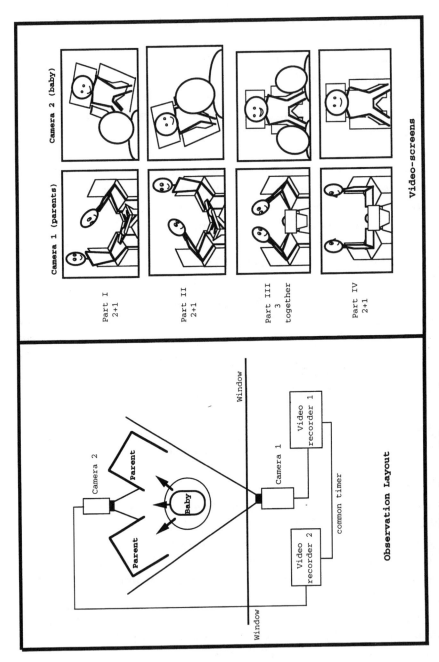

FIGURE 1.2   The LTP setting and four parts

tion. Attaining and maintaining a stance that is both empathic and noninter-fering is no simple matter—in some ways it is more difficult for a coparent than for a professional. Likewise, improvising under the eyes of a close, fa-miliar partner requires some detachment from the context.

There are, to be sure, individual differences in personality or style that make it more or less comfortable for parents to assume one or the other po-sition. Yet, beyond these, mutual influences are at play between the third party and the dyad's members. Smooth dyadic play facilitates noninterfer-ing empathy whereas difficult dyadic play puts it to the test.

Indeed, what about the task of the infant? Certainly it requires some adap-tation to adjust to the new setting and to meet unknown people. Whereas three-month-old infants usually are interested in the novelty, eight-week-old babies are more dependent on their current state and vary more in their abil-ity to adapt.

In any case, when operations run smoothly on both sides, feedback is gen-erated: The noninterfering empathy of the third party will continuously rat-ify and enhance the dyadic process, and vice versa. Likewise, failures on either side will increase the likelihood of missteps, which in turn are bound to register with the other party. For instance, imagine a baby's reluctance to play on that particular day; or a parent's repeated awkward stimulations of the baby; or a third-party mother letting her affective resonance overflow to the point of distracting the baby, if not the father, or plainly interfering and showing contempt. Careful observation reveals the influence of these pat-terns on the other parties.

Note that the physical setting enhances the triangular effect. The closeness in itself heightens affective resonance; in particular, and in spite of facing their baby more directly than each other, the parents are close enough to continuously detect each other's moves through peripheral vision. At first sight, it would be easy for an observer to construe the two-plus-one config-uration as a twosome, forgetting that the presence of a third party makes it a threesome that has to work together.

Part 2: Switching to Father–Baby Plus Mother

We will have ample opportunities to continue imagining the father's reac-tion when his turn has come to play. It is not infrequent that in this second part the baby is less excited and engaged, regardless of who is her partner; she may be tired or merely bored. This situation provides observers with a different perspective on the family. How do the parents deal with a less involved, perhaps even negative, baby? Still supposing it is father's turn to play, will mother as third party really entrust him to deal with the situation? Or will she feel an urgent need to help out, taking the risk of interfering? Or will she feel like withdrawing, perhaps precisely in order not to interfere, but then abandoning the father to his difficult task?

Part 3: Father–Mother–Baby

At some point, you, let us say father, as the previously "active parent" (the one who was playing), have sensed that your daughter is tired and have suggested the three-together play. Mother has reengaged and soon you both experience how narrowly you coordinate your moves, almost as if you were a single person in spite of the baby's selecting only one face at a time to look at! Then comes the other parent's turn, perhaps when the mother takes one of baby's hands and suggests that father take the other one. Soon enough the three of you are dancing and laughing together.

For observers, the three together adds yet another dimension to the triangular process: the direct interaction between three partners. It is noteworthy that it is more complex than the two plus one: Matching and synchronizing the acts of three direct partners requires a much higher number of coordinations. It follows that this configuration is most prone to false steps or "miscoordinations" and most sensitive to distress and conflict between the partners.

Indeed, as a result of the symmetry between the parental roles, the three together allows us to observe clearly the cooperation between the parents to engage the infant, perhaps their competition for exclusive interaction with her, or even the plain confusion in coordinating their actions. The obviously asymmetrical nature of the interaction between parent and infant introduces a bias in the three together. It is only potentially that the infant has an equal say, yet it tells much about the infant's investment in interacting with both parents. As a matter of fact, infants as young as twelve weeks enjoy the challenge; that is, if the parents (1) clearly display their conjoint availability and (2) flexibly accept the temporary selection that their child makes by orienting herself toward one or the other. On the other hand, young infants are easily stressed in conditions of parental competition or disorganization. Thus, the three-together configuration is the most complex in the family process and therefore highly significant clinically as well as developmentally.

Part 4: Mother–Father Plus Baby

With father and mother directly interacting and baby watching, we return to a two-plus-one configuration, this time with baby in the third-party position. The process is more complex in this configuration than in the previous two plus ones. On one hand, the infant's watching has a different status than the adults' watching. Very young babies will often devote most of their efforts to self-regulating and will possibly even need momentary direct help. Nevertheless, they also frequently attain a watching stance. The best conditions are when the parents engage in a lively interaction with each other. It makes the scene more enticing for the infant. On the other hand, the parents have to maintain their caring for their child's well-being in addition to, and in spite of, having to constitute a separate dyad. Moreover, triangular influences are still at play. In short, this part is the most sensitive to the dialectics by which the parents and the infant create boundaries between their subsystems, and multilaterally negotiate their potentially conflictual tasks.

To summarize, we can consider that the four configurations of the scenario are indeed four facets of family interactions. Both the two-plus-one and the three-together configurations include multilateral influences. Their sequencing in four parts provides the backbone of a narrative-like play trilogue. There is yet another element built into the scenario: the transitions between configurations.

TRANSITIONS

Parts imply transitions; how the partners move from a part to the next—for instance, from a two plus one to a three together—is intrinsic to the scenario. Imagine the family going from mother interacting with baby, with father watching, to all three interacting together; the manner of the transition tells much about how the parents minutely coordinate in order to switch from complementary to symmetrical roles. Likewise, the family going from the three interacting together to father and mother in direct interaction, with baby watching, tells much about how they coordinate in order to "separate" into parents/infant subsystems. The objective is to change configurations smoothly and clearly while keeping the interaction going.

Remember, the parents are free to change configurations when they want. Therefore, they need to warn each other of their readiness to change and ratify this plan before actually implementing it. Moreover, if they want the infant to understand what is expected of her, they have to make the change contingent on her readiness and make their own moves clear. Suppose that the third-party parent enters prematurely, without having obtained previous ratification from the active parent; the move is likely to be perceived by the coparent as an interference rather than as a proposition to change, with all kinds of consequences not only for the parents (from repair to plain retaliation) but also for the infant (stress and confusion).

Practically, these sequences are rather brief (about fifteen to thirty seconds) and clearly marked, which is our concern here, but later in the chapter we return to transitions in greater depth in the process reading section. There we uncover a microcosm with definite steps and coordination requirements that are extremely demanding.

To this point, we have dissected the LTP in parts and transitions in order to more fully understand it. Now it is necessary to put the pieces back together. Indeed, the play may be viewed as listening to the family telling their story together. The questions of interest are: Does this story-line contour stand out clearly or is it fuzzy, perhaps plainly flat? Is the story line continuous or does it suffer breaks or a deadlock? Are the high points neatly brought about, with the gradations that make the story more captivating, or are they abrupt? In this process it is essential to look for our own echoes to the family's affective communication as they progressively draw this story line of their play.

ASSESSING FAMILY ALLIANCES

The analysis of the LTP task clearly demonstrates that the three partners have to continuously work together as a team if they are going to attain the goal of trilogue play. They do not have to be perfect at all times, but they must "play it together," for better or for worse. The other issue is how the partners help each other in their capacities of framing versus developing parties: Are the parents guiding the infant and adequately facilitating his engagement given his state and his developmental stage? Is the infant responding to his parents' solicitations in a state- and stage-appropriate way and thus driving his parents?

The answers to these two questions lead to the quality that radiates from all the family interactions. We know from systems theory that the interactions between the elements of a system generate a new, unique property that is irreducible to its parts. It is sustained as long as the interaction lasts. And as long as it lasts, it will in turn contextualize the interactions of the elements. We assume that the two-faced quality of working together and helping each other is this emergent property.

The terms that capture the different qualities of the family alliances are *cooperation, stress, collusion,* and *disorder*. The cooperative and stressed alliances, A and B (see Fig. 1.3), are "good enough" in that the observer definitely has a sense that the family is working together as a team. Moreover, the parents are on the same track in framing the infant and the infant is driving them in a confrontational or straightforward way. This constitutes a favorable, protective context for a child's adaptation and a family's development. In contrast, the collusive and disordered alliances, C and D (see Fig. 1.3), are problematic in that the observer senses more obstruction than cooperation. Rather than working as a team, the family appears divided. It is as if the parents were working against each other and thus capturing the infant in a detouring coalition or excluding him. The problematic family alliances constitute a restricted, unfavorable context that puts the infant's socioaffective adaptation at risk. It prevents the parents from using their intuitive parenting skills effectively.

The differences between the cooperative and the stressed alliances mostly pertain to the challenge the family faces in working together and helping each other. In cooperation, liveliness and grace prevail over adversity, so the line of the play is well contoured, leading to many moments of playful mutual enjoyment. Suppose the infant happens to confront the parents rather than directly engage in play. Then humor will still prevail. When stress predominates, there are obstacles to harmony: A sharp difference in parental styles, a parent's respect for authority verging on fear, a sense of provocation in submitting to the procedure, an infant's refusal to engage that pushes the parents to their limits—all of these make it harder to work together and help each other. Grace yields to bravery. The line of the play is marked by accidents, but they will eventually be overcome, indicating that the partners kept up with their goal and positivity prevailed.

The differences between the collusive and disordered alliances pertain to the extent of the family's conflict. Collusion refers to a coalition of the par-

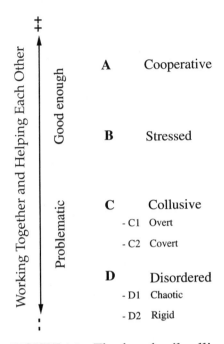

FIGURE 1.3   The four family alliances

ents to detour their unnegotiated conflict onto the infant. This coalition may be obvious, played out in a hostile, confrontational way (C1), or it may be hidden, played out covertly (C2). But in both cases, the result is the same: The infant is forced into a go-between or scapegoat position. The line of play is fragmented, marked by numerous interruptions, as if the theme had switched from working toward playful mutual enjoyment to overt or covert competition. Negativity prevails, though it is hidden by a civil front. As for disorder, it adds ambiguity to collusion. The observer is confused as solicitations to engage are mixed with withdrawal and exclusion. The line of play may be more chaotic (D1) or rigid (D2). It is utterly disconnected, no goals are detectable, and the play ends up in a breakdown or a deadlock. Affect is distinctly negative, though it may be covered up with pseudopositivity.

STRUCTURAL READING:
COCONSTRUCTING A TRIANGULAR FRAMEWORK

Remember that in the structural reading we map the family's nonverbal interactions in each part of the LTP, checking them against a model we have elaborated by means of microanalysis. We ask: Does the interactive framework a family has constructed advance playful mutual enjoyment or does it more likely impede it? In this way, we lay the structural foundations of the family alliances.

COCONSTRUCTING THE FRAMEWORK

Suppose your baby is sitting in his baby seat. He is cooing and you cannot resist approaching him to get into a round of dialogue play with him. You have spontaneously and automatically executed a number of nonverbal acts to help establish and sustain dialogue. H. and M. Papousek have extensively studied these phenomena (Papousek and Papousek, 1987), called "intuitive parenting behaviors," in order to underscore their biological foundation. Some of them are known in ethology as "signals of readiness to interact" (Stern, 1981) and were shown to be disturbed in the transactions between psychotic parents and their infants (Fivaz-Depeursinge, 1991). It is very likely that you have first placed your body at the specific distance for dialogue—closer with babies than with adults. You have also oriented your body inward to further adjust the distance at shoulder and face levels to present your face, still at dialogue distance. And meeting your baby's gaze, you have greeted him and he is engaged in matching interactions, the two of you exchanging smiles, frowns, vocalizations, and so on.

On close examination, it is apparent that these actions are much more complex than they first appear. They comprise several levels of interaction: (1) lower body, (2) upper body, (3) head and gaze, and (4) expressions. At each of these levels, the distances, orientations, and the other signals between you and your baby constitute formations (like birds or planes flying together) that define the interaction as a framework for dialogue.

When we introduce a third partner to the interaction, it may transform this dyadic framework into a triangular one. If you are not willing to include the third partner, you simply ignore him. No words are necessary; he will get the message. The framework remains dyadic. However, if you are willing to let him join in, he will know it immediately because you will modify the geometry of the interaction space quite automatically: First, you open up the space delineated by the placement of your lower body in order to provide him with an access, making this space roughly triangular. At the same time, you turn, changing from the straight vis-à-vis to an orientation that also includes him in the interactional space. In the meantime, he also positions himself to participate, aligning his location and orientation on yours. In other words, you have conjointly changed the formation between your lower bodies in respect to your baby's placement to make it triangular.

In fact, this is the primary function that you have to fulfill if you are going to engage in trilogue play: coconstructing a formation to participate so that everyone is included in the interaction. In the LTP situation, this operation is deceptively simple: For the parents, it merely consists of placing the infant in his seat, seeing that he is appropriately supported and inclined; then the parents align themselves on their seats so that together they draw an equilateral triangle whose size fits the distance required for face-to-face communication with the infant. It is this triangle that provides the optimal access to each other, ensuring that everyone is included. Note that this formation remains unchanged throughout the LTP: Playing requires participation from the beginning to the end.

That participation is basic is further demonstrated by distorting the triangular formation. Envision a triangle of a different shape, say with the father's pelvis turned outward and away from the mother and the infant. Throughout the play, the message "one excluded" or "two minus one" is conveyed rather than "all included" or "three together." As part of the most long-lasting context, this message will color the meaning of all other signals, be they mutual gazes, greetings, smiles, or cries, that are exchanged within this participation formation. Or suppose the infant is excluded. For instance, we sometimes observe interactions in which the parents fail to appropriately adjust the inclination of their baby's seat, for various reasons; the result is a sagging infant unable to participate. Yet, failing to understand the cause of this disengagement, the parents are liable to attribute it to a rejection on the baby's part.

Participation is only the first necessary condition to achieve trilogue play. The second condition is organization: You need to further organize the space of participation for your respective roles. Returning to our first example of free play, if you prefer to watch father play and remain in the third-party position, you lean back as he leans forward. On the other hand, if you prefer to coact, you align with him by leaning forward at shoulder level—that is, within the global triangular formation for participation, you coconstruct together a specific triangular formation for role organization. This is also the case in the LTP situation except that the roles of active partners versus third party are assigned for each part. Again, it is deceptively simple. It is first implemented at the level of the torso. In the first two parts, namely mother–baby plus father and father–baby plus mother, the active parent leans forward and the third-party parent leans back. In the three together, the parents lean forward and align; in the father–mother plus baby, the parents sit back and turn to face each other. Accordingly, they draw triangular formations that are configuration specific: Whereas the triangle is equilateral in the three together, it is oblique in the two plus one.

These triangles ensure the best perception of roles and the best implementation of them. For instance, it is easier for a third-party parent to stay out and watch by sitting back; the active parent needs to be close to the baby in order to play and also to avoid distraction by the view of the other parent; the baby can best perceive who is his partner and who is not; and so forth. In contrast, envision mother as the active parent leaning close to her baby whereas father hardly sits back; in this context, it is only natural for the baby to avert from his mother (perceived as too close to be looked at) and perhaps turn to father (he is sitting at a distance more adjusted for dialogue), keeping father engaged with baby. The result is that father interferes with mother's role. If the pattern is long-lasting, it constitutes a formation disadjusted for organization: The roles are not clearly marked and are reversed. Furthermore, a disadjusted formation fails to facilitate the formation construction in the service of the other functions.

The torso formations are sustained over a given part: Their "time constants" are of the order of duration of a part that is roughly four times briefer than those of the pelvis formations, which last over the entire session. Therefore, the torso formations are embedded in the pelvis formations and they in turn will embed the formations at the next levels. In summary, the four formations of organization constitute the second necessary but not sufficient condition for trilogue. Because this level mainly defines the parents' roles, it may not come as a surprise that it is in families with unnegotiated conflict between the parents that we observe deformations of this triangle level.

Corresponding acts follow at the levels of gaze and head signals and emotional signaling. Each of them partakes in the constitution of new formations and of their articulation within the overall framework. At this point, the third function you have to fulfill is shared focal attention, whether in spontaneous trilogue situations or in the LTP: You need to coordinate your attention with that of your partners in order to focus together on the games that the active partners are playing. If one of the partners avoids the games, clearly the goal of trilogue play cannot be reached.

Finally, affective contact must be achieved in order to establish trilogue play. It involves the meeting of expressive signals such as facial expressions, vocalizations, and gestures that the partners address to each other and share. Note that this sharing may as well be empathetic, when the infant's affective state is disregulated, then direct, when he is ready to play. Yet it may occur that the parents fail to be available for mutual playful enjoyment because they have difficulties in coordinating their signals with the infant or with each other. In this case, the goal of trilogue play cannot possibly be reached.

The higher we move in the framework, the more complex and the more variable in time are the signal exchanges, in that more exquisite and fine-tuned coordinations are required. The four types of formations that serve the four functions (see Fig. 1.4) at the four different levels of interaction constitute the triangular framework. Its treelike structure determines the directions of influences. On one hand, all levels of interactions and all formations are connected and therefore influence each other. On the other hand, the force of their influence depends on their place in the hierarchy: stronger from participation to affective contact than from affective contact to participation.

ASSESSING THE FRAMEWORK

The framework provides a blueprint for observing and assessing functional versus dysfunctional family process. Indeed, it is this hierarchy that allows us to assess the level and degree of difficulty a family experiences in attaining trilogue play: The higher the level of coordination attained with respect to the formations that implement the four functions, the most likely it is that trilogue play will succeed.

In chapter 3, the assessment scheme derived from this model is presented. Basically, it categorizes the triangular interactions that manifest exclusion in the participation formations in the least coordinated type of frameworks—the "D frameworks"—namely those that characterize D (disordered) family alliances. It is primarily but not always in families with heavy parental psychopathology that we observe exclusion of one or the other partner from participating in trilogue play.

The family interactions that are coordinated for participation but not for organization are categorized in the "C frameworks" that characterize C (collusive) family alliances. It is mainly in families with unnegotiated conflict between the parents and problematic triangulation of the infant that we observe the interferences in roles that characterize this type of framework.

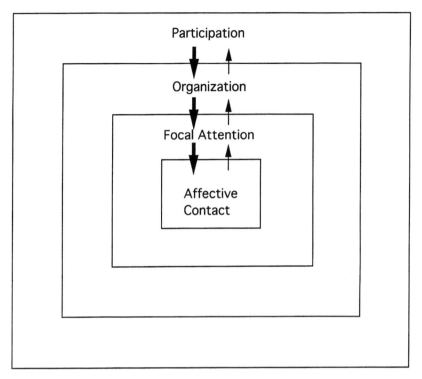

FIGURE 1.4   The hierarchical embeddedness of the four functions in the trilogue play.

The assessment scheme categorizes the interactions that manifest coordination for participation and organization but not for focal attention or affective contact in the "B frameworks." These interactions are mostly in the normal range and so are the ones that are coordinated for the four functions and categorized in the "A frameworks." B and A frameworks respectively characterize B and A family alliances (stressed and cooperative).

The ability to detect that a problem originates at a given level has both advantages and drawbacks. The advantage is the problem's relation to different levels of resources and difficulties is revealed. For instance, interfering with the coparent in a context of participation tends to be a matter of unnegotiated conflict, whereas the same process in a context of exclusion takes on much larger dimensions. The drawback is the reductionistic temptation: This categorization may be mistaken for a diagnostic device rather than for a global and clearly insufficient reading of the interaction. The most important information it provides is that a problematic formation originating at a given level sets the stage for additional problems at the next levels.

We end up with a graphical representation of this structure that is specific to each family alliance. It allows us to answer whether the triangular framework facilitates mutual playful enjoyment and, if not, where it derails. We discuss this issue further in Chapter 3.

Whereas the notion of hierarchy captures the ordered nature of the framework, it does not adequately convey its flexibility. As we are about to discover with the second microanalytic reading, the partners continuously and actively sustain the framework.

PROCESS READING:
COORDINATIONS, MISCOORDINATIONS, AND REPAIR

The brief sequences of play that require the most coordination are the transitions between the LTP configurations. How do the partners coordinate their actions from moment to moment? How do they miscoordinate their actions? How do they repair these false steps? Does the repairing help or does it amplify the miscoordinations? The processes of miscoordination and repair differentiate the family alliances.

What is the relation between structure and process? As Alan Fogel has stated, it may well be that rules are only inferred by the observer. They are "convenient metaphors that help us describe or label regularities" (Fogel, 1993, p. 13). Formations might actually result from a complex moment-to-moment process. A. Kendon insisted that formations are dynamic structures: Individuals partaking in a circular formation will compensate for each other's disalignments in order to maintain this spatial arrangement. Thus, in A. Fogel's terms, the "formation emerges spontaneously as a regular pattern" (Fogel, 1993, p. 11). From this perspective, formations are not only co-constructed but also coregulated; they are continuously (re) created and (re) elaborated over time. Coregulation provides us with a process reading of interaction. Consequently, it is our view that it takes the full understanding of the dynamics involved to be able to use productively the structural categorization we presented earlier.

Indeed, when we begin to search the moment-to-moment interaction for coregulation, we again uncover a universe of minute microprocesses. This world is most clearly revealed by "false steps," "errors," or "miscoordinations." Miscoordinations between partners are much more likely than smooth coordinations; after all, we are separate individuals. Consequently, as E. Tronick and his colleagues have emphasized, miscoordinations would not only be inherent in interaction but profitable for development; what counts is whether cooperative repair is initiated efficiently (Tronick and Cohn, 1989). Repair might reestablish the function or possibly amplify it.

Consider the following patterns of interaction: It may happen that the third-party parent, say the father, lets himself be "seduced" into engaging with his daughter as she happens to look at him. In itself this false step, or "organization error," which is a type of miscoordination, does not constitute a problem. What will make the difference is whether subsequent cooperative repair is initiated and proves effective. Father himself could initiate repair, trying to repilot the gaze of his daughter to her mother, or perhaps mother might protest and then accept father's repair without retaliation. In contrast, if repair is not initiated or effective, then the miscoordination would have generated a pattern of role interference, in turn advancing problems at the level of focal attention and affective contact. Suppose, for instance, that instead of initiating repair, mother gives in, letting father and daughter have their way in engaging in direct affective contact. In spite of mother's collusion, she may feel left out, with all due consequence. Or mother as third party might resonate so loudly to her daughter's joy in playing with father that she captures her into direct and lasting affect communion; father is thus left in the background in spite of his official role as active parent.

Steps in Transitions

A. Kendon was the pioneer in exploring these processes. Interestingly enough, he wondered how lovers sitting on a bench in a park coordinate their moves in kissing rounds (Kendon, 1976). The model behind the descriptions we are about to make owes much to his inspired work.

It should be emphasized that a smooth transition is so swift that it imposes itself on our perception as being obvious and simple. The coordinations that underly it go unnoticed. However, use your video-cassette recorder (VCR) slow-motion command and you will uncover a beautiful dance. Perhaps the easiest way to depict it is to start at the moment when the transition is actually being accomplished and then to go backward to examine how it has been prepared.

Take a family at the moment of moving from a two plus one—let's say mother playing with baby, and father watching—to the three together, that is, father, mother, and baby playing together. Mother, who was playing with baby, has backed away to make space for father to enter. Father has leaned forward a bit. At this point, baby is most likely looking elsewhere, pausing. (This is important because there was no interruption of gaze contact and the change to come will be contingent on baby's own initiative.) In this way, the three of them together have "deconstructed" the previous format. The parents then align their shoulders on each other, moving forward in concert to within dialogue distance of baby, ready to recapture her attention. At this point, they have "reconstructed" the interaction according to a new configuration, the three together; the parents are by now proposing this new framework to their child. The deconstruction and the reconstruction phases constitute the step of the actual transition.

How come the parents were able to execute this dance together at this precise moment? They "announced" and "ratified" the actual transition before implementing it. Let us move backward to this previous step. It might appear at first sight that a simple verbal announcement—"Let's move to part two"—and a verbal ratification—"Okay"—would suffice. Actually, this is not what we observe in most smooth transitions. In this preparatory moment, we observe that the partners also go through the moves of making a transition but in a weak edition. For instance, at the onset of baby's pause, mother may sit up a bit, father may move forward slightly, perhaps beginning to turn the table to set it in the middle. This phase corresponds with the ulterior deconstruction phase. Then comes the reconstruction phase but with a difference with respect to the ulterior reconstruction: They return to the previous two plus one, reconstituting it only for an instant. For example, mother may briefly reengage a round of dialogue with baby as father, about to finish fixing the table, watches benevolently. Together, these two phases constitute the preparatory step. Although these moves may well be associated with verbal announcements and ratifications, they are not always.

Why this preparatory step? For the time being, let us simply state first that this is the syntax of action, of nonverbal interaction; and second that this is a language that the baby can understand. And indeed, it is important for infants to be able to detect an interactional transition and learn how to make one. Chapter 4 discusses the notion that this step is a truly general phenomenon in social interactions.

How come the parents were able to execute this dance together at this precise moment? They preannounced the transition. Toward the end of the previous part, father as third party may have made a distinct circling body move as he was checking his watch, keeping track of time. Mother as active parent may have gotten the message, although at first it looked as if she did not: She was in fact engaging in a new, more intense round of play. But a bit later, she may have ratified father's move by addressing baby in baby talk: "Yes, you are going to play with your daddy, yes. . . ," and then, continuing to play, she may have addressed father in parallel, translating her sentence into adult talk. From this point, both parents knew they were ready to make the transition. They just had to wait until baby would give the signal, by pausing (or, at a later age, by deliberately turning to father).

But how would baby be in a position to anticipate that something different was about to happen? There are cues that may have contributed to moving her to a transition-ready state: First, perhaps she also perceived father's distinct move—in contrast with his most inconspicuous stance to that point; second, she may have heard her mother change from baby talk to adult talk; third, and most important, it is not unusual for play to close on an apex, for instance, a laugh shared not only by mother and baby but also by father, constituting a threesome affective event, which in this case is triangular. Here the threesome affective event has occurred at the precise boundary between the end of two-plus-one play and the onset of the transition step. Not only does this shared affect mark the closure of the previous part but it also marks the onset of something new, allowing the partners to proceed in step.

To summarize, the model of transitions just exposed comprises two main steps: the preparatory step and the actual transition step. Each step has two phases: deconstruction and reconstruction. In the first step, we obtain a weak edition of the transition, with a deconstruction that returns to the previous configuration. These two phases respectively stand for an announcement and a ratification. In the actual transition, it is the subsequent configuration that is reconstructed. In addition, main steps may be marked by affective events to mark boundaries. Finally, we can regress and find many events that preannounce the approach of the transition, until everyone is in a transition-ready state.

Interestingly, this sequence corresponds to the one that A. Kendon drew out of his study of "kissing rounds." In analyzing the interactions of lovers sitting outdoors on a bench, he noted that changing routines, such as going from kissing each other's necks or cheeks and touching noses to kissing each other's lips, was negotiated: Who would take the initiative, who would accomplish the approach, and what would be the type of routine was hinted at during a brief phase of involvement that preceded the routine itself. During this preparatory phase, the partner who would take the initiative in the next round would announce his or her approach and the other one would show his or her acceptance; for instance, he would sketch out an approach by means of a partial approach and she would tentatively lean her head on his shoulder, thus displaying her receptivity. It was the woman's facial expressions that determined the routine: When she displayed an "open smile," with her mouth and eyes open, the routine would be necking and touching; when she displayed a "closed smile," with lips and eyes closed, the routine would be kissing on the lips.

COREGULATION IN TRANSITIONS

By now it should not come as a surprise that this minute world of coordination is most vulnerable to tension and conflict. Accordingly, it opens up wide for the scrutiny of miscoordination and repair. Furthermore, as we stated at the outset, miscoordination and repair are indeed a normal and constructive part of the very work of coordination.

All the same, failing to execute the required steps in concert demands particularly swift repair during a transition. Otherwise, the specific moves simply miss the point. For instance, suppose father moves forward, in the belief that mother is in step, but she is not. She remains behind. Then father finds himself alone to face baby—he finds himself in a two plus one rather than in a three together. On noticing it, he might initiate a repair move; for instance, by calling for mother instead of continuing his own move, and mother might ratify his request by finally moving in. Or she may have noticed her own delay and moved in, and father might have waited for her, delaying the moment he would begin greeting baby. In both cases, the repair is cooperative. Effective repair requires reciprocity.

There are types of miscoordination that are more costly to repair. Referring to the above example, suppose that instead of father calling mother and waiting for her to return, he engages in play with baby, who might have just turned to him at this point, leaving mother behind. Returning to three together will take more effort and possibly the overcoming of bad feelings. Nevertheless, it may eventually work. However, the interaction has been interrupted and reestablishing smoothness will take more time, making the line of the play less neat. Here we are in the realm of the stressed alliances. At the next false step, the bad feelings may reemerge more strongly and repair may be replaced by a process of escalation. This type of miscoordination and repair is usually observed in families with collusive alliances. We recognize in these interactions the striking process of negative reciprocity that J. Gottman described in the interactions of unhappy couples (Gottman, 1994). We return to this phenomenon when we describe problematic interactions.

Finally, there are processes of major miscoordinations with ineffective repair that are continuously at work, in that the more the partners try to repair, the more they amplify the problems. We observe this scenario in families with disordered alliances and explore these issues further in Chapter 4.

DEVELOPMENTAL READING:
TRIANGULATION OVER THE FIRST YEAR

Recall that we reconsider the development of affective communication between parents and infant over the first year in three-person rather than two-person interactions. Working on representative events, we explain the respective contributions of the infant and his parents in the social and intersubjective domains. We ask if and how the infant handles the four triangles in his interactions in key emotional situations with his parents, and how the parents facilitate this handling. This reading allows us to differentiate the family alliances.

CLINICAL TRIANGLES IN THE LTP

Because it is in clinical thinking that triangles are most prominent, we can begin with how the triangular processes described by clinicians would look in the LTP. The following example illustrates triangulation as defined in the family process field.

Frankie, nine months, is playing with his mother under the disapproving eye of his father because father blames mother for having introduced a toy in the play in spite of the researchers' recommendation to try to play without objects, at least for a while. But now comes father's turn to play with the baby, whereas mother takes the role of third party. Father exclaims to Frankie: "Your mom has given you this toy. What am I going to do with it?" He grabs it and in a serious voice explains to the baby that, "One does not play like that with a toy. . . . One has to play carefully." The disagreement between the parents has been displaced to between father and Frankie. In addition, we know that not only is mother the accomplice of father but Frankie has by now developed skills in acting as the go-between in his parents' conflict. This is a classical example of triangulation used in the description of family process: The parents collude in including their child in an unnegotiated conflict, which in fact pertains only to them.

Let us now consider an example of psychodynamic triangulation—that is, the child's subjective experience of being excluded from his parents' relationship. As explained in the Introduction, R. Emde argued that whereas a child at the oedipal stage feels excluded from his parents' intimacy, prior to that stage an infant may feel excluded from his parents' relationship in different ways: from their domain of control or from their field of attention.

Mike, also nine months, has been playing with both his parents and now the parents have changed to interacting directly together, leaving him in the third-party position. He looks at length at his mother with surprise; then, with the same expression, he also takes a long look at his father. He whines. Finally, he comes into action. He leans forward, grabs his mother's knee, and tries to get her attention. Then he turns to father. These bids for attention to each parent in turn indicate that Mike feels excluded from the field of attention between them and acts accordingly.

Clearly, both these notions of triangulation are clinically pertinent. But, as stated in the Introduction, the problem with them is that they are partial. Triangular process does not pertain only to problematic inclusion or the experience of exclusion but also to "normal" inclusion, and in fact to inclusion in every possible figure in a three-way relationship. Thus, both of these situations lack foundation in a general theory of triangular process—that is, covering all permutations in a three-person relationship.

Take the example of the "swing threesome game" we observed at three months—the social stage—and at nine months—the intersubjective stage. (Families tend to ritualize their games and replay them over the first year, blessing us with the opportunity to see what precisely changes with age.) First, we may well observe that the baby will be the one to initiate the end of part two. Perhaps she will clearly put a stop to playing with mother, her active partner in that part, by insistently turning to father, touching his leg and brightly looking at him. Then she will make her intention of interacting with both clear by looking alternatively at mother and father and circling her legs. The parents will follow her cue and begin swinging her legs. After the first round, during the pause, she will thoughtfully look in turn at her mother and at her father to initiate the next round by pedaling with her legs.

This example illustrates another triangular process at work: including the third party, but in a functional context rather than in a problematic one, and leading to a three-together configuration (in which the infant is an active initiator; indeed, as infants recruit their new skills to coregulate triangular interaction, parents proportionally diminish their own control).

FAMILY TRIANGLES IN THE LTP

We also noted in the Introduction the importance accorded by the developmentalists to the triadic interactions that appear around nine months: Interactions between mother and infant about an object mark the advent of coordinated attention and referential communication about intentions, focuses of attention, and inner feelings. Perhaps the most studied of these processes is social referencing. In its experimental version, the infant is surprised by an event that she has trouble interpreting; she turns to read her mother's facial expression and acts according to her mother's response. When mother smiles reassuringly, baby proceeds; when mother's expression is negative, baby avoids the situation.

Imagine how social referencing might look in the LTP: The baby is surprised, say by an unexpected act of her father during trilogue. Perhaps mother and daughter were very much involved with each other and father tried to imitate mother's forceful style in order to introduce himself into the play. His act appeared awkward. Uncertain and somewhat fearful, daughter turns to look at her mother, searching for guidance in interpreting the event (social referencing). In the positive version, the mother smiles reassuringly and thereupon the baby reorients to her father and they all resume play. In a negative version, the mother, unnerved by father's awkward imitation, gives a negative look with a touch of contempt, and baby does not engage with father. Perhaps she resumes play with mother. Now, clearly, this event is inscribed in a network of dynamic relationships, and it makes a difference way beyond mother's response and baby's ensuing action: Among other things, father is actively excluded by a coalition between mother and daughter, which adds another step in the conflict between the parents–spouses; daughter develops a prototypic experience of being with her parents where father is excluded and invalidated by mother.

In addition, social referencing in everyday family process usually is accompanied by other key intersubjective processes, such as affect attunement, moral elaboration, affect sharing, and signaling. In the version where mother smiles reassuringly, she may add an affect attunement to let baby know that she knows how baby feels inwardly; for example, by translating baby's facial display of surprise or fear into a vocalization that she returns to baby; she may also address a humorous or affectionate message (affect sharing) to father, for repair. As the direct interaction resumes between father and baby and their animation rises, baby may briefly turn to mother in order to share her joy and then return to father (affect sharing). And the story goes on! This is the essence of intersubjective communion in the threesome.

In another negative version, the mother also smiles reassuringly; she also attunes to her daughter's inner feeling, but in an exaggerated manner that amplifies its negative tones and thus modifies her daughter's message ("modifying attunement"; Stern, 1985), to let her daughter know that she should inwardly feel more unnerved than what she has conveyed. There is probably also a message to father, but a disqualifying one. Here, it is less likely that the baby would reengage with father. And the story also goes on!

Note that these intersubjective processes are inherently triangular; they are continuously at work within the primary triangle and they uncover a complex interplay of influences. Moreover, they occur extremely rapidly, generally unnoticed by the subjects. We examine them in detail in Chapter 5 and see that the context in which they take on their meaning varies with the family alliances.

The introduction of a person as the third party instead of an object suddenly broadens the scope of the infant's emotional and psychic universe, making it immensely richer and more complex. Our task is to describe these interactions if we are going to have a clinically and developmentally pertinent theory of triangulation. But, as stated in the Introduction, there is even more to it. This is the world in which the infant lives and this world is there from the start. Consequently, what about the infant's handling of triangles before the advent of intersubjectivity and referential communication? Is there, as the classical view has it, a developmental line from the dyad to the triad? That is, does the infant learn to regulate dyadic interaction first, to progress to triadic (and perhaps triangular) interactions next? Or is this view an artifact of the setting in which adult–infant interaction has been studied up to now, excluding third parties (in particular, fathers), instead of building them into the situation? Chapter 5 examines in detail the cues to nonreferential, direct triangulation at the social stage.

When the infant is studied within the father–mother–infant triangle, a different view of development emerges, where the infant develops triangular interactions in parallel with dyadic ones (and possibly too in parallel with her relationship to herself and to objects; Trevarthen and Hubley, 1978). Indeed, the ethological skills infants use in dialogue play may be adequate for trilogue play, right from the beginning, even if they do stretch the infant's attention capacities (see Stern, 1985). Therefore, there may not be a reason to make a special developmental provision for trilogue.

REDEFINING TRIANGULAR PROCESS

We now propose a new definition of triangular process. Its goal is to preserve threesome relatedness in the midst of affectively loaded situations, such as harmony, uncertainty, and conflict. Triangulation is the handling of the four-configuration system in a three-person relationship. From the infant's perspective, these four triangles are the triangle of two with mother plus father; the triangle of two with father plus mother; the triangle of three with father and mother; the triangle of one (the infant herself) plus father and mother together.

Therefore, an infant's "triangular strategies" are precisely her manner of handling these four triangles by communications involving herself and her two partners. These triangular strategies manifest themselves in referential affect sharing and signaling and social referencing at the intersubjective stage, and in their prefigurations at the social stage. The parents validate their infant's bids for threesome relatedness in more or less differentiated ways, depending on the type of family alliance.

It is important to acknowledge that three-party relationships involve not only the interactional aspect of triangular process but its imaginary or mental counterpart. "Interactional triangular process" thus refers to the behavioral aspect of this process; its mental counterpart is the "imaginary triangular process." The interactional and the imaginary triangles work in close connection. Although the imaginary aspect is beyond our present scope, we want to mention that we owe much of the present reflection to collaborative research conducted in the interfaces study group (see Fivaz-Depeursinge et al., 1994), where experts in both domains attempt to conceptualize the connections between the interactional and the imaginary aspects. We discuss this important issue in Chapters 4 and 7.

THE READING OF OBSERVER–FAMILY WORKING ALLIANCES THAT LEADS TO FRAMING INTERVENTIONS

The focus of this study is on observing trilogue. However, it is the clinical research context in which the trilogue is observed that gives it its meaning. Therefore, functioning on stage is inherent in the task. With the reading of the observer–family interactions, we return to real-time observation and thus the connection with the functional/clinical reading of the family's interactions. We also recourse to elements of the microanalytic readings in scrutinizing a brief but significant sequence of their interactions. These assessments lead to the characterization of the working alliance between observer and family. Not surprisingly, it turns out that the working alliance is tinged with the nature of the family alliance. It is functional when the family alliance is cooperative or stressed (A and B) and difficult when the family alliance is problematic, namely collusive or disordered. In turn, the working alliance opens up the prospect of framing interventions, whether with volunteer families or clinical families. Finally, it poses the question of the effects of these framing interventions on the family alliance.

We elaborate on these issues in Chapters 6 and 7. As an introduction, let us revert to the observation of the LTP to examine how it may be experienced by the family. Then we examine the clinical and practical implications this experience has in designing the setting, conducting the session, and envisioning the relationship with the family.

FUNCTIONING ON STAGE

Playing out the drama between the family and the observers as "authority figures" is not only for father, mother, and baby to get close while having fun together; it is necessary to act within the confines of the LTP script for the benefit of the experts and in front of the silent audience of "ghosts," however benevolent or malevolent. As Fraiberg and coauthors stated, there are "visitors from the unremembered past of the parents; the uninvited guests at the christening." In the worst cases, these parent and grandparent figures have "taken up residence in the nursery." That is, they put the parent–infant relationship in peril by imposing the repetition of the tragedies from the childhood of the parents (Fraiberg, Adelson, and Shapiro, 1975, p. 387).

Playing out this drama comes in different versions according to the present disposition of the baby, the dynamics of the nuclear family, and its current relationships with the origin families and other significant milieus. And, as we want to emphasize here, it also relies on the actual relationship established with the team.

The volunteer families make the commitment to come to a clinical research center at a crucial time in their life cycle. They meet the experts, creatively play by their rules, authorize the experts to scrutinize their performance, and confront themselves with this performance. This situation is even more complicated for clinical families, in that their very label of "problem family" may be loaded with feelings of guilt. Hopefully, they will have a growth-enhancing experience for the benefit of their baby's well-being as well as their confidence as parents. Remember, parents of babies are highly motivated people.

In the best of cases and days, the drama turns into a success and a wholesome celebration: The characters allow themselves to cocreate a beautiful dance emanating from the LTP framework, to share pleasure and show it. Baby experiences pleasure and mastery in swinging, taking turns at vocalizing, charming his parents and the experts. The parents are proud of their child's performance and beauty—to be contemplated on TV with the observers, to be scrutinized by the experts. Probably, this story and video will be shared with extended family and friends. To be sure, this experience could be validating for everybody involved.

Yet baby might not be willing or able to cope on this particular day and time; perhaps he prefers showing up his autonomous fiber or he is preoccupied with a toothache. Then another version of the drama is played out, which is obviously not for the better. The parents are frustrated and perhaps are forced to end the task for the sake of their child. This situation may demand more support from the observers to show the parents the proper value of this experience.

To continue with distressed families, whether volunteer or clinical, say a couple going through a crisis, the drama takes on less positive tones and the tension rises. The burden of conflict has to be dealt with in some way, which will be felt by the baby and the audience. Many strategies are available, from containing the tension within the couple to spreading it around, drawing in the baby and the observers. The observers will have to rely on their clinical skills to help the family elaborate on the experience, adjusting the procedure to the parents' readiness. Then, whether the family is volunteer or clinical will make a difference in the way the observer/consultant intervenes.

Sometimes the malevolent ghosts of the family invade the stage, making it impossible for the characters to bond and work together. The question before the team is whether the experience is beneficial to the family and, if not, how to make it beneficial. Direct intervention may be needed to "scaffold" a family that is not sufficiently supported by the regular format and its relationship with the observer team.

THE WORKING ALLIANCE

Each scenario involves a different relationship between the observers and the family, and this is the key variable in the working alliance. Here, the family is part of a larger group that they form with the observers. This group is a system that evolves together. Like the parent–infant coevolutive system, it is composed of two subunits: the observer subunit, which functions as the framing party, and the family subunit, which now functions as the developmental party.

From this perspective, the observer–family interaction would indeed merit a study in its own right. But it would require a different setting, where the group of observers would also be observable under research conditions. However, we see in Chapter 6 that the LTP setting allows for systematically observing and microanalyzing the "preparation," a small piece of quadratic interaction between the facilitator/consultant and the family during the instruction and as they separate. It reveals the underpinnings of the working alliance.

Theoretically speaking, much has been said about the mutual influences between observer and subject. The aspects we wanted to make apparent in the previous descriptions are the importance of the working alliance and the fact that observation is a major intervention in itself, the consequences of which are considerable. Not only do we need to very carefully analyze the context in which families are observed but we also need to carefully design this context in order to facilitate trilogue as much as possible, given the constraints of scientific observation. We have an ethical contract to provide a context that furthers beneficial experiences and involves intervention if necessary. Our success in implementing these tasks must be carefully evaluated.

FRAMING THE FAMILY

The team is composed of a facilitator/consultant, assisted by a supervisor, and several researchers attending to the technical aspects. The physical setting is the most facilitative we could think of, ethologically and clinically speaking, which also meets the technical requirements of recording. As stated earlier, it is not a simple matter to obtain adequate records for micro-analysis of three people interacting.

The facilitator / consultant and her supervisor conduct the clinical operations: establishing a trusting relationship, "warming up" together with the family to the LTP, asking for feedback on the situation, and providing feedback on their performance. The overall session, whether defined as a research one (for volunteer, nonclinical families) or as a systems consultation (for clinical families brought by their therapists), follows the same order.

Gina's parents, who have volunteered for our study, come to our center when their baby is eight weeks old; they meet with the consultant, are shown into the lab, and feed their baby—a time to warm up and chat. When they feel ready, they are introduced to the setting and given the LTP instruction, and then they are left alone until, having concluded the play, they call the facilitator. After a pause for discussion between facilitator and supervisor, they all review the tape-recordings together, doing a "videoscopy," as S. Lebovici likes to call it (Lebovici, 1992). In this feedback session, the primary focus is on the parents' experience as subjects, the interrogations they might have, and comments on the infant's competences and the corresponding parents' intuitive parenting behaviors. The detection of where the working together and helping each other derails is of great help. It will determine the points of entry that the facilitator will select during the video review. At the end, they sign an authorization for the specific use of their video records and will later receive a copy of these records.

Suppose the observation has uncovered tension between the parents and distress in the infant. The art of the facilitator then resides in giving support and feedback adjusted to the often implicit demand of the parents. It is indeed our experience that a fair proportion of volunteer families come in with latent expectation of support. We describe these framing interventions in depth in Chapter 6.

When a clinical family and their therapist(s) come in, the therapeutic team is invited to assist the entire observation and to formulate a focus for the ensuing consultation; the observer team addresses the issue during the reviewing of the tapes with the family and the team. We conceptualize this review as a therapeutic systems consultation in that we may choose to intervene while also attempting to provide feedback that takes into account the interaction between the family and the accompanying therapeutic team. We describe detailed examples of systems consultations in Chapter 7.

Observing a new family in trilogue is always a fascinating and emotionally loaded experience that may also cause us to question our own ways. We readily see ourselves in the position of neutrally benevolent grandparents, whether we act as mere facilitators or as clinical consultants. In a way it is quite similar to the task of the parents in respect to the child. To facilitate the implementation of the LTP implies a readiness to frame or scaffold the family—however benevolent or malevolent their "ghosts" may be. The amount of support needed is a vital indication of the nature and intensity of the treatment required.

REFERENCES

Corboz-Warnery, A., Fivaz-Depeursinge, E., Gertsch-Bettens, C., and Favez, N. (1993). Systemic analysis of father–mother–baby interactions: The Lausanne triadic play. *Infant Mental Health Journal 14*(4), 298–314.

Fivaz-Depeursinge, E. (1991). Documenting a time-bound, circular view of hierarchies: A microanalysis of parent–infant dyadic interaction. *Family Process, 30*(1), 101–120.

Fivaz-Depeursinge, E. Stern, D. N., Bürgin, D., Byng-Hall, J. Corboz-Warnery, A., Lamour, M., and Lebovici, S. (1994). The dynamics of interfaces: Seven authors in search or encounters across levels of description of an event involving a mother, father, and baby. *Infant Mental Health Journal*, 15 (1), 69-89.

Fogel, A. (1993). Two principles of communication. Coregulation and framing. In J. Nadel and L. Camaioni (eds.), *New Perspectives in Early Communicative Development* (pp. 9–22). London: Routledge.

Fraiberg, S., Adelson, E., and Shapiro, V. (1975). Ghosts in the nursery. *Journal of American Academic Child Psychiatry, 14*, 387–421.

Gottman, J. M. (1994). Why marriages fail. *The Networker* (May–June), 41–48.

Kendon, A. (1976). Some functions of the face in a kissing round. *Semiotica, 15*(4), 299–334.

Lebovici, S. (1992). *En l'homme, le bébé.* Paris: Eshel.

Papousek, H., and Papousek, M. (1987). Intuitive parenting: A dialectic counterpart to the infant's integrative competence. In J. D. Osofsky (ed.), *Handbook of Infant Development,* 2nd ed. (pp. 669–720). New York: Wiley.

Stern, D. N. (1974). The goal and structure of mother–infant play. *Journal of the American Academy of Child Psychiatry, 13*, 402–421.

Stern, D. N. (1981). The development of biologically determined signals of readiness to communicate, which are language "resistant." In R. E. Stark (ed.), *Language Behavior in Infancy and Early Childhood* (pp. 45–62). North-Holland: Elsevier.

Stern, D. N. (1985). *The Interpersonal World of the Infant.* New York: Basic Books.

Trevarthen, C., and Hubley, P. (1978). Secondary intersubjectivity: Confidence, confiding and acts of meaning in the first year. In A. Lock (ed.), *Action, Gesture and Symbol. The Emergence of Language* (pp. 183–229). New York: Academic Press.

Tronick, E. Z., and Cohn, J. F. (1989). Infant–mother face-to-face interaction: Age and gender differences in coordination and the occurrence of miscoordination. *Child Development, 60*, 85–92.

CHAPTER 2

The Functional/Clinical Reading of Narratives That Results in a Typology of Alliances

In the functional/clinical reading, the goal is to capture the quality that radiates from the partners' interactions in order to identify the family's type of alliance: cooperative, stressed, collusive, or disordered. The partners are continuously assessed to determine whether they are working together and helping each other while following the progression of the play. Intuition and common sense are essential, as well as the intimate knowledge of how families travel the course of the Lausanne triadic play (LTP).

This chapter presents commenting narratives of four constructed interactions prototypic of the four alliances. Mike and his parents, representing the cooperative alliance, go through the motions of the procedure with grace, allowing us to picture how a smooth and beautiful play may emerge, and spell out the work it involves. We recognize in Nancy's family the effects of a considerable, if normative, complementarity in parental style corresponding to the stressed alliance. We recognize in Frankie's family the influence of irrepressible parental competition that characterizes the collusive alliance. The tension and conflict in Tania's family divert from the goal of establishing playful mutual enjoyment and disorganize the interaction to the point of chaos and absurdity. Before proceeding with these narratives, we present a brief scheme to guide this assessment.

HOW TO ASSESS THE FAMILY ALLIANCE FROM A FUNCTIONAL/CLINICAL PERSPECTIVE

The scheme consists of assessing each of the successive configurations and transitions as they unfold, and wrapping them up in an overview. The following questions are answered:

1. In observing each configuration and transition, and in looking at the family as a unit, do we get the sense that they work as a team or that they are divided?

2. In observing each configuration and transition, but then in looking at the framing and developing parties, do we get the sense that the parents work together, as a solid coparenting subunit, and that the infant is both following and driving them? Or are the parents working against each other, and in which position is the infant?

3. Taking in the evolution of the play in time, what is the overall affective climate? Does positivity and playfulness prevail over negativity, even in the face of the infant's adverse reaction? Or does negativity take over, either openly or under a civil front?

Finally, in looking over the sequencing of the configurations and transition from the beginning to the end, do we get the sense of a clearly contoured story line, with high points neatly brought out and then faded? Or is the story line broken or not perceivable?

With these interrogations in mind, the good-enough family alliances can be differentiated from the problematic family alliances, as well as the cooperative from the stressed ones and the collusive from the disordered ones. The difference between the cooperative and the stressed resides in the free-flowing and steady versus the somewhat rough or unsteady nature of the patterns, in the face of the challenges confronting the family as they coordinate their actions.

The difference between collusion and disorder is related to the extent of the division. Collusion entails division in the coparenting party and, as a consequence, an overt or covert detouring coalition for the infant. In addition, disorder entails a sense of confusion or perplexity conveyed by the mutual exclusion between the partners yet in parallel with their straining to cooperate.

In good-enough family alliances the family members are helping each other in their capacities of framing and developing parties. The infant is engaged and driving. Positivity and playfulness prevail over negativity and the story line is contoured and continuous.

In problematic family alliances the family is basically split and the framing and developing parties fail in helping each other. The coparenting subunit is divided and the infant is on the defensive. Negativity prevails, be it open or covered up, and the line of the play is flat or going downwards, fragmented or even winding up in a deadlock.

MIKE'S FAMILY: A COOPERATIVE ALLIANCE

Mike's family gracefully plays together, making their dance look deceptively simple. However, when examined closely, the amount of coordination involved in the face of the inevitable false steps and likely divergences in a three-party interaction is impressive.

NARRATIVE

The father is a mechanic and the mother is a secretary. As a nonclinical, volunteer family, they are simply open to collaborating with the study if it may be of help to their family as well as to others.

Mike is a very attractive, active, and expressive three-month-old with a happy disposition. As the facilitator closes the door, mother, who plays first, immediately makes contact with Mike.

Father follows the dyadic interaction closely, by looking mainly at Mike; the highs and lows of the dyad can be seen on his face, because he is continuously resonating to their interaction. Yet in spite of the wide variations in affect tone that we will observe in the dyad, father continuously maintains his benevolent mirroring albeit noninterfering stance.

The play between mother and Mike is very close and intense indeed. There is a lot of affective sharing and almost no pauses. Mother, although sensitive to Mike's cues, gives him little time to recuperate. And Mike intently tries to keep up with her, averting only briefly. But with many returns to highs, on the whole, his vocalizations progress toward more lows. The end of their play naturally takes place in this evolution.

It is typically after a most intense high of affectionate sharing that Mike switches to more distinct complaining, thus triggering the transition. "Oh, yes, you are going to cry with your daddy. Oh, yes, we are going to see whether it works with him [stressed tone]. . . . Hey, baby!" says mother, and Mike is crying. She sits up and turns to father with a mock guilt expression. Both take the time to laugh together, apparently not troubled by their child's crying. Only then does father lean toward Mike.

Mother, now the third party, sits back and, like father in the previous part, continuously keeps in touch and resonant with the dyad. Father and Mike have readily engaged in a vocal dialogue: "Ya, tell your miseries to your daddy." Father progressively integrates an imitation game of tongue protrusion. We observe a progressive deescalation of Mike's agitation, accompanied and sustained by father's stepwise changes in voice tonality.

The episodes of threesome affective sharing follow each other to an apex like a firework, with continuing resonance, yet with brief reminders of the previous distress. The pauses are few and rather brief. The episodes have various themes (clicking tongue, sticking out tongue, vocalizing, pushing for bowel movement). In the final fireworks, Mike progresses to laughter, rejoined by his parents.

Then they recede and father concludes by congratulating Mike. He adds: "What are we going to do now? Are we going to let you by yourself for a short moment?" (He has doubts about which part comes next and is also requesting mother's help.) Mother reminds him of the three-together part and, an instant later, the parents synchronously move to play together and Mike reorients toward them in the typical way of infants in part three: rapidly looking back and forth toward either parent.

This part is commanded by Mike's relative indisposition to play. Accordingly, the aim switches from playfulness to regulating the infant's state. For a while, Mike stays on edge; he works hard, but his generous vocalizing progressively turns to fussiness. The parents set out to help him, each holding or caressing Mike's hand and smiling; they synchronously address him, albeit in somewhat different styles: Father mostly imitates Mike's vocalizations, whereas mother talks to him; the impression is that of a rich, multimodal, synchronous, and attuned accompaniment that is intense yet not overstimulating.

After a while, Mike tries to comfort himself by bringing his hand to his mouth several times; when he does not succeed in keeping it in, he becomes fussy. But the parents continue encouraging him to try again. From there on, the cooperation between the parents becomes more complementary. Mother holds out the pacifier to Mike (father exclaims: "This is cheating!" for the parents apparently think that this is contrary to the rules of the LTP and they keep trying to distract Mike from it). This scene is particularly impressive: father doing a "vocal/suck" dialogue with Mike, imitating his sucking sounds very skillfully and carrying him along, while mother inconspicuously withdraws the pacifier and Mike tries to replace it with his own hand, to no avail. On receiving the pacifier again, Mike vigorously sucks on it and keeps it, in spite of his parents' renewed attempts to draw it away. Actually, it helps him to calm down, reengage in a "vocal/suck" dialogue with father, and eventually even attend to mother for a little while.

The transition itself is triggered by a sharp gaze aversion by Mike. Mother announces: "We are going to take leave of you." Father: "We are going to leave you for two minutes, darling." Mike reorients toward mother and then toward father. Mother adjusts the pacifier with her left hand.

Soon afterward, the parents are sitting up, looking at each other and facing each other. Mike is calm, sucking, with an unfocused gaze. After a brief comment on how hard this task of "ignoring" Mike is, the couple playfully engage in a dialogue. The main topic is their agenda of the day. They make plans; they are animated and more and more involved. Their dialogue is intermingled with short comments on Mike's state; their monitoring of him is amazingly synchronized with their dialogue.

For a while, Mike appears content to suck on his pacifier and to slowly recuperate. Then he starts to vocalize, becoming more active; as he happens to drop the pacifier, breathing hard, he succeeds in overcoming the loss by sucking on his lips and concentrating on manipulating the belt of the seat. He continues to emerge from drowsiness, eventually focusing on his parents. Soon afterward, mother sits up and announces: "Okay, let's tell Ms. X that we are finished . . . ," and father answers, "Okay." Having briefly reengaged with Mike, mother then turns to the observation room and calls for the facilitator.

Working Together and Helping Each Other

From the onset of the mother–Mike plus father play, the family is clearly working together in a highly intense, resonant style that fits in with the physical closeness between them. It is all the more remarkable in the face of the variations in tonality in the mother–baby dyad. Globally, the affective involvement is optimal. No opportunities for affective contact are missed, either when Mike is agreeable or toward the end when he is more restless. The two-plus-one organization holds throughout.

Perhaps most striking is the closeness yet clear boundaries between the parties. By virtue of its very noninterference, the third-party father's intense but contained resonance can in no way be incriminated in amplifying the varying tonality of the twosome's play. On the contrary, it may well contribute to its regulation. Mother and Mike are continuously in close and intense touch, and this very resonance requires much regulation on the part of the infant, even stretching it to its limits. Indeed, by clinical standards, it would be regarded as moderate hyperstimulation.

In the face of the intense style of the dyad, the solidarity between the parents plays a major role. Its interplay with the infant's active attitude generates a continuously positive cooperation in the threesome.

The way the parents have negotiated the transition between parts one and two shows their capacity to overcome a potential conflict with humor and cooperation. The interplay between the parents' solidarity and the infant's positive stance toward recovery and play continues to give evidence of the constant cooperation in the threesome.

During the father–Mike plus mother play, the family continues working together; the affective participation is optimal. The two-plus-one organization holds, making repair unnecessary.

The third-party mother's intense and overtly contained resonance in no way interferes with the dyad's play. It supports it in a highly empathic style, which is furthered by the notably successful recovery of Mike and the amazingly attuned dialogue with father. Indeed, more than mother as active parent, father is effective in stimulating Mike and helping him to regulate himself. Interestingly, mother in no way appears to feel downgraded by the success of her husband in comparison with hers; to the contrary, she thoroughly enjoys it.

During the three-together part, the family continues working together. Again, despite the father's lapse of memory about part three, this couple playfully overcomes the "error" at the moment of the transition. By now, they focus mainly on helping the child regulate his state; their availability remains optimal, but the affective contact is empathic rather than playful. It is notable that the parental cooperation works just as well in the face of the infant's indisposition to play. However, they clearly have not forgotten the main goal of the LTP, and they actively work at reestablishing it.

The forms of cooperation between the parents are flexible. We see them change from coaction to complementary roles and back to coaction. To be sure, the infant's stance to recovering and playing helps them greatly in this endeavor as well. Note this infant's remarkable capacity to clearly display his states and needs and to actively work at their regulation.

Finally, during the father–mother direct interaction, with Mike as third party, the acute interactive awareness and synchronization of the parents with respect to their child as well as to each other is remarkable. And, even though Mike does not actively participate in episodes of affective contact, he clearly furthers them by successfully autoregulating himself.

Although not a single move of their child has escaped the parents' peripheral monitoring, they smoothly conduct their dialogue in parallel; in fact, they are also quite entranced in it and support each other in not breaking the two-plus-one rule of this part when distracted by their child. There is much affection, humor, and support in their interaction, marked by complicity and playfulness, as testified by numerous microepisodes of affective contact between them. This positive climate likely contributes to Mike's successful regulation of his own state in the face of the change in interactive format and its evolution from drowsiness to attending to his parents.

In summary, there is no doubt that the family continuously works together and helps each other. Positivity prevails even in the face of potential conflict between the parents and distress of the infant. Humor and empathy then take over direct positive affect sharing. Overall, the story line of this trilogue play definitely has its aesthetic quality, starting off very intensely with mother–Mike play and reaching its high point with father–Mike play. Then it recedes to a slower and quieter pace in the three together and reaches a second high point during the father–mother dialogue. Yet it is not for lack of false steps that it is aesthetic. On the contrary, the way the family deals with false steps makes the story fascinating. Therefore, it is not an overstatement to categorize this type of play in the cooperative family alliance.

NANCY'S FAMILY: A STRESSED ALLIANCE

This family successfully plays together; however, they have to work fairly hard to continue through ups and downs and in the face of sharp contrasts between the styles of the parents. It is interesting to observe how they do it.

NARRATIVE

Nancy's parents are in their late twenties. The father is a nurse and the mother is a teacher. Their professions play a role in collaborating with us to help other families. Nancy is a tiny, attractive, impetuous three-month-old with a happy disposition.

The preparation proceeds smoothly. Mother plays first. Her play with Nancy lasts longer than is usual at this age. She conducts it at a fast pace. Nancy vigorously struggles to cope and father watches attentively. His attitude is slightly withdrawn, as if not to intrude, but perhaps also to keep his reactions under control. In effect, he resonates clearly albeit very discreetly and his facial expression reliably reflects what is going on in the dyad.

In contrast, mother's affectionate, playful, physical, and notably teasing style tests her partners. In a way, Nancy's reactions are in style: She holds her ground with strength too, averting herself and protesting if necessary, but reengaging as soon as she can afford to. Mother never fails to react to her daughter's signals, thus preventing a breakup. But she may choose to increase the teasing rather than decrease it. Accordingly, it is not surprising that Nancy already prefers the kind of play that infants begin to enjoy during the second trimester: play that is mediated (here by her hands and feet) rather than direct face-to-face play. Interestingly, on averting from her mother, Nancy tends to orient to her father. He silently laughs, lowering his head until Nancy has reoriented to mother, for instance, owing to mother's laugh at Nancy's overstepping of the two-plus-one rule.

About midway into this part, we observe that father joins forces with Nancy by subtly but firmly signaling the need to move to the next part. Wary of the time, he ostensibly checks his watch and makes his presence more obvious, whereas Nancy amplifies her aversions from mother and orients several times in a row to her father. He eventually openly responds to her in a last attempt to make his point. Mother responds to these actions in her own way: She ignores her husband's implicit requests, but in the meantime she somewhat adjusts her play to a more acceptable level for Nancy. Accordingly, we observe a few longer episodes of coaction between mother and daughter. And it is seemingly on her own terms that mother initiates the transition to the next part.

The father's play with Nancy is much briefer and less animated. We observe short-lived moments of contact between father and Nancy, but father's low-key style of play fails to sustain Nancy's interest for long. When she pauses, father promptly voices his sadness at Nancy's lack of interest. This negative tone could not possibly escape Nancy's perception and she predictably increases her pauses and turns to mother. Mother's stance is literally outstanding: On the one hand, she physically distances herself by ostensibly turning her body away; on the other hand, she closely follows the action and resonates to every move between father and Nancy—smiling, commenting in an off voice, laughing, coughing, picking at something—yet never directly interferes. Her responses become more and more conspicuous. Whether father experiences this manifest resonance as supporting or interfering, it is not long until he initiates the transition to the three-together play and mother follows his lead.

The parents are more effective together than separately. In fact, father, mother, and Nancy enjoy their playing three together so much that the part lasts a long time and includes a number of games, both in coaction and in alternation.

Perhaps the best illustration of this process is the first game: Mother, in her provocative style, points her index finger on Nancy's tummy, and father, in his subdued style, talking softly, points his index finger in the direction of Nancy's chin. Nancy orients herself to father. As they look at each other, father begins to make faces and mother backchannels with tongue noises. Nancy responds by opening and closing her mouth, smiling and vocalizing. And so on.

When they finally proceed to part four, Nancy is tired and fussy; she characteristically fights to regulate her state by herself, repeatedly bringing her fist to her mouth. Father is definitely turned toward Mother, intent on implementing the two-plus-one rule, whereas mother freely alternates between turning to him and to Nancy; they talk about her together. The parents put an end to the play after a reasonable amount of time.

Working Together and Helping Each Other

Overall, the family works together and helps each other. They are ready to participate in the LTP, to play by the rules of the successive parts; they playfully sustain affective contact with each other, moving from one part to the next in an orderly and clear way.

There is no doubt that the interactive styles of the parents with Nancy work better together than separately. On the one hand, mother's provocative, teasing style poses a challenge that Nancy pursues, but not without tension. Likewise, it poses a challenge for the third-party parent, and we see how father, initially withdrawn, joins forces with Nancy and skillfully sets out to press mother to terminate the play. On the other hand, father's subdued style and pessimistic attitude also create tension for his partners, causing Nancy to lose her animation and search for stimulation elsewhere while pushing mother to the edge in checking her resonance and sticking to her third-party role.

In a way, Nancy's style, which definitely resembles that of her mother, not only underlines but also contributes to exaggeration of the difference between her parents. It is all the more remarkable that the two-plus-one organization holds and that Nancy's involvement does not break it up definitively. Clearly the key is the unfailing cooperation between the parents, going beyond their differences. Cues to this cooperation, however discreet, pave the way for the first two parts and become obvious in the three-together part, when the parents synchronize their moves and combine their styles. This joint effort allows Nancy to balance the mannerisms of both parents.

Thinking in terms of feedback loops about the framing and developing parties helping each other, there are two different processes in the first part: When father as third party stays away, mother's provocative style stretches Nancy's capacity to her limits. In contrast, when father, intent on adhering to the LTP rules, slowly and discreetly but firmly pressures mother to terminate, it has a regulating influence on mother's stimulations. This situation in itself prefigures the cooperative process at work in part three.

What may be the regulating influence of mother as third party on the father–Nancy play is less clear. Mother's conspicuous resonance could be experienced by father in positive as well as negative ways. In any case, the part comes to a decent closure before any breakdown occurs.

The feedback loop is utterly changed in the three-together part. Joining forces has a major bonus effect on Nancy's sustaining affective contact. Nancy can mitigate her mother's intense solicitations and thus keep up with them by orienting toward father and maintaining contact with him. In turn, stimulated by Nancy's responses, father rises to a higher level of animation, which feeds back into mother's stimulations. No longer challenged by Nancy's aversions, she lowers the level of these solicitations. This benefit is only possible because the parents coordinate their moves.

Positivity prevails in the affective climate of the play, even if it is mitigated by tension in the first two parts. The line of the play is somewhat irregular, because it is only in the three-together part that the dance takes off. Before that, the play mainly has ups and downs: ups in the mother–Nancy play and downs in the father–Nancy play, with tension throughout—to the extent that after these highs in part one and lows in part two, the observer is in doubt about what will become of this play. The rise in the three together is all the more striking. The coda in part four makes sense in view of the work involved in keeping up with the procedure. Stressed cooperation emerges from this threesome's interactions.

FRANKIE'S FAMILY: A COLLUSIVE ALLIANCE

In this family, the parents strive to play by the rules and to reach relatedness with their baby. However, there are definite obstacles: The parents continually contest with each other about these rules and interfere in each other's interaction with the infant, with the result that the dance definitely does not take off.

NARRATIVE

Frankie's parents are in their late thirties. The father has his business office at home; the mother works as a statistician and travels quite a bit. They have a live-in nurse. They collaborate with us because they have an intellectual interest in research and research on the family may be helpful.

Frankie is a vigorous, large, somewhat overweight three-month-old with a rather flat expression. He appears to be in a fair disposition, whereas during the previous session he was pretty fussy.

During the preparation, the parents ask several questions about the research, intent to show their interest, but interrupting the delivery of the instruction. Otherwise, the preparation proceeds smoothly.

Mother plays first. She turns the table and father disapproves. She keeps it turned. Just as she succeeds in attracting Frankie's attention, father interrupts, asking whether she signaled to the researchers that she was beginning. She does not seem to mind, complies, and starts again. Her style of engaging is affectionate, physically close, yet surprisingly uninspired and stereotyped. It is more adultlike than babylike. Thus, she does not easily capture Frankie's attention. In fact, the more she tries and the closer she leans toward him, the more he averts from her, turning in father's direction.

Considering his third-party role, father is rather close too, as if he were ready to engage. At best, his response to Frankie's gaze is not discouraging.

A loop is created in which the more mother tries to capture Frankie's attention, the more Frankie turns to father, who more often than not encourages Frankie's orientation to him rather than helping his coparent to regain her role. Moreover, we note that when an episode between mother and Frankie does take off, in that she has at last enlisted his attention, father most likely interferes by making gestures that reattract the baby's attention. Again, mother does not seem to mind. However, she terminates her part in less than two minutes, turns Frankie over to his father, and sits back to watch. It is important to note Frankie's stance: While keeping vigilant, continuously monitoring one or the other parent, he remains sober and almost motionless except for chewing movements of his lips.

The play between father and Frankie is different. Father and son are visibly partners and they engage in an intense, excited, perhaps somewhat forced play. Frankie even gives out a few half smiles. Yet he keeps chewing on his lips. At some point, when Frankie happens to gaze at mother, he gets an engaging response from her, just as he got from his father when father was the third party. She remains at a distance, but she smiles and makes faces, imitating his characteristic sucking movements in a somewhat mocking way that resembles pouting. Frankie's attention is captivated and father progressively draws back.

Mother does not stop this provocation short of father's exclaiming to Frankie in a sad and angry voice: "You are not interested in me today. . . . I will not call you anymore." Mother laughs and proposes to proceed to the three-together part. The escalation comes to an end and repair seems to finally take place. But, rather than proceeding, the parents engage in a contest: What are they supposed to do in part three? This creates a rather long, tense, animated aside and consequently a cutoff from the contact with Frankie. By the time they agree, Frankie, who has intently watched them argue, switches his chewing movements into a pouting face. On seeing this, the parents laugh in concert and finally set out to play together, each holding one of Frankie's hands.

However, the dance does not take off; the parents are definitely not in it together. They soon reverse to their previous two-plus-one styles, taking turns in doing their own thing. Note that Frankie's response does not induce them to act otherwise, in that he is by now on the edge. Having taken a few turns, the parents abbreviate the three-together part and quickly proceed to part four. Although the mother decidedly turns toward the father and tries to engage him in a conversation, he remains turned toward Frankie. How could this infant understand that he is expected to be the third party? In any case, the parents rapidly put a stop to their own interaction and call for the facilitator.

Working Together and Helping Each Other

Again, love is in no way in question. The observer is somewhat perplexed in watching this type of play. On the one hand, we are perceptive to the intent drive of the parents to collaborate with us and to cooperate in engaging Frankie. On the other hand, we perceive the somewhat forced and often inappropriate solicitations of the parents to a three-month-old infant, such as moralizing or exaggerating Frankie's negative signals by imitation rather than helping him quiet down and return to a positive state. Finally, we observe Frankie's energy in actively fighting the tension—sucking and pouting but not breaking down. His vigilance and attention to his parents' contests is outstanding.

In spite of this drive on the part of the three partners that conveys they are tightly knit together, it is difficult to view their interaction as a unit. Likewise, the complicity between the parents is in sharp contradiction with their blatant escalation of interferences with each other in playing with Frankie. Although Frankie is a driving infant, his energy is devoted to monitoring his parents' interaction and he hardly engages in play, which is not surprising in view of the divergent stimulations he gets from his parents. The dynamics enter a complicated feedback loop when Frankie's efforts at regulating himself are misinterpreted and he receives a negative, blaming, or mocking response from the parents. These negative signals alleviate tension between the parents.

Thus, the contrast between the affective tonality of the parents and that of the infant becomes less perplexing. With the exception of one event (when father tells Frankie, "You are not interested in me today. . . . I will not call you anymore"), the conflict between the parents does not visibly affect their mood; they remain at least superficially playful and positive, yet not in an empathetic way. It is Frankie who affectively expresses the tension manifested by the contests and interferences. This tension is displaced from the interaction between the parents to their interaction with their child. In such a split-affective climate, negativity is bound to prevail over positivity.

The line of the play is drawn by the numerous contests and interferences rather than by the evolution of the play itself. We can sketch this evolution:

After a dull start in the mother–Frankie plus father play, it rises to a higher level of animation in the father–Frankie plus mother play and progresses toward tension in the three together and during the father–mother direct interaction. But what really captures the observer's attention—and probably the subjects' too—are the events around the contests and interferences, that is, the high points of conflict.

We are observing a detouring coalition of the parents onto the infant and the making of a scapegoat, however beloved. Collusion evolves from this threesome's interaction.

TANIA'S FAMILY: A DISORDERED ALLIANCE

In this family, the attempt to cope with the task is fierce yet utterly inefficient, as if the parents were caught in a vicious circle.

NARRATIVE

The father is a businessman and the mother has given up her work as a clerk to take care of their daughter. Tania is a tall but underweight infant with pretty features, albeit a tired expression. We know from the first-session interview that she has sleeping and eating problems.

As the facilitator closes the door after a lengthy preparation, the parents are negotiating. Mother prompts father to sit down, but he remains standing for fear that Tania will cry as she did during the first session. While waiting, mother throws herself into activities around the infant's seat; without consulting father, she changes its inclination several times. Eventually the parents succeed in settling down Tania and themselves.

In order to visualize this play, it is important to keep in mind the ambiguous quality of the three partners' signals throughout the entire play, as if to simultaneously indicate involvement and noninvolvement. For instance, Tania sits in a sagging position (because the seat is too straight); leaning, she gazes sideways, not straight ahead. She tends to stare without blinking. Mother typically sits sideways too and as far away as possible from father and Tania. She addresses her baby in baby talk and touches her with the tips of her fingers, as if not to hurt her. When mother interferes in father's interaction with Tania, he ignores it, by continuing his solicitations, yet responds to it, by lowering his voice. A sense of utter ambiguity is conveyed, confusing the observer and presumably the partners as well.

Against this background, and observing the mother–Tania play, the salient story of this first part is concerned with the evolution of a conflict: The parents interfere with each other in trying to engage a baby who is not participating. The story begins with an intense but abrupt episode of greeting and vocalizing; it falls off just as quickly with Tania gazing down and catching her fist to suck on it. Thereupon, mother distinctly switches to a plaintive tone. Tania gazes sideways at father, who immediately responds with a silent but broad smile. Mother complains: "Is it your daddy that you are looking at . . . mommy doesn't interest you [sad tone]." Father cracks up; greeting Tania, smiling, he exclaims: "Look at your mom!" Yet he takes no action to enforce his request such as redirecting the infant's gaze toward mother. Tania keeps staring at him. Mother turns to father: "Perhaps it would be better if she would not see you." Father protests, looks up with an angry and contemptuous expression, and thereafter keeps a tense, frozen smile. Forty seconds set up the conflict.

From this point on, the two-plus-one organization remains tense. Father is silent and immobile, with a forced smile. Tania looks away. Mother keeps trying, but appears more and more defeated and unanimated. After a particularly painful laugh, she sets out to announce the transition to part two: "Do you want to play with daddy? You haven't seen daddy this afternoon. . . . Do you want to play with him, yes? Yes? Do you want to?" This long, indirect request draws no visible reaction from father. Next, mother acts: She abruptly sits up, cutting off gaze contact with Tania, and turns to face father. This time, father turns to meet her gaze, listening, otherwise motionless and mute.

Still without a word, father begins to move. Tania immediately responds by orienting to him. Yet as he leans forward, calling for her, she averts herself, as far as possible. Father withdraws.

The story of part two is in many ways a replay of part one but amplified. The tension and the parental conflict escalate. Tania is leaning further and further out, in her attempt to suck on the belt. Then she starts crying. From then on, the parents take her in and out of the seat.

In this confusion there is no way to recognize a given configuration. Tania is working at soothing herself by sucking on the belt that she can sometimes reach and that sometimes escapes her. It is worth mentioning a pattern that again illustrates the ambiguity of these interactions. As father attempts to help Tania bring the belt to her mouth, we observe three repetitive events in close succession. At the very moment that Tania is reaching her mouth, father diverts her action by giving her a slight push aside, on the grounds that Tania would put the belt up her nose. Needless to say, Tania's frustration escalates. It brings her to a spell of yelling and sobbing that forces father to take her out of the seat.

But, amazingly, when the parents take Tania out, she quiets down very rapidly. As soon as she stops crying, one of the parents declares that she should be in the seat and they promptly settle her down again. Tania appears ready to try again, intently looking at the belt that one of the parents dangles in front of her as the other one settles her down. But she soon cries again.

The parents go through shorter and shorter bouts of helping her, but most of the time they sit back not sure what to do. However, they are intent on accomplishing the LTP. What it might mean to them at this point is not clear—perhaps that Tania should be seated. At some point, we see father engage mother in talking with him (this might be the transition to part four), on the grounds that Tania might calm down if they do not attend to her. Finally, it is the facilitator who ends the loop.

In comparison with the first two parts, the affective tonality between the parents is less negative during the last two parts. The confrontation yields to a more conciliatory tone and even to some moments of complicity and planned cooperation: "You put her in the seat while I show her the belt." And they do it.

WORKING TOGETHER AND HELPING EACH OTHER

The family strives to establish positive contact, but if they succeed in sharing a few brief positive moments it is only in twos, never in a threesome concert.

From the beginning, the roles of third party and active parent are blurred and Tania is in no position to clearly distinguish who is her partner in dyadic play. She is excluded from the interaction by the way her parents set her seat and her consequently ambiguous signals fail to indicate to the parents the path to clarifying their roles.

To understand the disorder that reigns between the partners, it is important to grasp the dramatic dimension in the story—that is, to empathize with the subjects' experience. Let us try and confront these inner experiences with the effects they have on the triangular interaction.

Take first the father as third party. He clearly tries to keep to his role, yet he is utterly disarmed when Tania looks at him. He appears to attempt a response to both demands at the same time; hence his ambiguity: not moving, presumably to keep to his role, and giving the broadest but silent smile, presumably to ensure Tania of his affection. As a consequence, he fails in both endeavors and his response can only be confusing.

Now consider mother as active parent. After the initial, brief, almost abrupt and intense episode of greeting and vocalizing together, Tania inevitably has to pause. This is most painful to mother, for she interprets it as rejection ("Mommy doesn't interest you"), causing her to switch to a negative tone that in turn will draw Tania further away from her and cause her to turn to father. The point is that these patterns likely feed into father's preoccupation with keeping Tania from crying—even at the cost of interfering and certainly at the actual cost of aggravating mother's sense of failure. This is a vicious cycle.

Finally, look at Tania, in between her parents, her sagging posture, her sideways glances from behind a fist, staring without blinking, smiling and averting, displaying her utter confusion. On another level, these actions may be her way of adjusting to the contradictory requests she receives from her parents. This "go-between" strategy in infants faced with unnegotiable parental conflict is often observed.

This ambiguity feeds back into the parents' perceptions of what their child communicates to them. In the context of the two plus one and in the perception of each parent separately, the message is "I am with you/I am not with you." We have to read these two signals simultaneously. In this sense, an infant inevitably adds to the confusion and the vicious cycle is triangular.

In spite of the role change between the parents, the story of the father–Tania play with mother as third party is in many ways an amplification of the story of part one. For father too, it appears difficult to cope with Tania's pausing. It seems that the fear of crying immediately creeps in. As for Tania, her style is also different with father, in that she averts herself further but also engages longer—and there are even hints of playfulness. Yet, as with mother, she drains herself in one blow, so to speak, and would certainly need a very long pause to recuperate.

By the time they reach the three-together part, it is clearly Tania who is in charge: Everything depends on her state. Again, the most effective strategy in uniting the parents, if only for a while, is Tania's sucking or crying. The parents watch her helplessly. Sometimes they devise coping strategies that are difficult to comprehend. Most striking is their blindness in the face of Tania's discomfort, which is by no means an inability to perceive this discomfort. A few times, father or mother appear to come to their senses, commenting on Tania's state and acting on it, albeit making it worse.

In summary, this story is painful. We get no sense of this type of family as a unit. Rather, we get a sense of three separate but bonded beings, who share the same ambiguous mode of communication, and this is confusing. Negativity has invaded the scene. The story line of the play is marked by a downslope toward loneliness and distress. It appears that if the goal of the LTP—mutual playful enjoyment—were clear at the beginning, it has become obscured. By the end, the interaction appears senseless. The parents oscillate between two short-term goals: When Tania is crying, their priority is comforting her. As soon as she quiets down, the goal is to keep her in the LTP seat. The switching between these two goals is endless and it is eventually up to the facilitator to stop the vicious cycle. Disorder is prevalent in these interactions.

DISCUSSION

We have reached the first global perspective on family alliances. We can intuitively recognize whether the group is together or divided. In the two plus ones where the active dyads are in the foreground, the third party's resonance makes the difference.

When the partners evolve in concert, the four configurations are integrated into a whole. The family keeps the triangular thread over the four parts and transitions. If division creeps in, instead of distinct but connected configurations, the split pattern is invariably repeated from part to part. If disorder is added to division, the thread is increasingly loosened and even the repetition of split patterns becomes senseless (Cronen, Kenneth, and Lannamann, 1982).

The focus on helping each other in turn underscores key ingredients of the family alliances: on the one hand, the solidarity and cooperation between the parents that make for a solid framing of the infant; on the other hand, the driving force of the developing infant that implicates the parents and allows them to fine-tune their framing. The narratives of the two problematic family alliances illuminate the disturbing effects of a divided coparenting party. The two against one makes the infant a hostage to her parents' conflict regulation and thus inevitably diverts her development from its "normal" course.

Affect regulation is clearly at the center of the family alliance. Playfully sharing positive affects as a threesome is not only the goal of trilogue play but it is the engine. When positivity and fun prevail even in the face of adversity, cooperation is possible. When negativity and sternness take over, division invades the scene.

At this early age, sharp differences in autoregulation between the infants are already recognizable. They have learned to cope with widely different conditions. Both Mike and Nancy strive hard to cope with the demands of the play and the solicitations of their parents that may at points submerge them or fail to enlist their attention. But both of them bathe in an atmosphere of prevailing positivity. Their parents support them in regulating their affects. After having experienced the differences in styles of dyadic interactions with their father and their mother (Nancy much more than Mike), they also experience how these styles reconcile when their parents are united with them in the three together. Finally, they even get to witness the complicity of their parents as a twosome.

In contrast, it is in a tense, if not hostile, atmosphere that Frankie and Tania experience their interactions with their parents. Rather than receiving appropriate support for regulating their affects, they are forced to be on the defensive, to the point of withdrawal or distress. In addition, they are confronted with the confusing effects of their self-protective signals on the relationship between their parents. Indeed, Frankie's stressful signals end up alleviating the tension between his parents, as do Tania's withdrawal or distress signals.

Because of this sober style, the hard work that Frankie is accomplishing might be overlooked. On close examination, he is a vigilant and hard-driving infant. On the lookout for everything that goes on between his parents, he strives hard to regulate his affects, notably by means of his characteristic lip-chewing movements. As reported, when his tension mounts and as the parents amplify these movements by mock imitation, they take the form of a pout that will be misinterpreted as anger. It is this very signal that winds up reuniting his parents against him. We follow through this process of becoming a "beloved scapegoat" in the developmental reading (chapter 5).

The reader may recognize in Tania's interaction with her mother the dyadic patterns observed between depressed mothers and their infants (Cohn, Matias, Tronick, Connell, and Lyons-Ruth, 1986; Field 1984a, 1984b, 1986; Murray, 1992). This mother's forceful efforts and obvious affection for her child, and the subsequent draining and deanimation she exhibits, graphically correspond to these descriptions; so does the instant animation and deanimation of the infant (see especially Stern's description of an infant's ways of being with a depressed mother: Stern, 1994). Interestingly, although father is not depressed, his interactions with Tania, at least in the presence of mother, do not depart widely from mother's interactions with Tania; father is also unable to stand Tania's need to pause. Most of all, his attempts to make up for the mother's difficulties, such as responding to Tania when she addresses him as a third party, not only further undermine mother's sense of competence but also isolate and burden Tania.

It is notable that Tania's autoregulation seems well practiced: Chewing is preferred in addition to her incongruent ways, particularly averting yet keeping her partners in her peripheral vision. That is, until the tension between the parents reaches the point of confrontation. Then she cuts off, visually averting as much as possible from the scene. Finally, she bursts out crying. We understand these ways both as protective and as a coping mechanism for the paradoxical affective demands with which she is confronted.

Thus, the four plays yield a widely different picture. At one extreme, Mike and his parents gracefully travel through the LTP, playfully repairing their false steps. The play's contour is clearly drawn, harmonious, and continuous. At the other extreme, Tania and her parents intently fight to abide by the LTP rules and suffer at failing in relatedness. It is difficult to trace a thread, for the action is confused to the point of absurdity, the goal is diverted, and the actors as well as the spectators lose their sense of coherence. In between, Nancy and her parents eventually balance their style differences in the three-together play. The sense of a line is conserved; in some way, the doubts that were brooding during the first two parts eventually make the play all the more fascinating after the three together takes off. In contrast, Frankie and his parents get caught in escalations of parental competition that definitely prevent the dance from taking off, making Frankie a hostage to his parents' conflict.

Love is not in question in any of these cases. In fact, it is the most beautiful aspect of these stories when they run smoothly. Mike's family's playful and intense trilogue reveals a passionate love story. Mike is in love with his parents and they are in love with him and with each other. Nancy's family play also comes out as loving, but it takes on a most poignant, if not paradoxical, dimension when it drives the family into detouring coalitions and exclusions.

We have constructed these four narratives to cover fairly well the range of LTPs that families have offered us over the years. Note that Mike's and Tania's family interactions are probably more "extreme" as part of the nonclinical population. It is our experience that volunteering for research may stem from two rather different motives in our local culture: on the one hand, a prosocial motivation of curiosity and interest that leads happy families with good-enough alliances to seek opportunities to learn and help others; on the other hand, a motivation for distressed families to seek help in a research setting that appears less threatening and more socially acceptable than a therapeutic one.

To provide some perspective for the reader, let us report that the family alliances as measured by the triangular framework were fairly stable over the first year in this longitudinal sample. Practically, nine out of the twelve families maintained the same type of family alliance over the three-, six-, and nine-month LTP sessions. Three of them changed. Two of them initially categorized in D alliances stepped up to a C or B alliance by the nine-month session. One of them initially categorized in a B alliance stepped down to a C alliance at nine months. Assuming this result would be replicated in larger samples, it would indicate both that the family alliance is a stable property of the family and that it is amenable to change. The fact that it is stable would provide an early predictor of the family's resources or vulnerabilities. The fact that it is amenable to change would mean that it is susceptible to framing interventions. We analyze these results in detail in Chapter 6 when we take up the subject of the working alliance and of framing the family.

In constructing these narratives, we have touched upon a number of patterns and processes detected by intuition, common sense, and expert experience. They point to the inferences we make in our everyday life and in our clinical activities. They are working hypotheses that we make more or less explicit as we experience interactions, whether as actors or spectators. Our task is to attempt to test these working hypotheses by making a systematic, objective description of the patterns and processes that sustain them. The structural reading in Chapter 3 takes us into the domain of the patterns of triangular interaction.

REFERENCES

Cohn, J., Matias, R., Tronick, E., Connell, D., and Lyons-Ruth, K. (1986). Face-to-face interactions of depressed mothers and their infants. In E. Tronick and T. Field (eds.), *Maternal Depression and Infant Disturbance* (Vol. 34, pp. 31–45). San Francisco: Jossey-Bass.

Cronen, V. E., Kenneth, M. J., and Lannamann, J. W. (1982). Paradoxes, double binds, and reflexive loops: An alternative theoretical perspective. *Family Process, 21,* 91–112.

Field, T. (1984a). Perinatal risk factors for infant depression. In J. Call, E. Galenson, and R. L. Tyson (eds.), *Frontiers of Infant Psychiatry* (Vol. 2, pp. 152–159). New York: Basic Books.

Field, T. M. (1984b). Early interactions between infants and their postpartum depressed mothers. *Infant Behavior and Development, 7,* 517–522.

Field, T. (1986). Models for reactive and chronic depression in infancy. In E. Tronick and T. Field (eds.), *Maternal Depression and Infant Disturbance* (Vol. 34, pp. 47–60). San Francisco: Jossey-Bass.

Murray, L. (1992). The impact of postnatal depression on infant development. *Journal of Child Psychology and Psychiatry, 33*(3), 543–561.

Stern, D. N. (1994). One way to build a clinically relevant baby. *Infant Mental Health Journal, 15*(1), 9–25.

CHAPTER 3

The Structural Foundations of the Family Alliances

In discovering the four plays in Chapter 2, we had experiences that were fascinating but clearly different in each case: pleasure and beauty with Mike's family, tension and relief with Nancy's, irritation and frustration with Frankie's, and perplexity and pain with Tania's. These feelings emerged in the very first instants of the Lausanne triadic play (LTP) session and persisted throughout, for they were linked with the patterns that characterize these interactions. It is indeed a striking fact in our everyday life as well as in our clinical experience that we immediately perceive these patterns.

Still, it is another matter to make these patterns explicit, to communicate them, and to objectify them for scientific purposes. This is the goal of microanalysis, a method developed by ethologists and developmentalists to explore and objectify the complexities of natural interactions. The method begins with a detailed, systematic, frame-by-frame transcription of the video-records. It establishes a description of the patterns on which observers can agree; these are the very patterns that we implicitly capture, but it makes them explicit and objective. Whereas the method is systematic, it is also artful: Detecting patterns in interactions is similar to transcribing a piece of music in order to discover its structure and its main theme beyond its numerous variations. Moreover, it requires looking at the actions of all partners as a whole rather than as a set of individuals.

We know from microanalytic studies that interactive patterns form a highly ordered though flexible hierarchical structure, like a partition of music or a choreography. It is this architecture that we explore in this chapter. The triangular framework lays the structural foundations of the model of family alliances elaborated by our team as we microanalyzed the interactions of prototypic plays. It categorizes the interactions in four types of frameworks—A, B, C, and D—ordered according to their degree of coordination. A and B frameworks work in attaining the goal of trilogue play, whereas C and D frameworks do not. Exposing the main lines of this structural model will (1) indicate how the community could progressively establish an understanding of triangular interactions on a scientific foundation; (2) show how an objective and formal assessment of a trilogue allows for detection of the resources and the difficulties that a family experiences; and (3) allow for a proposal to help families develop new, more effective ways of communicating.

THE ASSESSMENT SCHEME

Figure 3.1 outlines the assessment of triangular frameworks in the LTP. We believe that these four functions must be fulfilled not only in trilogue play but also generally in face-to-face interactions. Participation assesses whether everyone is included. Then comes organization—that is, whether everyone is in their role. Joint attention, or whether everyone is attending to the games, is next. Finally, affective contact follows, or whether everyone is in touch with everyone else. Once these functions are in place, the patterns of interaction that we observe may be effective in trilogue play.

It is at the bifurcations between the functions that the different frameworks are located. At the first bifurcation are the D frameworks that make up disordered alliances (there is someone excluded, as exemplified by Tania's family). At the second point are the C frameworks that make up collusive alliances (there are repeated interferences or abstentions, as in Frankie's family). At the third branch are the B frameworks that make up the stressed alliances (the focus is fragmented and/or the partners are not sufficiently in touch, as in Nancy's family). At the last bifurcation are the A frameworks that make up the cooperative alliances (everyone is in touch, as in Mike's family). Only in the latter case are all necessary functions fulfilled, allowing for the emergence of repeated playful moments of affective communion.

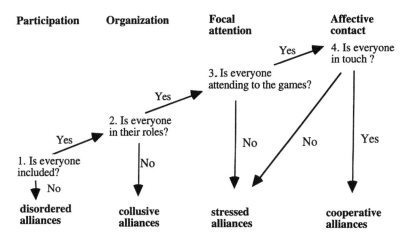

FIGURE 3.1   Assessing frameworks in the LTP.

THE FOUR FUNCTIONS IN TRILOGUE PLAY

PARTICIPATION (IS EVERYONE INCLUDED?)

From a theoretical point of view, participation is the simplest of the four functions: It requires only that everyone be included without specifying how—that is, it involves a relatively small number of coordinations, so complexity is low. We ask the partners to "play as a family," which is such an obviously necessary task that this important function is generally overlooked in the analyses of interactions. It is also the function that remains the least variable in time: It must be unchanged from the beginning to the end of trilogue play, making up a single and very long episode.

ORGANIZATION (IS EVERYONE IN THEIR ROLE?)

Organization is built into the LTP instruction in that the roles of active partner versus third party are prescribed for each part of the play. Only when each of the three partners is in his or her role is trilogue play likely to succeed. Organization is more complex and variable than participation: The rules that define who is addressing whom and when change with each of the four parts, making up four long episodes.

FOCAL ATTENTION (IS EVERYONE ATTENDING TO THE GAMES?)

The play will only be triangular if all three partners attend to the same focus, which is the current games. Focal attention is more complex and rapid than participation and organization, because following up and focusing together on every single game requires many different coordinations and involves many changes (three to six episodes per part).

AFFECTIVE CONTACT (IS EVERYONE IN TOUCH?)

Similar to dialogue play, trilogue play implicitly calls for establishing and sustaining emotional intimacy; out of this connectedness emerges shared moments of playful enjoyment. Affective contact is the most complex function and the most variable in time, because it involves conversational and emotional signals that require many coordinations in very brief episodes (about two to four episodes per game). For instance, the mutual greetings that initiate contact, say in the three-together part, involve nodding the head, opening the eyes and the mouth wide, vocalizing, and perhaps gesturing—all on a split-second basis and coordinated not only individually but interactionally.

THE FOUR LEVELS OF NONVERBAL INTERACTION: PELVES, TORSOS, GAZES, EXPRESSIONS

In the clinical descriptions we have observed that the partners use multiple physical modalities in playing: their pelves, torsos, heads, gazes, facial expressions, voice intonations, and gestures. Whereas these modalities come in "packages" (for instance, leaning the torso forward, orienting the face "en-face," and greeting [Beebe and Stern, 1977; Cohn and Tronick, 1988; Weinberg and Tronick, 1994]), they also constitute distinct layers or levels (Fogel, 1977). Indeed, the partners can delineate different interactive domains with their pelves, torsos, gazes, and expressions. We observe in trilogue play that the rate of movement of these body parts increases stepwise: When the partners sit to play trilogue, they position and orient their pelves and then hardly move them over the entire play period, whereas they reposition and reorient their torsos more frequently. Likewise, they reposition and reorient their heads and gazes even more frequently. Finally, the changes in expressions are extremely rapid. Practically, we distinguish four levels: the pelves,

four: expressions

three: gazes

two: torsos

one: pelves

FIGURE 3.2   The four levels of interaction in the LTP.

the torsos, the heads and gazes, and the expressions. They are represented in Figure 3.2.

FORMATIONS

In Chapter 1 we define and exemplify Kendon's F-formations as the transactional space that the partners sustain by means of their positions and orientations (Kendon, 1977). Formations are the building blocks of the triangular framework. There are two points to remember about formations; First there are four types of formations—one to implement each function. Second, each type of formation is introduced at a different level of interaction: participation formations at the level of pelves, organization formations at the level of torsos, focal attention formations at the level of gazes, and affective contact formations at the level of expressions.

Participation Formations

Participation formations physically display inclusion/exclusion in the three-way interaction. The conventional setting in which the LTP takes place serves as a reference to assess participation.

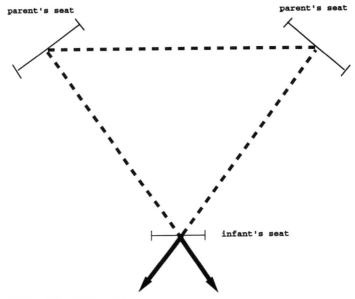

FIGURE 3.3   The LTP setting.
    The LTP setting outlines an equilateral but infant-oriented formation constituting
the reference for assessing participation formations. Connecting the center points of
the seats yields an equilateral triangle. The parents' seat orientations converge on
the infant's seat and determine an infant-oriented triangle.

    This setting was designed to ensure optimal access of the partners to each
other. The seats form an equilateral triangle to provide equal access (see Figure 3.3); however, the parents' seats are more oriented toward the infant's
seat than toward each other, which is necessary because play must be centered on the infant. It is interesting to note that with affective development
the physical orientation of the partners naturally moves toward the center of
the triangle and thus the triangle becomes equioriented. This situation coin-
cides with the advent of the infant's referential communication and the possibility to center on a shared external theme.

    When the play begins and the parents eventually settle down, they spon-
taneously center and align their bodies on their seats, thus espousing the reference triangle. However, some parents deviate from the reference triangle
and create a different one where their orientations exclude the infant.

    Participation formations originate at level one with the location and ori-
entation of the pelves. They are delineated anew at the other three levels,
mainly by orientation patterns of torsos, gazes, and expressions (details in

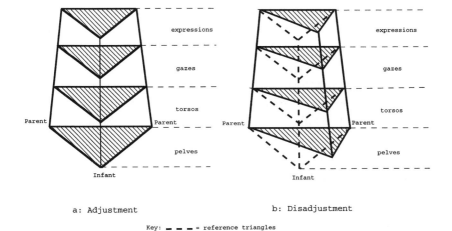

a: Adjustment   b: Disadjustment

Key: ▬ ▬ ▬ = reference triangles

FIGURE 3.4   Domain of participation.

To derive the participation formation at level one in an actual play, the middle points of the parents' pelvis positions are connected and the perpendiculars to their pelvis axes are drawn out, thus determining their intersection point. These three points yield a first formation. At level two, the middle points of their shoulders are connected by drawing out the perpendiculars to their shoulder axes, thus determining their intersection point. These three points determine a second formation. At levels three and four, the patterns of orientation of gazes and expressions of the three partners (the infant included) that fall within the setting's triangle are separated from the ones that fall outside, thus determining a third and a fourth formation. By connecting the formations drawn at the four levels, the geometric representation of the domain of participation is obtained.

Adjustment: The formations thus obtained are isomorphic to the reference triangle; in particular, they include the infant's seat. The domain of participation is adjusted.

Disadjustment: The formations are not isomorphic to the reference triangle; in particular, they do not include the infant's seat. The domain of participation is disadjusted.

Figure 3.4). By connecting the formations at the four levels, a three-dimensional pyramidal structure in four layers is obtained. The pyramid constitutes the domain of participation.

In Figure 3.4a the four formations are represented as isomorphic to the reference triangle and constitute a regular structure. Everyone is included and consequently the domain of participation is adjusted for trilogue play. It is not possible to overemphasize how fundamental this pyramidal construction is in understanding triangular interactions. Indeed, it lays boundaries between the family and its environment; it separates the "between us" from the "out there"; it circumscribes the three-dimensional domain in which the partners are free to move in order to implement the other functions—that is, it is the "container" of all productive interactions.

In Figure 3.4b the four formations diverge from the reference triangle. The figure represents one of the many ways in which the participation domain may be disadjusted: It fails to include the infant because the parents orient away from her. It goes without saying that under these conditions no other function can possibly be implemented. It is this D framework that characterizes disordered alliances.

ORGANIZATION FORMATIONS

Organization formations display the roles of active versus third-party partner. We must take into account the social rules that specify the distances in addressing a direct partner versus being a participant observer during an interaction. In addition, these rules make special provisions for dialogue distance with an infant, which is shorter than with an adult. Figure 3.5 depicts the triangle of reference for each part of the play resulting from these rules.

On the left of Figure 3.5 we see that the active parents turn the table in order to face the infant (also a special provision for the infant) when they set out to play in parts one and two. Then they lean toward the infant at a distance that facilitates dialogue (18–25 cm; (Papousek and Papousek, 1987; Schoetzau, 1979). The third parties sit back, at "watching" distance—that is, far enough not to interfere but close enough to perceive what is going on in the dyad. In part three, both parents align at infant dialogue distance from the infant; they stay at intimate distance between themselves in order to be able to closely coordinate. Finally, in part four, they both sit back so that the infant is at watching distance, while they position at adult dialogue distance from each other. On the right of Figure 3.5 the criteria for the specific distances between the partners are defined. It is mainly by their distal positions in relation to each other that the partners show who they address directly and who is watching. These address patterns constitute new triangles that are part specific and are the references for assessing actual organization formations.

Organization formations originate at level two. They are delineated anew at levels three and four by means of complex patterns combining distal positions between the heads with gazes and expressions (see details in Figure 3.6).

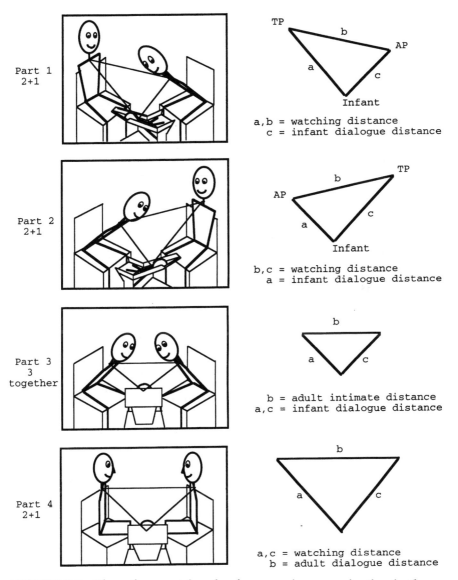

FIGURE 3.5 The reference triangles for assessing organization in the four parts, at torso level.

On the left, pictograms of the distal positions in each part. By connecting the middle points of the parents' shoulder positions with respect to the infant's, reference triangles are obtained that are oblique (parts one and two) and isoceles (parts three and four).

On the right, criteria of distances between the torsos corresponding to the three sides of the organization reference triangles.

64

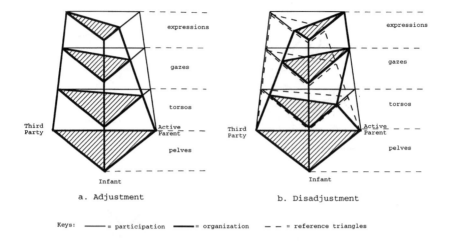

FIGURE 3.6   The domain of organization in part one and its insertion within the domain of participation.

To derive the actual organization formations at level two, the middle points of the parents' shoulders are connected with respect to the infant's (see Figure 3.5). At level three, it is by means of the distal positions between the partners' heads combined with their gaze orientations that the organization formation is derived. At level four, it is by the addresses of the expressions that the formation is derived (i.e., to whom the partners address their facial expressions, vocalizations, gestures, and who they touch). By connecting the organization formations at the three levels, the representation of the domain of organization is obtained.

Adjustment: The formations at the three levels are isomorphic with the reference triangle. At torso level, the distances are adjusted. At gaze level, the distances between heads are adjusted to infant/adult dialogue and watching distance. The gaze orientations are reciprocal between the active partners but unilateral between the third parties and the dyads. At the expressive level, the signals are also reciprocal between active partners but unilateral between the third parties and the dyads. Under these conditions, the domain of organization is adjusted.

Disadjustment: The formations at the three levels are not isomorphic to the reference triangle. At level two, the distance between the active partner and the infant is shorter than infant dialogue distance, and the distance between the third party and the infant is infant dialogue distance. At level three, the distances between the heads are also too short. At levels three and four, there is too much gaze and expressive contact between the third party and the infant, and too little between the active parent and the infant. Under these conditions, the domain of organization has a distorted, irregular aspect that graphically depicts its disadjustment.

Figure 3.6 shows the domain of organization obtained when the formations at the three levels for part one are connected. In addition, the figure shows how this domain neatly inserts itself within the domain of participation.

In figure 3.6a, the formations are isomorphic to the reference triangle for part one and constitute a regular structure. This domain of organization shows everyone in their roles; consequently, it is adjusted.

In contrast, Figure 3.6b represents one of the main ways in which the domain of organization may be disadjusted. Globally, it shows that the initial formation at level two diverges from the reference, in that it is too small because the dialogue distance and the watching distance of the parents are reduced; then the second and third formations, at levels three and four, are inverted, in that the third party directly addresses the infant and the active parent is left watching. Practically, it corresponds to the situation where the active parent leans too close to the infant, invading her space; consequently, the infant orients her gaze toward the third party who, also leaning too close, responds by an encouraging gaze and expressive contact, thus interfering with the active parent.

Of course, when the organization formations are distorted, focal attention and affective contact cannot be implemented to satisfaction, even though participation is kept intact. This C framework characterizes the collusive alliances.

FOCAL ATTENTION FORMATIONS

Focal attention formations display the joint focuses shared by the partners as they play the face-to-face games. These games are face-to-face in the literal sense as prescribed by the LTP instructions, asking the parents not to use objects. The active partners' faces or body parts are the references for assessing focal attention formations.

Focal attention formations logically originate at level three, with head and gaze orientations. The possibility is introduced not only to globally address each other but to specifically co-orient together on some point, manifesting that the partners have a joint focus. These patterns of co-orientations constitute a new type of formation. Of course, focal attention formations are redelineated at level four. Indeed, it is also in reference to the current focus of the play that the partners display most of their expressions: for instance, a third-party parent looking and smiling at the dyad smiling at each other.

A single oval surface in each part is used to symbolize co-orientations, indicating that the partners continuously attend jointly to the appropriate focuses. Figure 3.7 shows the domain of focal attention that is obtained when the two formations are connected and how it inscribes itself within the other domains.

In Figure 3.7a the domain of focal attention is adjusted and in Figure 3.7b it is disadjusted. As indicated by the two oval surfaces that only partially overlap, more than one focus at a time prevails at the level of gazes and the expressions manifested at level four refer to more than one focus at the same time. For instance, whereas the active parent mother and the infant focus together on their playing, the third-party father is rapidly altering his gaze between the focus of the game and mother; he is as preoccupied with controlling her actions as with following up the action. At level four, the tense smile on his face (not shown in the figure) also reflect this dual preoccupation. Or, the active parent mother fragments the games, interrupting them prematurely and forcing new focuses on the infant's attention by means of distraction strategies, thus creating only partially overlapping focuses. It follows that trilogue play cannot be implemented to satisfaction, but participation and organization remain intact. It is this type of B framework that characterizes the stressed alliances.

AFFECTIVE CONTACT FORMATIONS

Affective contact formations display the sharing of affects between the partners, which is the goal of trilogue play. They appear at the level of expressions and insert themselves within the domain of joint attention.

Indeed, at the level of expressions the partners are able to communicate specific affects to each other by means of vocalizations and brief movements of the face, hands, head, and body—movements that are contingent and resonant with each other. Remember that these signals are not exclusively positive. The parents also stay in tune with the baby when she is disregulated by means of empathetic signals that typically involve blends of negative-resonant and positive-entraining displays.

Figure 3.8a symbolizes affective contact formations by three positive and overlapping smiles. These symbols stand for either direct, playful, and positive exchanges, or empathetic ones; they are contingent on each other and reflect a communion of affects. The figure also shows how they neatly insert

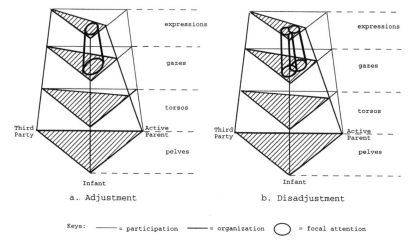

Keys: ——— = participation   ━━━ = organization   ◯ = focal attention

FIGURE 3.7 Domain of focal attention in part one, its insertion within other domains.

The focal attention formations at levels three and four are symbolized by means of an oval placed between the active partners. At level three, this oval contains the center points of the three partners' gazes (on faces or body parts)—that is, their co-orientations on the focus of the game. At level four, this oval "contains" the facial, vocal, and gestural expressions that refer to the focus of the game. By connecting the focal attention formations at the two levels, the representation of the domain of focal attention is obtained.

Adjustment: The formations at the two levels are isomorphic to the reference oval and appropriately located. The partners co-orient their gazes on the focus of the game, which is located on faces or body parts.

Disadjustment: The formations at the two levels are split in two focuses that only partially overlap. At level three, the gazes are not sufficiently co-oriented, because one partner is dividing his or her attention ("flickering gaze") or fragmenting it (see text for examples). At level four, the expressions are not referring to the same focus.

themselves within the other domains. This A framework characterizes the cooperative alliances. All functions are implemented to satisfaction.

Figure 3.8b symbolizes the disadjustment of the domain of affective contact through positive, neutral, and negative smiles that do not overlap, indicating their dissonance and nondependency on each other. For instance, the third-party parent, in contrast with our previous example, follows the action, but does not visibly resonate to it; or the active parent mother overshoots or undershoots her stimulations, generating incongruity with the

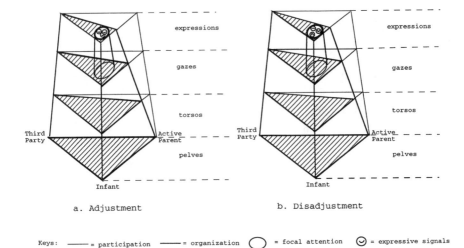

a. Adjustment   b. Disadjustment

Keys: ———— = participation ———— = organization ◯ = focal attention ☺ = expressive signals

FIGURE 3.8   Domain of affective contact in part one, its insertion within the other domains.

The affective contact formations at level four are symbolized by smiles that overlap to indicate that they are contingent and reflect affective communion.

Adjustment: The smiles overlap; they are positive (direct or empathetic sharing). The three partners are in playful or empathetic communion.

Disadjustment: The smiles do not overlap and do not have the same valence. Although the three partners share the same focus, their affective displays concerning the focus are dissonant with each other and/or are not contingent with each other.

infant. However, more often than not, this type of disadjustment goes hand in hand with disadjustment in the domain of focal attention. Then the dissonant smiles are distributed in two ovals rather than one. This B framework corresponds to stressed alliances.

THE INTERPLAY BETWEEN PARENTS AND INFANT

Up to this point, we have specified the conditions in which triangular interactions are structured without considering that the partners are unequal in their capacities to implement them. We know that the parents have to substitute for the infant in many respects. Structurally speaking, they implement for her the controls she cannot yet execute herself, for example, controlling her body posture. They settle the three-month-old in the seat, verifying that it is appropriately inclined, tying her with the belt to keep her from falling. These details are essential since an improperly inclined seat would radically exclude the infant. Likewise, orienting the seat to face either of the parents (parts one and two) or both of them (parts three and four) is imperative.

It is important to emphasize that although the infant cannot implement these controls on her own, she can follow up on them once they are secured for her. An alert three-month-old placed in a vis-à-vis position, with her body and head adequately supported, understands perfectly that this setting is for dialogue: She can activate her postural tonus and further implement dialogue by means of the signals she has under better control, namely head and gaze orientations and expressions, even though she also needs her parents' framing in sustaining her attention (Kaye, 1982; Camaioni, 1989) and in regulating her affects (Trevarthen, 1984; Tronick, 1989).

Suppose the baby responds to her mother's calling for her with a change of her head and gaze direction and a brightening up of her face. In doing so, she marks her inclusion and her role by respectively placing her signals within the domain of participation and addressing them to her direct partner. Suppose she also follows up by joyfully vocalizing with her mother. The infant shows her readiness to attend to a specific face-to-face game and falls in tune with her partner. As the infant matures, the balance of control will shift to a more equal repartition. Chapter 5 examines the moves observed when the baby is nine months old.

The parents and the infant thus assume their guiding and developing functions, which are necessary conditions in trilogue play. Therefore, we need to integrate them in our assessment and to modify the criteria in this balance of control between parents and infant as the latter develops new skills.

THE TRIANGULAR FRAMEWORK OVER THE ENTIRE PLAY AND THE INTERPLAY OF INFLUENCES WITHIN IT

We have mainly discussed the structural frameworks in the first part of the LTP. Considering the succession of the four parts adds yet another dimension to the framework. The partners have to sustain their coordinations in each of the four domains over the entire play with the flexibility necessary to adjust to the changes in roles, focuses, and variations in affect.

Figure 3.9 shows the triangular framework of the four parts in succession. Note again the constancy in the "container" provided by the domain of par-

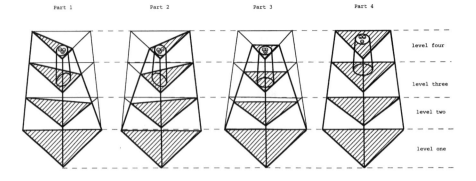

FIGURE 3.9   The triangular framework in the four parts of the LTP.

ticipation in the face of the modifications of the organization domain according to the two-plus-one or three-together formats. The same relation holds for the domain of organization with respect to changes in the focal attention domain, and so on.

The importance of these invariant/variant relationships cannot be overemphasized in order to understand the interplay of influences in the triangular framework. This understanding enables us to precisely assess the resources versus the disturbances a family experiences when working together. The full structures of each part represented in Figure 3.9 graphically depict that operations become distinctly more complex and variable in time as we move up from the pelves to the expression levels. This is precisely what defines a hierarchical structure (Fivaz, 1989).

Regarding the directions of hierarchy influences, two principles are at work: circularity and asymmetry. On the one hand, all components are coupled and therefore influence each other. On practical grounds, it is necessary that all formations at all levels work in concert. On the other hand, when systems are hierarchically organized, the interplay of influences is asymmetrical (Fivaz-Depeursinge, 1991). The most encompassing and invariant components (the participation formations) exert a stronger influence on the least encompassing and most variant ones (the affective contact formations). We refer to the stronger forces as *contextual* and to the weaker forces as *implicative* (Cronen, Kenneth, and Lannamann, 1982).

Consequently, in assessing triangular patterns, we consider that distortions in the participation formations are more taxing for achieving trilogue than, say, distortions occurring only in the joint attention or affective contact formations. The former are more contextual and the latter are more implicative.

THE FRAMEWORKS THAT WORK

None of the actual interactions we have observed strictly and continuously conform to the optimal functioning we have just sketched. First, infants never unfailingly cooperate throughout the LTP, especially at three months. And it is important to remember that what the task calls for primarily is to establish the appropriate balance between the needs of the baby and the collaboration with the research team. This requirement manifests the autonomy of the parents with respect to the authority of the researchers. Second, perfect coordination is not the rule. As we shall see in Chapter 4, what counts in the long run is how families repair miscoordinations.

Therefore, and not surprisingly, the actual criteria we use for our assessment are relative rather than absolute: Is everyone sufficiently included? Is everyone sufficiently in their roles? Is everyone sufficiently attending to games and sufficiently in touch? The child did not agree to cooperate with the researchers. Furthermore, opposing her parent's goal may enhance the infant's development provided this goal is clearly presented by means of their nonverbal displays. Therefore, an infant's refusal to cooperate in the face of her parents' clear, well-coordinated, and benevolent offer to engage in trilogue would not hinder the framework categorization.

A Frameworks

Returning to the assessment scheme laid out in the earlier part of this chapter (see Figure 3.1), we have arrived at our categorization by answering positively to the four requirements: Everyone is sufficiently included, is in their roles, is attending to the games, and is in touch. This situation also implies that the parents fill in for their infant as needed.

However, as already emphasized, the drawing of the actual four types of formations at the four levels for type A frameworks would only approximate the ideal framework. There would inevitably be minor and temporary irregularities in some of the formations, yet congruence and adjustment prevail.

Mike's family play is typical in these respects. In Chapter 2 we note that in the first part, mother tends to overshoot her stimulations and that in spite of his brilliant efforts to cope Mike finally has to put a stop to them and cry. However, when we examine how the four functions are implemented in this part, we see that everyone is included, in their roles, focusing on the games; it is the process of affectively fine-tuning that partly derails, yet only in the mother–baby dyad. The third-party father empathetically stays in touch. This type of structure readily falls within the range of sufficient adjustment. This is confirmed in the next parts when father takes over as the active parent, helping Mike to recover, and then carrying him along in a very intense imitation game. Everyone is not only included in their roles and paying attention but is in tune. In particular, mother as third party thoroughly enjoys father's success.

However, father too has overestimated Mike's endurance in engaging, and by the time they get ready for the three-together play, Mike is drawn out. In the three-together part, the front-stage goal switches from engaging in play trilogue to helping Mike regulate his affects. Structurally speaking, everyone is included and in their roles. But their joint attention is by now focused on Mike's state rather than on games and the parents are empathetically in tune with Mike—and Mike responds to that. Again, the parents' flexibility in giving priority to their infant's needs (rather than rigidly sticking to the instructions) falls within the range of sufficient adjustment.

Interestingly, the strategy pays off. During part four, Mike, who is by now in the third-party role, continues his efforts at self-regulating and finally succeeds in reengaging by watching his parents' lively interaction. Everyone is included and in their roles; in addition, the primary focus is reestablished and the three partners end up being in touch again.

In fact, all of these minor mishaps are growth-enhancing not only for the infant but for the parents. One of the goals of observational research is to provide the family with an enriching experience and see how they take advantage of it.

B Frameworks

Like the A frameworks, the B frameworks are pretty effective. The main resources are the goal is discernible from the beginning to the end and these frameworks allow for playful affect sharing. The main difference is that reaching this goal requires hard work and it happens only occasionally because the task is stressful for the family. In particular, the parents experience difficulties in helping the child regulate her attention and her affective states. Thus, the outcome of our assessment of the four functions is sufficiently positive for participation and organization, but it is at the bifurcation to focal attention and/or to affective contact that problems arise.

The patterns of Nancy's family have been constructed to illustrate the resources as well as the stress and hard work that characterize these frameworks. Recall that in part one mother as the active parent adopts a style that is mostly teasing, though she is very quick in perceiving Nancy's aversive reactions. Therefore, she moves rapidly, sometimes abruptly, from one game to the next. Nancy is vigorously holding her ground, alternating between engaging and disengaging, and sometimes turning to her father. He keeps strictly to his third-party role. However, he is visibly stressed not only by the happenings in the mother–baby dyad but also to keep up with time, checking his watch repeatedly.

In structural terms, it is where focal attention is concerned that we observe a clear difference with the ideal framework, in that the focus on games is fragmented and thus not sufficiently jointly attended. It follows that mother and baby can reach only rare and brief moments of playful enjoyment, with third-party father resonating. Most of the time, the affective contact is marked by antagonism between the infant and her parents, which in turn stresses the third-party father, who also gets out of focus, checking his watch and being momentarily distracted.

In part two, the father as the active parent adopts a very contrasting style—so low key, in fact, that it fails to enlist Nancy's attention. On the other hand, mother resonates so intensely that she unwittingly makes herself too conspicuous. Whereas this type of interaction is very different in style and content from the interaction in part one, it matches the latter's structure in most respects.

In Chapter 2 we note an interesting change in part three, in that the parents' conjugated resources enable Nancy to better regulate her affects. Basically she looks at her low-key father and gives him affective signals while responding in fact to mother's still vigorous stimulations—that is, she mediates each of her parent's styles with the other by crossing them over, so to speak.

As a consequence, in part three, the family is better able to jointly attend to the games and to keep in tune with each other, to the point of attaining several, though brief, episodes of playful affect sharing. In comparison with parts one and two, we can now draw a single oval to symbolize a shared focus and inscribe in it happy smiles to symbolize affective contact, such as in A frameworks. The drawing of the part four framework generally matches that of part three.

Roughly speaking, the framework is maintained throughout in spite of the stress that the situation imposes on this family and the lows in parts one and two. The resources for playful affect sharing are there, yet attaining it requires the three partners to join forces in handling this stress in the face of their sharp differences. It is fascinating to observe the strong cooperation between the parents that not only allows them to play by the rules in spite of their differences but to happily conjugate these differences in the three-together scene. Likewise, it is wondrous to watch a three-month-old infant's ability to combine two styles that are not separately suited for her into a whole that fits her better.

THE FRAMEWORKS THAT DO NOT WORK

The other two types of frameworks are problematic in that they stop any sustained experience of mutual enjoyment no matter how much the partners strive for it. Yet we should not overlook the strength that characterizes these interactions. The very striving toward the goal and the collaboration with the researchers are witness to the enormous motivation that animates families at the stage of infancy.

C Frameworks

Altogether, in this type of framework, participation is intact. It is when organization is at issue that the deviations appear. Then all other functions are compromised as well.

Typically, Frankie and his parents are unfailingly engaged. With respect to organization, we observe that mother, who is the active parent in part one, leans very close to Frankie—too close in fact—and father, who is the third party, hardly sits back. The result is that Frankie tends to gaze away from his mother toward his father. As no repair is attempted, the actual gaze contact takes place mostly between the infant and the third-party father. Finally, the expressive signals between the parents and Frankie are not addressed to the appropriate partner either. In fact, they are scarce. Mother as active parent does not have much direct contact with Frankie anyway. Father, when addressed by Frankie, responds with mixed signals because of his third-party role. In any case, Frankie himself hardly smiles at all. These patterns closely match the model presented in Figure 3.6.

The same patterns of competition between the parents prevail in part two. In fact, the distortions in the organization formations remain invariant over the four parts as do the distortions in the joint attention and affective contact formations. Practically, it is when they move to part three that Frankie tenses up, making sucking movements, and the parents are able to momentarily overcome their competition by focusing together on what they call his anger or discontent: mother by imitating somewhat mockingly these movements and father by moralizing. By part four, Frankie is very tense and vigilant.

Structurally speaking, the framework remains distorted throughout the LTP. It derails invariably at the bifurcation to organization, compromising focal attention as well as affective contact. If the parents adequately fill in for Frankie's participation, they do not sufficiently support him in keeping to his role, in sharing a focus, and in keeping affectively in touch with them.

In Frankie's family, the competition is overt (C1: overt collusive alliance). In contrast, other families in the C frameworks may avoid competition at all costs (C2: covert collusive alliance). The parents remain distant from each other and from the infant. They rigidly divide their roles, and when they have to act together in part three, they continue to alternate rather than coact. They typically abbreviate part four. Due to the distance they maintain, their stimulations of the infant are below his threshold of arousal, and if anything happens, it is probably on his own initiative. The result is eventually the same as in the open competition in that the infant progressively disengages. He loses interest and focuses on objects or parts of his body.

D Frameworks

For the four issues of our assessment we have four negative results: (1) regarding participation, exclusion prevails; (2) regarding organization, abstaining and/or interfering prevail; (3) regarding focal attention, it is hardly possible to detect a joint focus much less one that might relate to play; and (4) regarding affective contact, most attempts at getting in touch are failing. There is no way the goal of trilogue play could be reached, the goal is not discernible, the four types of formations are distorted, and the parents fail in sufficiently substituting for the infant while supporting and protecting her. In spite of these extreme difficulties in trying to coordinate, the family nevertheless fights to reach the goal and cooperate with the researchers.

In Chapter 2 we emphasize two typical features in this type of alliance. First, the unfailing courage of the parents in pursuing the task in spite of their fear of the baby's crying—a fear that materializes at the end of part two. Second, we also note the endless contest between the parents about the inclination of the infant's seat. Settled too straight, Tania sags while seated;

interestingly, she happens to be leaning on father's side yet turned toward mother. This is just one example of the ambiguity that prevails in these family members' signals. For instance, in part one, as she tries to engage Tania, mother is seated as far away as possible from father and also sits far away from Tania, not turning the seat toward her. She addresses her solicitations from a distance, with a monotonous but high-pitched voice, touching Tania with the tips of her fingers. Father's signals are ambiguous too, particularly when he is in the third-party role and Tania turns to him. Keeping distant and silent, he nevertheless addresses her with exaggerated smiles and expressions.

Let us attempt to untangle these observations and put them in structural terms. The first and most determinantal element is the structural implication of settling the infant's seat at an inappropriate inclination. There is no way for the infant to participate without proper support of her body. Therefore, no triangular coordination is possible unless repair is effected. And we know that the parents repeatedly try to redress the seat to no avail; on the contrary, each repair makes it worse. The model states that the deviation from participation formations prevents the sufficient adjustment of all other formations.

Continuing to trace the participation formations at the other levels, namely torsos, gazes, and expressive signals, we find that there are but a few fleeting episodes where all partners' signals fall within the participation domain. Indeed, a partner's ambiguous signals preclude participation and exert a perplexing effect on the other partners, which is interpreted as negative.

Perhaps more conspicuous are the distortions of the organization formations. A distant stance at all levels, such as mother's as active parent, is hardly compatible with this role. Likewise, an interfering or withdrawing stance, such as father's as third party, also fails to fit this role. Finally, a twisted posture and sideways glances such as Tania's as active partner are not fitted to her role. Nor are her rare affect signals that she addresses ambiguously or not at all.

There is not much left to consider regarding focal attention. In any case, the observer is in no position to detect a focus. Finally, what of affective contact? Most of the time, no one manifests that they are in touch with each other. The rare signals expressed are tinged with negativity or are blatantly negative, and they are almost never triangular.

Again, there is not much to add to the structural description when we examine the other parts of the play. As reported in Chapter 2, part two is an amplified replay of part one, with the dispute about the infant's seat rising to new heights; so was Tania's sucking and leaning out, until she broke down in sobs. Parts three and four are endless alternations between taking Tania out to soothe her and putting her back in the seat to watch her suck.

Therefore, the framework becomes even more distorted with each part; the goal of the interaction turns into an absurd preoccupation with keeping up with a meaningless and painstaking task. Most taxing in structural terms is the parents' increasing inability to appropriately fill in for their child by providing her with the most basic holding. It goes hand in hand with their inability to protect and relieve her from pain.

Within D frameworks, we distinguish this type of rigid interaction (D2: rigid disordered alliances) from those that are also unproductive but vary, as if the partners were testing various alternatives and thus striving for a change (D1: chaotic disordered alliances). In our clinical experience, this subtype has a better chance for change than the rigid subtype. We return to this topic in Chapter 6.

CONCLUSIONS

In this chapter we propose a model to describe the structure of triangular interactions in the LTP. It assesses in succession the implementation of the four nested functions we fulfill in face-to-face interactions in general and in trilogue play in particular: participation, or whether everybody is included; organization, or whether everybody keeps to their roles; focal attention, or whether everybody attends to the games; and affective contact, or whether everybody is in touch.

The method for assessing these issues draws on the procedures we intuitively use in our daily interactions: checking on the gestaltlike formations that we create together by coordinating our displays, at the four physical levels of interaction that we activate in trilogue play (level one: pelves; level two: torsos; level three: gazes; level four: expressive signals). In the LTP, these formations result in a pyramidal structure. The wider structure serves participation; it is drawn by the participation formations that delineate the transactional domain and that the partners display from level one up. Nested in these and displayed from level two up are the organization formations by which the partners manifest their roles; in turn, nested in the organization formations and displayed from level three up are the joint attention formations that designate the focus to which the partners are attending; finally, nested in the joint attention formations and displayed at level four are the affective contact formations by which the partners show their being in touch with each other.

Together, the formations constitute the triangular framework. They form a four-level hierarchical system characterized by influences that are both circular and asymmetrical. The more contextual the formations, the stronger their influence on the others (e.g., the participation formations in relation to the organization ones). In contrast, the more implicative the formations, the weaker their influence on the others (e.g., the affective contact formations in relation to the focal attention ones).

Given this interplay, we can categorize frameworks by detecting which formations are adjusted or disadjusted, and therefore which functions are appropriately implemented versus which functions eventually derail. Repeating this operation for each part, we end up with a full framework that indicates how the partners travel the course of the entire play.

In all four framework types the main objective is for the partners to attain trilogue play and to cooperate with the researchers. In the A and B frameworks the goal is attainable and the tonality of the play is mostly positive, whereas in the C and D frameworks the goal is definitely out of reach and the tonality of the play is mixed or negative.

In the A frameworks, all functions are implemented; in the B frameworks, focal attention and/or affective contact derail to some extent. In the C frameworks, organization also derails. In the D frameworks, all functions, beginning with participation, are jeopardized.

The crucial test with respect to the validity of the framework model is the actual hierarchical embeddedness between the four functions. When disadjustment occurs, say in participation formations, then all the formations serving the other functions should be disadjusted too. When focal attention formations are adjusted, then participation and organization formations should be adjusted. The model proved to fit all families' observations in the sample, with minor exceptions (for details, see Frascarolo, Fivaz-Depeursinge, and Corboz-Warnery, under review). We discuss the meaning of these exceptions in Chapter 8. On the other hand, as reported in Chapter 1, types of frameworks remained fairly stable over the first year.

In our view, this model has main assets over previous ones: First, it accommodates three interactants and focuses on how they relate rather than on the addition of their separate behaviors. Second, the model accommodates the multiple modalities that the partners activate in play and it orders them into levels of increasing complexity and variability over time. Third, the model accounts for the directions of influences between the different levels, combining the asymmetrical directions with the circularity between the components. Fourth, the model differentiates degrees of adjustment/disadjustment to the task—that is, it applies both to functional and dysfunctional interactions. Fifth, it is potentially applicable to other types of triangular interactions. We return to these issues in more detail in Chapter 8.

At this point, it is important to recall that we propose this model on the basis of exploratory studies, however microanalytical it may be. Therefore, further research by independent teams on representative samples is needed for validation. In the meantime, it is the clinical and developmental pertinence and plausibility that plead for the triangular framework.

REFERENCES

Beebe, B., and Stern, D. N. (1977). Engagement–disengagement and early object experiences. In N. Freedman and S. Grand (eds.), *Communicative Structures and Psychic Structures. A Psychoanalytic Interpretation of Communication.* New York: Plenum Press.

Camaioni, L. (1989). The role of social interaction in the transition from communication to language. In A. de Ribeaupierre (ed.), *Transitions Mechanisms in Child Development: The Longitudinal Perspective* (pp. 109–125). Cambridge: Cambridge University Press.

Cohn, J., and Tronick, E. (1988). Discrete versus scaling approaches to the description of mother–infant face-to-face interaction: Convergent validity and divergent applications. *Developmental Psychology, 24*(3), 396–397.

Cronen, V. E., Kenneth, M. J., and Lannamann, J. W. (1982). Paradoxes, double binds, and reflexive loops: An alternative theoretical perspective. *Family Process, 21,* 91–112.

Fivaz, R. (1989). *L'Ordre et la Volupté.* Lausanne: Presses Polytechniques Romandes.

Fivaz-Depeursinge, E. (1991). Documenting a time-bound, circular view of hierarchies: A microanalysis of parent–infant dyadic interaction. *Family Process, 30*(1), 101–120.

Fogel, A. (1977). Temporal organisation in mother–infant face-to-face interaction. In H. R. Schaffer (ed.), *Studies in Mother–Infant Interactions* (pp. 119–152). London: Academic Press.

Frascarolo, F., Fivaz-Depeursinge, E., and Corboz-Warnery, A. (Under review). The evolution of the family alliance over the first year.

Kaye, K. (1982). *The Mental and Social Life of the Baby: How Parents Create Persons.* Chicago: Chicago University Press.

Kendon, A. (1977). Spatial organization in social encounters: The F-formation system. In A. Kendon (ed.), *Studies in the Behavior of Social Interaction* (pp. 179–208). Lisse, IN: Peter DeRidder Press.

Papousek, H., and Papousek, M. (1987). Intuitive parenting: A dialectic counterpart to the infant's integrative competence. In J. D. Osofsky (ed.), *Handbook of Infant Development,* 2nd ed. (pp. 669–720). New York: Wiley.

Schoetzau, A. (1979). Effect of viewing distance on looking behavior in neonates. *International Journal of Behavioral Development, 2,* 121–131.

Trevarthen, C. (1984). Emotions in infancy: Regulators of contact and relationships with persons. In K. R. Scherer and P. Ekman (eds.), *Approaches to Emotion* (pp. 129–157). Hillsdale, NJ: Lawrence Erlbaum.

Tronick, E. Z. (1989). Emotions and emotional communications in infants. *American Psychologist, 44,* 112–119.

Weinberg, M., and Tronick, E. (1994). Beyond the face: An empirical study of infant affective configurations of facial, vocal, gestural and regulatory behaviors. *Child Development, 65,* 1495–1507.

CHAPTER 4

Process Reading, or the Dynamic Foundations of Family Alliances

In understanding interactions, making out a structure is only one task. It is similar to adopting a gestalt vision and focusing on the main contours in order to better discern them. But it necessitates leaving aside the multitude of fluctuations inherent in the coordination dynamics. The very substance of this coordinating is movement between states that mismatch (e.g., mother is smiling and baby is neutral) to states that match (e.g., both are smiling) and vice versa.

Think of the considerable work mother and infant have to accomplish, until they reach a shared smile or vocalization. On initiating play dialogue, the mother looks at the baby and the baby is averted. The mother calls for the baby's attention: "Honey?" and the baby orients to her. Mother greets her by making a mock surprise face, but the baby remains sober; the mother cocks her head in one direction, then in the opposite one, and the baby brightens up. As the mother repeats, "honey, honey," the baby begins to circle her arms and legs; the mother continues calling her, smiling, until the baby finally rises to a smile too. This series of calibrations and recalibrations reflects a process of progressive matching. It may look like a dance, but nevertheless it takes a lot of work. In fact, it is known from several sources that we spend more time in states that mismatch and in movement between states than in states that match. For instance, Tronick and colleagues have shown that mother and infant in dialogue play do not spend more than 30 percent of their time in states that match (Tronick and Cohn, 1989).

These interactionists refer to the movement between matched and mismatched states as "miscoordinations," interactive "errors" and "repair," or "disjunction" and "rerighting" (Beebe and Lachman, 1994). It is important to understand that these terms do not have a negative connotation. Indeed, authors consider that "reparations are typical features of the interactions" (Tronick and Cohn, 1989, p. 90). The point is that we all miscoordinate and repair in our daily interactions, infants included.

Still, S. Duncan prefers the terms "ratifications" for movement toward states that match and "failure to ratify" for movement toward states that mismatch. For this author, interaction is a process by which every move by A is either ratified or not ratified by B (Duncan and Farley, 1990). Despite some interesting differences in outlook, the perspective is close to that of Tronick and his colleagues.

Consider a couple in the midst of an argument. They are obviously in mismatched states. As the argument heats up, the spouses are caught in an escalation process. One way to exit it is to stop and share a positive affect. For instance, at some point, one of them laughs wholeheartedly and comments, "Here we are again!" and the other one laughs too. They pause and proceed with their discussion. This humorous metacommunication has allowed them to move from a mismatched state to a matched state where they repair the interaction. It is known from John Gottman's programmatic research on marital interaction that repair, by means of validation, expressing affection, humor, or interest, is one of the main predictors of a healthy evolution of the marital relationship. Sharing positive affect in the midst of conflict presumably has a buffering effect (Gottman, 1994).

In this chapter, we approach the processes of miscoordination and repair as they manifest themselves in transitions between the configurations of the Lausanne triadic play (LTP). But let us first reacquaint ourselves with how these processes manifest themselves during transitions by taking a brief detour via other nonverbal interactions.

MISCOORDINATION AND REPAIR DURING TRANSITIONS IN MEDICAL INTERACTIONS

Exemplary indeed are the miscoordinations in physician–patient consultations, particularly at the juncture between the interview and the physical examination. At this time, it is critical that the partners keep up their relationship and cooperate while avoiding any ambiguity concerning intimacy. This explains the radical change in behavior that they adopt: In proceeding to the physical examination, the physician switches to a much more neutral stance, narrowing the focus of his or her gaze on the part of the body that he or she is to inspect. The patient ceases to move and looks to the side, keeping the physician's gestures in her peripheral vision field (Heath, 1986). This is in sharp contrast with the rules of interaction that prevail during the interview, where physician and patient face each other, look at each other, and perhaps smile. Hence the moment of transition between the two agendas is most critical to allow the partners to attribute meanings devoid of ambiguity to their behaviors, particularly with respect to a gaze directed at a naked part of the patient's body. As a consequence, any miscoordination in conducting this transition is liable to generate problems, mainly embarrassment in the patient and puzzlement in the physician.

A. Heath, a specialist in the study of physician–patient interactions, reports in detail the observation of such an episode (Heath, 1988). The physician has just asked the female patient to undress when the telephone rings. She is waiting, undressed from her waist up. Upon finishing the phone conversation, the physician and the patient reorient to each other. As she looks up at him, she finds him looking at her chest. She rushes into a seemingly chaotic behavior; looking down, she begins to pass her open hand back and forth over her chest, blinking and shaking her head; she stops only when she perceives in her peripheral vision that the physician looks up again. She looks up too, only to find the physician again looking at her chest. She repeats the same gestures. It is only when both physician and patient mark a cutoff by averting their gazes and rearranging their seating positions that the normal course of interaction is reinstated. According to Heath, the patient's apparently chaotic gesturing may be understood as a response to a paradoxical situation in which the meaning of the gaze has become ambiguous. Recalling that both modesty and cooperation are required from a patient, these gestures may be interpreted as having a double meaning: On the one hand, they display her sense of modesty (by hiding her chest), and on the other hand, her willingness to cooperate with the physical examination (by uncovering her chest).

In this case, the partners repair the interaction by marking a cutoff. Such cutoffs serve as stop actions and as synchronizers to begin a new sequence. But a mutual smile or laugh, even with mixed overtones, may also occur—that is, an affective event.

It is not surprising to find such major miscoordinations at the junctures between different agendas of the medical consultation. The coordinations in moving from a given configuration to the next are so numerous and demanding that transitions are vulnerable points, especially at times of tension and conflict. Miscoordinations are most likely to occur at junctures in daily routines such as greetings, departures, or changing the subject of a conversation. Once they occur, they may be difficult to repair. In bad cases, the repair action itself may be ineffective, if not self-defeating, generating embarrassment, perhaps even shame (Emde and Oppenheim, 1995; Miller, 1996).

In studying the course of the transitions between the interview and the physical examination in a number of medical consultations, we have found that physician–patient dyads routinely go through the two-step four-phase sequence of the transition that Kendon described in kissing rounds (Kendon, 1976), which is reported in Chapter 1. Note that this sequence is mostly implicit. The partners begin with phase one, the announcement, in which one of them in some way hints at the change to come; for example, the patient might glance or point to the body part to be examined, or the physician might look in that direction. In phase two, the ratification, the partner signifies agreement; for example, the physician briefly co-orients on the body part to inspect, or the patient follows the physician's gaze. In phase three, the deconstruction, the partners dismantle the previous interview configuration; for example, they stop looking at each other and one of them turns away. In phase four, the reconstruction, they initiate the new configuration; for example, having walked to the examination bed, the physician assumes the neutral stance and the patient adopts the peripheral gaze orientation. In this study, we did not observe the major missteps that generate embarrassment, presumably because it involved experienced and sensitive physicians. However, we found that minor miscoordinations were more probable in the interactions that the physicians evaluated as difficult than in the ones that ran smoothly (Graf, 1997; Guex, 1992).

Kendon did not put forward the process of miscoordination and repair in his study of kissing rounds. But we can easily imagine the kind of disastrous consequence a misstep in this type of transition might cause, notwithstanding embarrassment. On the other hand, the lovers might successfully repair the event, perhaps by means of humor, and by integrating the event in the story of their relationship. This is an important point: What may appear as a major miscoordination might be promptly repaired and what may appear as a minor miscoordination might entrain an escalation and an endless process of problematic repair.

MISCOORDINATION AND REPAIR IN INFANT INTERACTIONS

That infants as young as three months actively work at repairing miscoordinations is demonstrated by the dramatic still-face experiments. Tronick and colleagues ask mothers, after a two-minute regular face-to-face play period, to pose a still face: They continue to face their baby but remain facially, vocally, and gesturally unresponsive. After two minutes, they resume the face-to-face play. Most striking during the still-face episode is the three-month-old babies' effort at reestablishing contact. After briefly averting, they typically reorient to their mothers, signaling with smiles, coos, and gestures to resume play. They actively attempt to repair the violation of the rules of dialogue. When their actions repeatedly fail to reach this goal, the babies become wary, possibly distressed, and they finally withdraw (Tronick, Als, Adamson, and Wise, 1978; see also Beebe and Langman, 1994; Murray and Trevarthen, 1986).

By six months, infants respond in a more mature way. Although they show when they are disturbed, there is little fussing and crying; besides, they also display interest in the situation (Toda and Fogel, 1993). Some babies will even laugh at their mother, certain that this behavior does not fit (Cohn and Tronick, 1983) and that it is playful.

Repair of this major violation of dialogue rules is hard work, which is best demonstrated by the babies' mixed patterns of positive and negative affect in the third phase when the mothers resume playing (Weinberg and Tronick, 1996). The authors observe a carryover effect from the still face to the reunion, with increased negative affect such as crying and fussing. However, they also observe a rebound of positive affect, in expressions of joy, increased looking at mother, and vocalizations.

Although these authors have not described in detail how mother and baby jointly go about repairing the interaction, they consider that the complexity of the infant's affective reactions "reflects the dyad's attempt to renegotiate their typical interaction and to cope with the negative intra and interpersonal aftermath of the still-face" (Weinberg and Tronick, 1996, p. 912). Furthermore, they argue that the experience of repair has an important developmental function. It induces the development of interactive skills. Indeed, coordination significantly increases over the first year (Tronick and Cohn, 1989). Repair provides the infant with a sense of his effectiveness (versus helplessness when he is unable to repair) and strengthens his sense of self (see also Trevarthen, 1993, for reports of similar types of experimental perturbations).

TRANSITIONS AND MISCOORDINATIONS

It is only in reference to a given structure that we can detect miscoordinations and repair. Rather than exposing these processes as they manifest themselves during the parts of the LTP, we have elected to examine them during the transitions between these parts. There is a systematic correspondence between the two-step four-phase microstructure of the transition and the macrostructure of the triangular framework. For instance, take the two-plus-one and the three-together organization formations in Frankie's family. We see that they are distorted because of competition between the parents. When we look at the transition between these two parts, we observe corresponding distortions in the phases to the extent that microanalyzing transitions constitutes another pathway to characterize the triangular framework.

Statistical analysis of interactive patterns by means of a program that not only detects patterns but also analyzes their temporal orchestration or their complexity clearly differentiated the transitions of satisfactory versus problematic alliances (Magnusson, 1988). Generally, the patterns of transitions in good-enough alliances were highly complex, coherent, and effective in implementing transitions. The patterns of transitions in problematic alliances were less complex; they were laborious and inefficient in implementing the transition (Besse, 1997). In good-enough alliances the transitions are clear and succeed in marking and implementing the change in configuration. In problematic alliances the transitions are tortuous or abrupt, failing in marking and implementing the change.

The last two parts of the LTP are the most sensitive to parents' coordination, and the transition to the first of those—the three-together configuration—is the most telling. Assessing process during two-plus-one to three-together transitions takes us to a more subtle aspect of the triangular framework and reveals the dynamics that sustain it. We draw on data from other families in our longitudinal sample. While broadening the reader's perspective, we report on the extensive work done with Xerxes's family. In addition to collaborating with our longitudinal study, Xerxes's parents allowed multiple interviews by several people and actively participated in a collaborative research team, the Interfaces study group (Fivaz-Depeursinge et al., 1994). Thus, additional data are also available on the parents' inter-subjective experiences during miscoordination and repair, or their representations and childhood memories.

Much of the work presented has been stimulated by this study group. Like Mike's family, Xerxes's is representative of the cooperative alliances. We begin by examining in depth the structure of their two-plus-one to three-together transition to get a clear perspective of how the Kendonian structure manifests itself in the LTP. An incursion into this structure at other ages shows that it is conserved across developmental changes in the first year. It is against this structure that we describe the processes of miscoordination and repair. The results of the entire sample are reported in Appendix A.

A Alliances: Swift Repair

Remember that in order to change from the two-plus-one to the three-together configuration, the partners preannounce the transition until they are in a transition-ready state. Then they prepare (step one) the transition before actually implementing it (step two). Each step is in turn constituted by two phases. During the preparation, the partners begin by announcing the change (phase one) and ratifying it (phase two) before proceeding to the actual implementation by deconstructing (phase three) the two-plus-one configuration and reconstructing (phase four) the three-together configuration. The sequence of all the moves in Xerxes's family transition is represented by pictograms in Figure 4.1. It lasts 24 seconds.

The two-plus one state (pictogram a): We start at the end of the two-plus-one part in which mother is the active parent, more precisely at the final high point of the "perfect face game." Mother sings as she successively touches her baby's cheek, forehead, other cheek, chin. Xerxes is very involved and father follows closely. The threesome, looking at each other, are smiling and laughing. This high point in affective contact marks their togetherness as well as synchronizes the end of the two-plus-one part. Note that the formations represented on this pictogram correspond to the type A framework that prevails over the entire session: Everyone is included, in their roles, attending to the game and in tune.

Preannounce (pictogram b, 1 second): Xerxes is tired. Though mother is about to begin another round, father moves forward, signaling his readiness

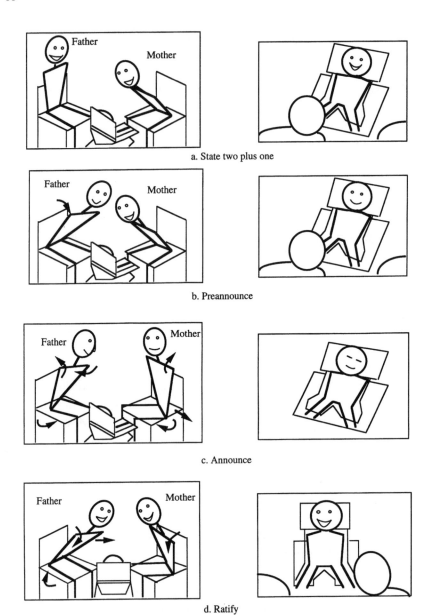

a. State two plus one

b. Preannounce

c. Announce

d. Ratify

FIGURE 4.1 (a–d)   Pictogram transitions in the family of Xerxes

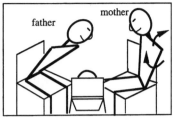 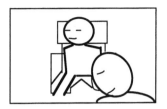

e. Deconstruct

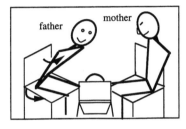 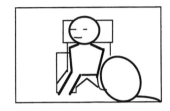

f. Reconstruct with miscoordination

 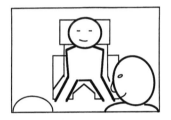

g. Reconstruct with repair of miscoordination

h. State three together

FIGURE 4.1 (e–h)   Pictograms of transition in the family of Xerxes

to proceed to the next part. This preannouncement alerts mother to approach the end of her play.

Preparation Step

1. *Announce* (pictogram c, 6 seconds): Father and Xerxes simultaneously mark a pause as they both look away. These cutoff signals finally register with mother; she stops the game and sits up. Then father turns his body toward mother, saying, "Shall we play together?" and mother acquiesces, complying with father's move to turn toward him. By partially dismantling the two-plus-one configuration, these actions announce the change and thus initiate the preparation step of the transition.

2. *Ratify* (pictogram d, 5 seconds): As father begins to set the infant seat in the middle position, mother keeps at a distance from Xerxes, but as he looks at her, she smiles at him. A dialogue takes place between them; it culminates when the threesome gaze at each other, laughing and smiling. Father reorients his body toward Xerxes. These moves reinstate the two-plus-one configuration, but only partially, thus constituting the ratification phase of the preparation step. Again, the triangular affective event functions to mark togetherness in the face of change as well as to precisely synchronize for the next phase.

Actual Step

1. *Deconstruct* (pictogram e, 5 seconds): Xerxes turns away, still smiling. Mother leans back and to the side, inclines her head, running her hand on her forehead, looking off, whereas father focuses on fixing the infant seat. The two-plus-one configuration is now definitively dismantled. The deconstruction phase of the implementation step is executed.

2. *Reconstruct, including repair of miscoordination* (pictograms f, g, and h, 7 seconds): Having turned his body slightly inward, father is ready to reengage. He sits up, leans toward Xerxes, and extends an arm to touch him. But mother does not follow up. She keeps on looking off, her head on her hand, as if having left the field of action. So father calls again for her to join in— "Shall we play?"—in a soft and warm voice, glancing at her. She begins to lean forward, turning her body to mirror father's position. Both look at the baby, leaning forward, their shoulders aligned as they call for him. Xerxes starts shifting his face toward his parents. These moves complete the actual step of the transition by reconstructing the interaction in the three-together configuration.

But a clear miscoordination occurs during this phase, revealing the very minute nature of transitions. In fact, it only lasts one and a half seconds, but it counts as a significant delay with respect to the pace adopted. In merely suspending her reengagement, mother falls out of pace and thus fails to coordinate in due time with father, so for a moment he finds himself alone in proceeding to the reconstruction. We are at a critical moment in terms of dynamics. In fact, it constitutes one of those crucial bifurcations that will determine to a fair extent whether the interaction to follow will work.

Suppose, on the one hand, that father resents his wife's uncoordinated behavior and goes for some kind of retaliation, perhaps mainly by acting alone. Remember that at this point he has already, appropriately enough, begun to call for Xerxes's attention. When visual contact occurs, breaking this contact in order to address mother would add miscoordination to miscoordination. Suppose, on the other hand, that in taking note of her husband's unilateral action, mother feels rejected and, overlooking her own responsibility in initiating this state of affairs, she settles to remain disengaged. It is known that bad feelings grow exponentially as seconds go by to the extent that reengaging will then become problematic.

As it turns out, in this family, father gracefully calls mother in a tone that is bound to facilitate her emergence from whatever inner experience delayed her. It is with good grace that she ratifies father's request by moving forward and reengaging along with him. Since the baby has not yet actively responded to his father's stimulations, he will find both parents facing him when he reorients. Thus, the miscoordination between the parents has been repaired effectively, not only cooperatively, in a climate of positive affect, but also swiftly enough for the transition's order not to be disturbed. Globally, the family moves from the two-plus-one to the three-together configuration by changing their structure in a coordinated and orderly way.

It is interesting to note that when the parents were interviewed in the Interfaces group by Daniel Stern about their subjective experience during this transition, they reported significant representations and childhood memories relating to this moment of miscoordination and repair. Mother felt she had "done her share, her job was over. It was how she was, as the oldest child, in having to take care of the younger siblings. When she did it, she did it. When she stopped doing it, she stopped" (Fivaz-Depeursinge et al., 1994, p. 81). In other words, she was a demarcator. Likewise, father's interview revealed that "he was a watcher, a waiter, a reader of signals, maintaining a high degree of sensitive vigilance as to how to act so as to adjust to the actions she [mother] and others in his life have made" (p. 81). He was the diplomat in the family.

This example effectively illustrates how parents' sharp personality differences may complement rather than antagonize each other. In this family, as well as others in the sample, the personal ways continued over time. Indeed, from other analyses of similar transitions at five, nine, and twelve months, we found the exact same patterns (Sacco, Fivaz-Depeursinge, and Corboz-Warnery, 1995). In Xerxes's family, the series of phases within the transition were repeated in the same orderly way, although with time they were streamlined and became briefer. The manners of the father as diplomat and the mother as demarcator continued. For instance, although it was mother who was the active parent, the transition was invariably preannounced by father in the face of her tendency to stretch the baby's attention to its very limits. Then it was also the vigilant father who proceeded to announce the transition, by means of a gaze cutoff that was contingent on the baby's gaze cutoff. Mother then proceeded to ratify their move by closing the game, but more than once only after a delay. Yet again the parents promptly repaired the miscoordination in a climate of positive affect.

However, we also observed an important change over time, in that the baby contributed more and more actively in the transition. We have seen that at three months the parents made their announcement contingent on the end of the baby's gaze cycle, when Xerxes markedly turned away from his mother. It made him an agent in this operation, at least a posteriori. This was also the case at later ages, but by then his actions had a deliberate quality to them.

By six months, Xerxes had become uninterested in playing the LTP. He sat, quietly looking down, sober and perfectly regulated. His parents were not only unperturbed but amused, perhaps even proud of what they interpreted as an independent stance. They playfully and patiently went through the entire motions of the LTP, offering their baby numerous opportunities to engage, but not intruding. They were helped by Xerxes, who at times would benevolently grant them a glance with a faint smile. The parents could not fail to reciprocate and this signal of Xerxes was integrated into a triangular affective event that in turn marked the initiation of the transition. Surely, the pattern was repeated during the reconstruction phase of the transition, when Xerxes's seat was turned and he modestly exhibited pleasure.

At nine months, Xerxes was reconciled with the LTP and he was a full party to play. On the other hand, and characteristically for this age, he deliberately called for a stop when his interest in a game declined. Again, the parents ratified these actions by making them an integral part of the transition.

Finally, at 12 months, the session turned out to be merely a long negotiation between Xerxes and his parents. Xerxes had just started walking and had one goal in mind: getting out of his seat. The parents succeeded in distracting him during the first two parts, but settled for a compromise at the inception of part three. They made out their own version of a three-together play with Xerxes out of the seat and adopted a laissez-faire policy during the last part when he was in the third-party position. Consequently, the climate was tense when the parents conducted the two-plus-one to three-together transition. Yet the pattern remained intact; the phases were clear-cut, miscoordinations were swiftly repaired, and Xerxes's stop signals were still an integral part of the sequence. However, the pace of the transition was slowed down because of his negativity.

In conclusion, the pattern of the transition is maintained in the face of the contrasting infant conditions. The miscoordinations do not disrupt the order of the transition, thanks to the swift and flexible cooperative repair by the parents in a climate of positive affect. It is hardly possible to overemphasize the importance of this pattern's invariance as well as the swift repair in order for the infant to learn how to conduct transitions and how to cope with the particular styles of his parents.

B ALLIANCES: COSTLY REPAIR

The most important result concerning B alliances is that repair is possible. However, the conduct of the transition is somewhat difficult. The first possibility is that the transition itself may serve as a reparation for the preceding interaction. For instance, Nancy's parents avoided a breakdown of the play just in time. Consequently, the affective climate was more tense than playful. The second possibility is that miscoordinations occur during the transition as a natural follow-up to the derailments of focal attention and affective contact that characterize these alliances. Then the transitions become irregular, miscoordination adds to miscoordination so that the phases are delayed, and a temporary interruption of the interaction occurs, which was the case in John's family.

John's parents bear some resemblance to Xerxes's parents, in that the partners' personalities are very different. In John's family, father is the demarcator and mother is the diplomat. In the first parts, mother is very low-key, whereas father plays forcefully. Yet both have difficulties in structuring and modulating the games. Mother's games are too flat and dull to be sufficiently arousing, whereas father's are too fragmented to sustain a smooth play line. Four minutes into father's play, but not long after an especially high point, it appears as if father has lost track of time; mother takes it upon herself to propose the three-together part: "Shall we play together?"

Mother's announcement comes at a time when father cannot overhear it (he is noisily kissing his baby's knees). Father asks mother to repeat, which she does. This first miscoordination is thus quickly repaired. Then father hurries to ratify mother's announcement by promptly turning the table, yet he again fails to coordinate precisely. Whereas he sets the table appropriately for the three together, he tells his son to "go say hello to your mother," as if for a two plus one (beginning of deconstruction). These contradictory signals have alerted mother. As he redresses and starts searching his pockets for a handkerchief, she moves forward and speaks up: "We have to play together!" Father replies, "I know," in a somewhat tense voice (deconstruction achieved). The affective climate is at risk.

As father continues his search, mother leans forward and talks to John in a soft voice. She is presumably trying to quiet down John in the middle of tension (repair). But now it looks as if she might find herself in a two-plus-one configuration, leaving father behind (miscoordination). Yet father, having found his handkerchief, leans forward and aligns with mother (repair); however, the beginning of the play is delayed, for father now has to blow his nose; he does so noisily and John turns to look at him with concentration. As father terminates, mother redresses, as if anticipating father's move; indeed, he redresses too, in order to put his handkerchief in his pocket. This joint move marks a new starting point for the actual three-together play. Mother moves forward, father follows her, and they are finally ready to begin. In the three-together configuration, the parents cooperate, but the games they structure together are somewhat fragmented and affective contact varies from time to time.

This transition is undoubtedly irregular, with effective but costly and delayed repair. Successive miscoordinations occur because the signals lack clarity and their pacing is irregular. Repair nevertheless eventually succeeds. Even though it lacks the precision and swiftness it has in A alliances, it is effective in reestablishing the interaction at least at its previous level.

C Alliances: Aggravating/Elusive Repair

In the realm of collusive alliances, transitions are particularly aggravating points given their marked changes in roles. It is then up to the infant to be the guardian of the parental couple's unity. When competition is overt (C1 collusive alliances), transitions are tortuous and miscoordinations not only end up unrepaired but amplified. The affective tone is negative, which was the case in Frankie's family. Full-scale escalations with interferences regularly occurred during transitions, with much negative affect. During the two-plus-one to three-together transition at three months, the escalation was closed by an affective event with the parents mocking Frankie's pout. Needless to say, the parents escalated to a higher level of competition.

Conversely, when the competition is covert (C2 collusive alliances), transitions appear regular at first sight; the phases follow in strict order. However, they are exceptionally parsimonious and swift; they occur in an affectively superficial context where the foremost preoccupation is to get them over with quickly while keeping up a civil front—that is, elusive repair. In this case, it is up to the infant to animate the interaction, which is the case in Bob's family.

Bob is one of the most vocal three-month-old infants we observed in the LTP. His vocalizations are modulated but of low intensity. He avoids gaze contact with his parents even when not vocalizing (infants may look away when they work at vocalizing; D'Odorico and Cassiba, 1995). He restricts gaze contact to glances and rather circles his gaze around his parents' faces. In any case, these faces are rather far away; though affectionate, the parents maintain a distant and passive stance. They prefer to speak to him in adult talk rather than baby talk and answer his vocalizations with words. Mother's manner is reminiscent of Tania's mother and is characteristic of clinically depressed mothers. Father hides his self-consciousness by joking loudly about the cameras and the setting.

Mother plays with Bob before the transition to the three together. Even though Bob takes many initiatives, she is run down after one and a half minutes of play. She turns toward father: "Let's put it in the middle?" (announcement phase). She sits back. Father swiftly turns the table (ratification phase). Then he looks up, joking, and mother laughs (deconstruction phase). Finally, they lean forward, but they are disaligned, with mother behind (reconstruction phase). In the meantime, Bob keeps circling his gaze. Thus, it takes no more than ten seconds to implement the four phases of the transition. But it is more than parsimonious, in that it is restricted to the barest unilateral signals. Moreover, the preannouncements and the affective events are lacking. Preannouncements might be superfluous due to the parents' urge to finish. As for affective events, there is simply no time and energy for them. The next three-together part is done in no time, giving the family no chance to develop a single game, which is the situation during the last two plus one with Bob as third party.

In summary, the transition is civil and as devoid of visible miscoordinations as it is of actual coordinations, threesomeness, and actual repair. The parents take no chance at confronting each other or Bob. Thus, the pattern of problematic triangulation of the child is as present—even if less conspicuous—in the covert competition as it is in the overt form.

D ALLIANCES: ABSURD REPAIR

Transitions to the three-together configuration in disordered alliances mark a turn for the worse. Whereas families in collusive alliances may still keep up a front during the last two parts, in disordered alliances the breakdown is certain.

The transition in Tania's family may be called a pseudotransition. On the one hand, the parents clearly have the goal of moving from a two-plus-one to a three-together state, and they express it with words. Father: "Let us play together." Mother: "Yes." On the other hand, their actions defeat this goal. Both the initial and the end states are disordered, as we already know from the description of this family's D framework: In the two plus one, Tania sits sagging, excluded from the interaction, father as active parent is sitting at a cautious distance from her, and mother as third party sits back, but as far away as possible from father. There is no game and the affective tone is tense and negative. In the three-together end state, Tania is sagging even more and most of the time the parents sit back and watch her suck on the belt.

In between these two states, the transition steps and phases hardly correspond to the regular pattern of transitions. If attempts to announce, ratify, deconstruct, and reconstruct are detectable, the phases are blurred, coordination is continuously delayed, miscoordinations are amplified, and repair is self-defeating. Microanalysis yields the following sequence of phaselike moves in between the two states (Fivaz-Depeursinge, Duncan, and Stern, 1995):

1. *Interrupting by way of announcing:* Tania reorients toward father, looking at him sideways. She is sucking hard on the belt. Father greets her, smiles, and raises his level of engagement. Without moving, mother cuts in to address Tania: "Is it good?" Tania immediately gazes away. This interruption is probably mother's way of initiating the three together, which she may feel is long overdue since they have put Tania back into her seat after a long period of crying. However, her timing operates as a major interference, causing the infant to avert away from her direct partner. Repair is still possible, provided there is a playful affective climate, but this is not the case.

2. *Amplifying miscoordinations:* During the next period, the parents intensify the miscoordinations. They stick to their antagonistic positions, father increasing his caresses and mother calling again on Tania. Thus, father refuses to ratify mother's interruption as the announcement she intends, but this refusal does not cause mother to change her strategy either.

3. *Pseudoratification in the guise of repair:* Father gives in first. He sits up and proposes to play together. His face and voice are blank. Mother looks at him with a sad smile, but promptly acquiesces. We are at a critical moment. By proposing the transition, father eventually ratifies mother's interruption as an announcement in its own right and mother follows up. These actions have actually deconstructed the previous two plus one and might act as a new point of departure. However, the tense and negative affective climate of this repair attempt continues to linger, making both parents more miscoordination prone. They are clearly not on the same track. Father feels he has given in and mother feels she is working alone toward proceeding with the LTP in accordance with the instructions.

4. *Miscoordination and return to initial state:* Tania reorients toward father. She prefers looking at her parents when they do not look at her. Interestingly, this is one way in which Tania's behavior feeds into the parents' miscoordination patterns. Because gaze contact is a rare event, father is probably more oblivious to the context in which he is acting. On meeting her gaze, father reinitiates interaction, greeting her and leaning forward—and leaving mother behind. However, mother makes no attempt to follow his lead and she remains behind. The family returns to the initial state.

Not surprisingly, these moves form a closed loop that leads up a blind alley, so the cycle is repeated. It is only after two repetitions that the family exits to the end state in which the parents sit up and watch Tania suck on the belt.

There is a predictable, rigid pattern, albeit an absurd one. The phases are determined by delayed and contradictory moves of the three partners, as if they were tied together by their very aversive moves. They can count on the negative outcome of their attempts to coordinate. Needless to say, there is a destructive quality to this triangular pattern.

CONCLUSIONS

In this chapter, we unveil but a small portion of the dynamics of miscoordination and repair that sustains structure. However, it suffices to show extraordinary complexity.

First, by setting our microscope on transitions, we discover that these microstructures are analogues of the larger structures formed by the triangular frameworks: The degree of order/disorder is reproduced at all levels.

Second, the analysis of miscoordinations and repair reveals the moment-to-moment coregulation between the partners. Miscoordinations turn up mostly with respect to the functions that characteristically derail in each framework. Thus, repair works to preserve the framework—A, B, C, or D— from one configuration to the next.

Third, the process of miscoordination and repair actually extends to the entire interaction. In fact, it is possible to go backward from repair to miscoordination, to coordination, and so on, until the preceding transition is reached.

Fourth, the manners of repair clearly differentiate the types of frameworks and family alliances. Thanks to both the precision and flexibility of coordination in A alliances, repair is swift, causing no rupture in the flow of the play. In B alliances, though effective to preserve the framework, miscoordination is apt to create a momentary interruption and repair is costly. In C alliances, when the transitions are tortuous rather than abrupt, repair is problematic, since it tends to amplify miscoordinations rather than neutralize them, thus creating major interruptions and aggravating the disadjustment. Finally, in D alliances, repair attempts lead down blind alleys.

Fifth, and central to this reading, the conduct of the transition and repair appears as a key learning opportunity for the infant. Marking major changes, transitions are apt to raise the baby's vigilance and interest, at least when the parents time them appropriately. Thanks to the regularity of the phases and to the effect of repair, the infant can then construct a mental prototype of these key moments (Fivaz-Depeursinge, Stern, Corboz-Warnery, and Bürgin, 1997).

Our social life is paved with transitions and each of them is a potentially vulnerable moment from the standpoint of our inner experiences. When the parents inappropriately time the transition and then conduct it in a climate of conflict, the infant is bound to experience more uncertainty and tension than interest. These experiences also presumably register in the baby's mind as prototypes, however disordered they may be. Thus, from a clinical standpoint, repair is the key process that differentiates family alliances. The infant is an active part in the process and is sometimes also a hostage.

REFERENCES

Beebe and Lachmann (1994). Representation and internalization in infancy: Three principles of salience. *Psychoanalytic Psychology 11*(2), 127–165.

Besse, V. (1997). *L'orchestration des transitions révèle l'alliance familiale* (Mémoire de diplôme). Université de Lausanne.

Cohn, J., and Tronick, E. (1983). Three-month-old infants' reaction to simulated maternal depression. *Child Development, 54*, 185–193.

D'Odorico, L., and Cassiba, R. (1995). Cross-sectional study of coordination between infants' gaze and vocalizations towards their mothers. *Early Development and Parenting, 4*(1), 11–19.

Duncan, S., Jr., and Farley, A. M. (1990). Achieving parent–child coordination through convention: Fixed- and variable-sequence conventions. *Child Development, 61*, 742–753.

Emde, R. N., and Oppenheim, D. (1995). Shame, guilt, and the oedipal drama: Developmental considerations concerning morality and the referencing of others. In J. P. Tangney and K. W. Fischer (eds.), *Self-Conscious Emotions: The Psychology of Shame, Guilt, Embarrassment and Pride* (pp. 413–436). New York: Guilford.

Fivaz-Depeursinge, E., Duncan, S., and Stern, D. N. (1995). Two perspectives on family conflict: The interactive, the intersubjective. Paper presented at the Society for Research in Child Development Conference, Indianapolis.

Fivaz-Depeursinge, E., Stern, D., Corboz-Warnery, A., and Bürgin, D. (1997). When and how does the family triangle originate: Four perspectives on affective communication. Paper presented at the Affects and Systems Conference, Affective Foundations of Therapy and Counseling, Zürich.

Fivaz-Depeursinge, E., Stern, D. N., Bürgin, D., Byng-Hall, J., Corboz-Warnery, A., Lamour, M., and Lebovici, S. (1994). The dynamics of interfaces: Seven authors in search of encounters across levels of description of an event involving a mother, father, and baby. *Infant Mental Health Journal, 15*(1), 69–89.

Gottman, J. M. (1994). *What Predicts Divorce? The Relationship Between Marital Processes and Marital Outcomes*. Hillsdale, NJ: Lawrence Erlbaum.

Graf, D. (1997). La communication non-verbale dans l'interaction médicale. Unpublished Thèse de Doctorat en médecine, Lausanne.

Guex, P. (1992). Le formation psychologique des médecins. *Patient Care, 8*(4), 47–50.

Heath, C. (1986). *Body Movement and Speech in Medical Interaction*. Cambridge: Cambridge University Press.

Heath, C. (1988). Embarrassment and interactional organization. In P. Drew and A. Wooton (eds.), *Erving Goffman. Exploring the Interaction Order* (pp. 136–160). Cambridge: Polity Press.

Kendon, A. (1976). Some functions of the face in a kissing round. *Semiotica, 15*(4), 299–334.

Magnusson, M. S. (1988). Le temps et les patterns syntaxiques du comportement humain: modèle, méthode et le programme "THEME." In *Revue des conditions de travail* (pp. 284–314). Marseille: Octaves.

Miller, R. E. (1996). *Embarrassment*. New York: Guilford Press.

Murray, L., and Trevarthen, C. (1986). Emotional regulation of interactions between two-month-olds and their mothers. In T. M. Field and N. A. Fox (eds.), *Social Perception in Infants*. Norwood, NJ: Ablex.

Sacco, M., Fivaz-Depeursinge, E., and Corboz-Warnery, A. (1995). Transitions dans le jeu père-mère-bébé. Evolution au cours de la première année. *Journal de Pédiatrie et de Puériculture, 8*(6), 363–366.

Toda, S., and Fogel, A. (1993). Infant response to the still-face situation at 3 and 6 months. *Developmental Psychology, 29*, 532–538.

Trevarthen, C. (1993). The function of emotions in early infant communication and development. In J. Nadel and L. Camaioni (eds.), *New Perspectives in Early Communicative Development* (pp. 48–81). London: Routledge.

Tronick, E., Als, H., Adamson, L., and Wise, S., and Brazelton, T. B. (1978). The infant's response to entrapment between contradictory messages in face-to-face interaction. *Journal of the American Academy of Child Psychiatry, 17*, 1–13.

Tronick, E. Z., and Cohn, J. F. (1989). Infant–mother face-to-face interaction: Age and gender differences in coordination and the occurrence of miscoordination. *Child Development 60*, 85–92.

Weinberg, M. K., and Tronick, E. Z. (1996). Infant affective reactions to the resumption of maternal interaction after the still-face. *Child Development, 67*, 905–914.

CHAPTER 5

Developmental Reading: The Infancy of Triangular Process

The core developmental issue of the primary triangle is triangulation. Its goal is to secure threesome relatedness, which involves three aspects: first, relating in all four configurations of a three-way relationship; second, relating in negative as well as positive emotional contexts, notably in conflict and uncertainty as well as in harmony; third, relating in a stage-appropriate way—that is, communicating feelings at the intersubjective stage versus overt affective signaling at the social stage.

Then, practically, triangulation is the infant's and her parents' manner of handling the four configurations or triangles in their three-party interaction. Playful sharing of enjoyment as a threesome, negotiation of conflict as a threesome, and clearing up uncertainty among the threesome are achieved through specific triangular strategies on the part of the infant and the parents.

Not surprisingly, the degree of differentiation and the effectiveness of triangular strategies differ to a large extent according to the family alliance. *Differentiated triangulation* is observed in A alliances. The infant and her parents appropriately handle the four triangles so that threesome relatedness is maximized; strategies are diverse and effective in all emotional contexts and they are stage appropriate.

Restricted triangulation is observed in B alliances. The infant and her parents still suitably handle the four triangles, yet tension partially curtails opportunities for threesome relatedness; the range of strategies is reduced and may not be stage appropriate in the context of conflict and uncertainty.

Detouring triangulation is observed in C alliances. The infant's triangulation skills are colonized in the service of regulating the parents' conflictual relationship. Negative emotional contexts dominate. Thus, the handling of triangles is little differentiated; threesome relatedness is not only impoverished but distorted and often stage inappropriate.

Finally, *paradoxical* or *undifferentiated triangulation* is observed in D alliances. In both forms there is no meaning context against which to interpret interactions, so the handling of triangles is undifferentiated, the range of strategies is reduced, and threesome relatedness is beyond reach. In the paradoxical form, detouring of the parents' conflict is present, though blurred by confusion and negativity, and the infant's triangulation skills are used and distorted in a paradoxical way. In the undifferentiated form, it is the mere lack of triangular process that dominates.

There are surely many entries into these subtle processes. The entry we have chosen is at the level of expressive signals. We detected all the moments when the infant made visible bids at threesome relatedness, by sharing her attention between her parents and addressing them with the same signal. Then we examined how the parents validated these bids.

We decided to start at the intersubjective stage, at nine months, because developmental research on triadic interactions between infant and mother about an object already exposed the infant's strategies, namely coordination of attention, affect sharing, affect signaling, and social referencing. Likewise, the notion of affect attunement provided an anchor to the parents' responses.

Faced with a vacuum concerning the social stage, we decided on another course of action. We conducted a functional/clinical reading of triangulation in the longitudinal sample at three months. Then we set out to delineate the eventual triangular competence of the younger infants by designing an LTP with still-face situation. To some extent it allowed for control of the parents' responses and sharp observation of the infant's strategies. We describe this situation and the first results obtained at the social stage in the second part of this chapter. First we discuss our observations of families in the regular LTP at nine months.

INTERSUBJECTIVE TRIANGULATION

Let us examine in detail an *intersubjective triangular event*. It serves to review the main infant's strategies and to introduce the different types of parents' responses. Practically, a triangular intersubjective event evolves in four steps:

1. *Triggering event:* In a two plus one, Mike was playing with his mother and they laughed together; father was resonating.
2. *Infant's bid:* Mike turned to his father with a broad smile, bidding for father to share his pleasure about his game with mother.
3. *Parents' validation:* Rather than merely continuing to resonate, father distinctly intensified his smile in response to Mike's address. Mother also intensified her smile, showing that she shared in this experience and thus contributing to making it a truly threesome event.
4. *Closure:* Mike lowered his head and resumed his interaction with mother, who was prompting him to do so, whereas father regained his participant observer stance. The event took only a few seconds.

The sequence is the same for affect signaling (e.g., anger with mother, then with father) or social referencing (e.g., surprise/uncertainty with father, consulting with mother). See photos 5.1, 5.2, and 5.3. It is mainly the degree of intersubjective communion established by the responses of the parents that distinguishes the types of triangulation. We differentiate intersubjective validations—namely, the responses that address the infant's inner experience, such as in affect attunement—from responses that fail to capture this intersubjective nature (validation of actions) or even its triangular nature (misvalidations).

To put the following illustrations into context, note that the patterns of interactions of the families at nine months are amazingly similar to what they were at three months. To be sure, the infant's development has deeply transformed the ways the families implement the LTP procedure. But the forms are unchanged insofar as the triangular frameworks and the manners of transitions are concerned.

Thus, Mike's family style remains intense and affectionate. The parents flexibly play by the rules, which is especially important with a nine-month-

5.1: Nine-month-old playing with mother

5.2: Bidding for affect sharing with father, who validates

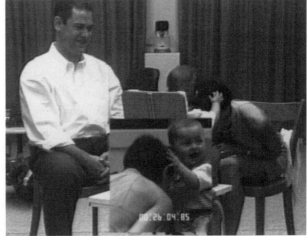

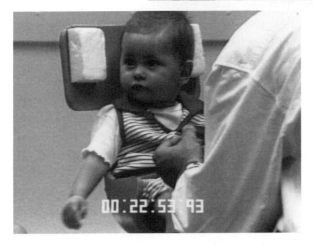

5.3: Surprised by an event having occurred with father, baby looks at mother with quizzical expression (social referencing)

Photos 5.1–5.3

old beginning opposition. This is also the case in Nancy's family. Nancy has become an impetuous baby. She replicates her mother's self-assertive and intense style; the contrast between them and father is even sharper than before. Similar to the play at three months, it is only when the parents join forces to play together in part three that the dance takes off. At nine months, Frankie is more actively involved in the prevailing detouring coalition of his parents and often deliberately colludes in the process. At the same age, Tania is in a better condition than at three months, insofar as she has gained physical autonomy and can better regulate her affects. Sitting by herself and manipulating objects makes a world of difference in negotiating the LTP task, for her parents' sake as well as for herself. But the parents' tension has not subsided, nor has the mother's depression. The father's anger, though contained, is still pervading.

INTERSUBJECTIVE TRIANGULATION IN A CONTEXT OF CONFLICT

Differentiated Triangulation

Envision the following sequence in Mike's family. At some point during their play together, father puts his index finger across Mike's lips and moves it for Mike to make different sounds as he vocalizes. Mike's level of excitation progressively rises, with his father exclaiming in a teasing but plaintive tone: "Ouch, ouch, ouch! These little teeth, they hurt. . . . Don't bite me. . . . You are such a genius. . . . Ouch, ouch, ouch." Yet as the excitement has come to its highest point, father turns to his wife and tells her on the side: "Next time I'll do that to you!" Mike then bites his father hard enough to startle him (affect signaling) and father, still looking at his wife, lets out a more distinctly painful "Ouch." Mike immediately stops and turns to his mother with a quizzical look (social referencing). Note that her response determines the realignment of all the interactions in the family. Staying back, she starts out smiling in a reassuring way. Then she moves forward, opening her mouth widely in a display of "I am going to eat you" (affect attunement); but she stops at a distance, closes her mouth, and then states in a soft but serious voice: "What have you done to your daddy, darling?" (moral elaboration). Mike turns away, briefly glancing at his father, then averting as father is holding his finger and comments: "Oh that hurts." Then, having reminded each other that they are now going to play three together, the parents encourage Mike to reengage by setting up a game in which they kiss each other in turn.

A fair case can be made in stating that Mike's biting his father when his father excludes him from his field of attention to attend to his wife at an untimely moment is a way to interrupt the interaction between them—that is, to intervene in the two-plus-one triangle when he is pushed into the third-party position against his will. Thus, Mike is experiencing exclusion from his parents' field of attention and he acts upon it by retaliating. Startled by his father's reaction, he calls upon his mother to help him in assessing his relationship with father. She responds with reassurance, empathy with his inner feelings, and limit setting; father confirms the limit-setting message. Then they work together at reconciliation by initiating the three together in which Mike experiences a happy threesome communion.

In summary, the parents pick up and validate the referential and triangular nature of their child's bid, without overlooking the conflict. Their responses are stage appropriate.

Restricted Triangulation

Envision a conflictual sequence in Nancy's family. At nine months, Nancy is still impetuous and her parents have to work hard at keeping her seated. She turns off many of mother's and father's game propositions and voices her protest by vociferating and orienting to the other parent. At some point, her mother succeeds in engaging her in a game of scratching on the side of the seat. Soon afterward, it is father's turn to play with Nancy. She shows little enthusiasm in adjusting to his low-key style. However, at some point, leaning in her mother's direction and glancing at her, Nancy spontaneously resumes the scratching game, in a bid for affect sharing. Afraid she will engage with mother, father lets out an anxious "no." Nancy screams and holds out her arms at mother (affect signaling); then she reorients to father.

It may be inferred from this sequence of events that Nancy's negative affect signaling refers to her frustrating experience of not having been understood in her bid for threesome relatedness. Had father acted less anxious about keeping roles, an opportunity might have arisen for engaging in a satisfying game and perhaps for triangular affect sharing. This example illustrates how tension may force a parent into overlooking a triangular bid, misvalidating it and thus curtailing a stage-appropriate opportunity for threesome intersubjective communion.

Detouring Triangulation

In play two with mother plus father, Frankie succeeds in bribing his mother to play with a toy at which he obstinately points (she is uninspired anyway). Father has been blaming mother for having introduced an object into the play. As the time comes for father to play with Frankie, he gets the toy along with his son, in addition to a frank laugh from mother: "Go to your dad and take the toy!" Father begins by greeting his son affectionately. Then he sobers, changing his voice and taking the toy in his hands: "One should not play like that with a toy. One should play carefully." At this moment, Frankie turns to his mother with a puzzled look, presumably wondering how to appraise this sudden change in tone (social referencing). Mother's previous pleasure in teasing father turns into uneasiness. She gives a mixed smile in response to Frankie's confusion. Thus, she fails to clear up his uncertainty.

Frankie reorients toward his father with a nascent pout on his face. He funnels his lips, wrinkles his nose, and raises his lips in an exaggerated display of disgust. He shows a touch of anger by lowering his brows. Frankie's negative affect is feeding right into his parents' detouring triangulation strategy. Pouting almost turns out to be the sole occasion to establish intersubjective communion with father. Indeed, father is about to make an affect attunement with Frankie. Shaking his head and using an empathetic voice, he continues: "Yes, I know you don't like it, but that's the way it is. You cannot do whatever you want in life." Note that father's affect attunement tends first to overshoot Frankie's signal by exaggerating it and to distort his experience (linking it to a "fault" that Frankie did not commit instead of referring it to the context of parental discord—that is, ascribing a meaning that is at odds with the context). In other words, it is a modifying attunement (Stern, 1985).

Second, the affect attunement is selective (Stern, 1985). We have observed that it is almost only in response to Frankie's pouts that father responds with affect attunement. Also, by nine months, Frankie almost exclusively expresses negativity by means of this display. The pout, which we had already observed at three months, has become his dominant facial expression, to the exclusion of the normal range of affect signals of a nine month-old. It has become his "guiding emotion" (Krause, 1982) or his "emotional bias" (Malatesta, 1990, cited by Thompson, 1994). It is bound to shape his inner experience as well as his affect communication with others. Moreover, it blocks and distorts the experience of other emotions.

The event is closed when Frankie lowers his head, in a display that evokes shame. Yet in spite of all the negative aspects of this experience, the fact that Frankie reaches some degree of intersubjective communion with his father should not be overlooked. A part of his inner experience, however distorted, may be shared with a significant figure, as pointed out by D. Stern (1985). This element, added to the major advantage implemented by the pout signal in resolving the tension between the parents, explains why Frankie repeatedly pouts, both spontaneously and deliberately. This example illustrates how detouring triangulation colonizes the infant's triangulation skills in the service of regulating the parents' conflictual relationship, as well as distorts and restricts the infant's opportunities to experience relatedness.

Paradoxical Triangulation

We are at the transition from two plus one to three together in Tania's family. Father unilaterally introduces a new toy—a brown duck—to play three together. But mother wants to play with the blue duck. For more than one minute, the parents compete in presenting Tania with the toys, with hardly any consideration for each other's actions. Tania's response speaks for her familiarity with this confusing situation. Rather than protest, she uniquely focuses on trying to get the two objects in her hands and is on guard when either parent withdraws his or her duck, presumably to be playful. As Tania's interest in the ducks subsides, father presents her with other toys and mother forces her way into the game by trying to cooperate. By the end of part three together, Tania is totally cut off from her parents, absorbed in cuddling a doll. The parents sit back in wonder, commenting, visibly relieved.

The parents' detouring strategy is utterly disconcerting, because their blatant competition is presented as if it were natural. In addition, the infant's response betrays little, if any, emotionality except for her concern to hold the two ducks—a situation of "strange loops" (Cronen, Kenneth, and Lannamann, 1982) or "paradoxical communication" (Watzlawick, Beavin, and Jackson, 1967). There is no context against which to afford meaning to the signals. Paradoxical triangulation is precisely beyond referential communication (Sluzki and Ransom, 1976).

No less disconcerting is the following situation. We know that infants will go to extremes in order to reach some form of intersubjective communion.

We see Tania gather her strength to attune to her mother's inner state. Characteristically, she does this at the moment of the transition when the tension between the parents typically rises. The mother terminates the song and, at a loss, she strokes Tania's face (always with the tip of her fingers), tickles her knee, and turns to father, asking him to take his turn. Her voice is high pitched yet flat. Father meets her request with his frozen expression and then withdraws to get a book for Tania. As mother terminates her sentence, Tania, who has watched her mother attentively, abruptly puts on an engaging expression and lets out a conspicuous sigh of relief. Mother turns to her, smiling, and they go synchronously together through two rounds of "communing coattunement": a sigh of relief, shoulder shrugging, and deflating. Note that this is the sole affect attunement or moment of communion we observe between Tania and mother. But then comes the counterpart—a "microdepression" (Stern, 1994): As mother sits back, Tania is going through an abrupt hedonic fall. She makes a cry face, fusses, arches her body, and swings her arms and legs, until father presents her with the book and eventually succeeds in calming her down. This scene is reminiscent of D. Stern's descriptions of the interaction patterns between infants and their depressed mothers.

INTERSUBJECTIVE TRIANGULATION IN A CONTEXT OF UNCERTAINTY

Uncertainty about the behavior of a parent is likely to trigger intersubjective triangulation. In two of the cases concerning conflict, social referencing is one of the strategies to which the infants enlist. Upon Mike hearing his father's pained response to his biting, he perplexingly consults his mother's face. The answer she gives him is apt to clarify the situation (intersubjective validation), as is characteristic in differentiated triangulation. Upon hearing his father's negative tone in receiving him with a toy in his hands, Frankie consults his mother's face. In contrast with Mike, the mixed answer given to Frankie leaves him to deal with his feelings alone in the face of his parents' collusion, as is characteristic in detouring triangulation.

The following scene illustrates typical patterns in restricted triangulation; moreover, it enlightens the diversity and subtlety of the strategies observed in families. The story begins as Nancy experiences pleasure in playing with her mother. Admittedly, it may be expected that this will not last because of her oppositional stance. Nonetheless, Nancy briefly looks up at mother and then turns to father, smiling, in a typical strategy of triangular affect sharing. But instead of father responding and then gently guiding her back to mother, he is wary of strictly keeping up his role of third party and thus fails to pick up her bid for threesomeness. Father raises his head and looks up at the ceiling, his face tense with the effort to keep from smiling (avoidant misvalidation). Nancy stares at him with a puzzling look. She briefly checks on her mother's face (social referencing), finds mother smiling, and continues staring and smiling at her father. Finally won over, he smiles back and she reorients to her mother. Father relaxes his face, but Nancy resumes the episode. And Father resumes his move too, looking up! Nancy stares, smiling even more broadly, waiting it out. She is not to be fooled by such an unusual display: It must be a game! This is how an infant's initiative for threesome affect sharing, mistaken for an organization "error," is misvalidated, engendering uncertainty. But it is eventually playfully and constructively put to use in another way, showing the resources typical of B family alliances.

There is something unusual about Tania's social referencing: the motive of her uncertainty. We are at the beginning of her play with mother and father is in the third-party position. In spite of mother calling her, Tania resists getting involved in the song play that mother proposes. She is visibly cautious of engaging with mother, presumably because of her mother's depressive style of interaction. She looks up at her father (social referencing). Turning to him with an anxious expression, she gets a noncommittal, civil smile. Between looking at mother's hands, ready for the song, and looking at father's face, she progressively lightens up and eventually lets herself be entrained by mother. But she will abstain throughout from fully engaging, keeping only one hand for playing and the other one stuck in her mouth for self-soothing. Mother bravely continues her forced playing. In summary, the mere prospect of engaging in playing with her mother arouses uncertainty in Tania. She references her father, getting enough reassurance to cautiously engage, but does not experience intersubjective relatedness.

INTERSUBJECTIVE TRIANGULATION IN A CONTEXT OF HARMONY

It is worth noting that Tania's expressions of pleasure globally take the form of a sigh of relief rather than a straightforward expression of joy. It may be assumed that her selected reactions are to establish affective contact with her depressed mother. Relief may have become her guiding emotion in the positive range—that is, an emotion that not only becomes prevalent in her psychic experience but that blocks and distorts the experience of other emotions, such as straightforward joy. This relief also serves to comfort mother in the absence of emotional support from father, as we have already seen.

We observe Tania to conduct on two occasions a relief-sharing bid in the two plus ones. These bids are validated in that the third-party parent responds with a civil smile, whereas in the three together, Tania finally takes refuge in cuddling a stuffed animal under the fascinated look of her parents. In other words, everyone colludes in establishing a pleasurable substitute for an unreachable closeness. It also provides them with a way out of the family conflict, although it is very costly in terms of Tania's development of intersubjective experiences. We are again reminded of Stern's description of the infant's schemes of being with a depressive mother, here as a background context in seeking stimulation (Stern, 1994).

Triangular relatedness in pleasure is also problematic in Frankie's family, but to a lesser extent than in Tania's family. Just before the most delicate transition from two plus one to three together, Frankie goes through another frustration. His father cannot be bribed into giving him the pen. We observe again the pattern of Frankie's pout, the father's modifying and selective affect attunement, and the infant's head lowering. Then, all of a sudden, Frankie accomplishes two affect signals: He substitutes an engaging face for his pout and, turning to mother, who has just moved to engage for part three, he begins to applaud. Both parents applaud with him, mother quite spontaneously, yet with father approving in a moralizing tone: "Yes, that is super; that is super." Then, reverting to father, Frankie switches to pouting again and looks back and forth between his parents until they laugh together and playfully comment on his anger. The difficult transition to the three together is accomplished. This is one of the preferred strategies of triangular affect sharing that Frankie uses—in fact, that he can now deliberately trigger. Yet his pleasure presumably is more in the experience of masterfully manipulating his parents' relationship than in intersubjective communion.

This situation with Frankie's family contrasts sharply with threesome relatedness in pleasure in differentiated triangulation. At the height of pleasure in playing with his mother, Mike turns to father, smiles at him, gets a smile in return, and reorients to the game; or as mother proposes a song,

Mike turns away conspicuously but with a slight smile, then laughs with mother, turns to father, and laughs with him. Make believe and teasing are part of his repertoire and Mike shares his pleasure with father in fooling mother. At the beginning of the three-together part, and as his parents seize each one of his legs, the infant pauses, alternatively looking with animation at father and mother, in anticipation of the pleasure in the three-together game. This is differentiated triangulation in a context of harmony. Affective communion is indeed the driving force in trilogue play.

QUANTITATIVE RESULTS OF THE LONGITUDINAL SAMPLE

We detected and microanalyzed all triangular events in the nine-month sessions of the longitudinal sample. The results indicate that the model of triangular process is promising and deserves further study. They can be summarized as described below (for details, see Fivaz-Depeursinge, Corboz-Warnery, and Frascarolo, 1998; Fivaz-Depeursinge and Darwish, 1998).

The first question was obviously whether all infants in the sample made triangular bids. Note that, on practical grounds, observation of many of them in a single LTP session cannot be expected, since it is mostly at the height of pleasure, frustration, or uncertainty, and especially during transitions, that triangular bids are likely to emerge. However, all infants in the sample addressed triangular bids to their parents. The mean number was eight per LTP session, but the variability was high. Part of this variability was accounted for by the type of family alliance. Indeed, in good-enough alliances (A and B), the infants made almost twice as many bids as in problematic alliances (C and D). Thus, greater coordination and flexibility may well be facilitative of this important developmental step.

The second question was whether infants handled the system of their three-way interaction with their parents. That is, did they make triangular bids in the four configurations of the LTP? We found that two thirds of the infants made triangular bids in at least three of the four configurations. The other third made them in two or only one of the configurations. This dimension was again related to the type of family alliance, showing that family coordination facilitates the differentiation of triangular process.

Next came the issue of the quality of the parents' responses to their infants' triangular bids. Not surprisingly, infants in good-enough alliances received an intersubjective validation to more than half of their bids, whereas infants in problematic alliances hardly had any chance of receiving such validation. Thus, threesome relatedness was much more stage appropriate in good-enough alliances than in problematic ones.

We then asked how families regulated positivity in their threesome intersubjective relatedness. The balance between positive and negative affect is known to differentiate successful functioning from problematic interactions, particularly in couples (Gottman, 1994). The theory is that positive affect exercises a buffering effect over the toxicity of negative affect. By examining the rate of positive bids (namely, affect sharing) with respect to negative ones (namely, affect signaling and social referencing), we could get a first indication about this dimension. Knowing that overall affect sharing was as frequent as affect signaling and social referencing taken together, we found that the ratio of positive to negative bids was well above one in good-enough alliances to much lower than one in problematic alliances.

Finally, we found a high correlation between the overall ways that each family regulated intersubjective triangular events and family alliances. This result confirmed that triangular process has essential clinical implications.

SOCIAL TRIANGULATION

The forms of triangulation observed at the intersubjective stage are in continuity with those observed at the social stage. The examples speak for themselves, at least as far as the parents' strategies are concerned. Chapter 2 makes this issue pretty clear. In summary, where triangulation was differentiated or restricted at nine months, it was also differentiated or restricted at three months. And where triangulation was detouring or paradoxical at nine months, it was also this way at three months, except in the families that changed their type of alliance between these two sessions. In these cases, the type of triangulation conformed to the type of alliance (see Appendix A).

Although we did not microanalyze the triangular events at three months, we observed enough prefigurations of infant triangular strategies in the LTPs to question the classical developmental views. Indeed, we observed that not only did the infants discriminate the different configurations by distributing their gaze accordingly but most, if not all, three-month-olds would now and then rapidly alternate their gaze orientations between their parents several times during an LTP. In the good-enough alliances, these triangular gaze coordinations occurred mostly in the contexts that were designed for them, namely in the three together, in the last two plus one with the infant as third party, and during the transitions between parts. In the problematic alliances, they also occurred, but understandably not as predictably in these contexts.

In addition, there were relatively rare but distinct occurrences where an infant would transfer an affect signal from one parent to the other during the gaze transitions. For instance, an infant would warm up to mother. Looking at her brightly, smiling and babbling, she would then turn to father while maintaining her smile and vocal gesture. Or, in a difficult moment, her face would cloud and she would turn with the very same expression to the other parent. Thus, we were observing prefigurations of the intersubjective triangular strategies. Finally, but more difficult to objectify, infants practiced "double addresses": In the configurations with both parents, they would use one modality to interact with one parent, say gaze, and another one to interact with the other parent, say vocal.

However, these observations were new and in contradiction with the classical developmental theories. The classical theories assume that triadic infant–caregiver–object interactions at nine months represent the culmination of a developmental sequence that begins with infant–mother dyadic interactions. Remember, at that stage, and in contrast with the referential communication of the nine-month-old, the three-month-old's communication is essentially expressive, nonreferential, or direct (Stern, 1985). She shares her pleasure, distress, or uncertainty with her mother directly by engaging, averting, or fussing. As D. Stern puts it, these signals are "purely social"; they are the very constituents of the relationship itself (Stern, 1985). Mutual imitation plays an essential role in this type of relatedness.

As we know from Meltzoff's studies, imitation is the infant's means of exploring and identifying people, just as manipulation is her means of exploring objects (Meltzoff and Moore, 1995). The parents respond in kind, by true imitation more than by affect attunement. Of great importance in connection to early triangulation, the infant's signals are not only direct but her attention is obligatorily confined to her direct partner. The developmental sequence continues with infant–object dyadic interactions, where again the infant's attention is mostly confined to the object. Her behavior provides "few indications that she wishes to share her interest with her caretaker" (Bakeman and Adamson, 1984, p. 1278). Other authors see this development as a more progressive process where "attention regulation and affective exchange are elaborated to include reference to objects during periods of mutual play" (Kasari, Sigman, Mundy, and Yirmya, 1990, p. 27).

It is interesting to note that E. Tronick takes a different position. He remarks that the classical criteria used for ascribing communicative intent imply the reference to an object. According to him, this requirement "fails to index the infant's communicative competence properly. . . . When the infant's acts are seen as performed with reference to interaction with a partner or the actions of the infant's partner, the communicative intent of the infant becomes evident long before there is reference to objects" (Tronick, 1981, p. 5). As the infant coregulates the interaction with her partner, she constantly refers to it (see also Scherer, 1992).

Whatever the developmental course of person–object coordination may be, another distinction was required to define our position. This distinction had been advocated by Trevarthen long ago. He posited that the infant is born endowed with three different types of motives: self-directed, object-directed, and person-directed (Trevarthen, 1984). Triangular competence is an integral part of the person-directed motive and should not be confused with the development of the coordinated practice between person and object (Trevarthen, 1984).

Evidence for the Three-Month-Old's Triangular Competence

We conducted two studies to explore the infant's triangular competence at three months. The data of two samples of nine- to fourteen-week-old firstborn infants and their volunteer parents were used. One sample involved twenty families observed in the LTP. The other one involved seven families observed in a special version of the LTP, with a still-face episode and follow-up at five months. In designing this special version with F. Donzé and D. Stern, we wanted to optimize the chances of observing the infant's coordination of attention and affect between her parents (see Donzé, 1998; Fivaz-Depeursinge, 1998). On the one hand, we took precautions to make sure that the parents would present their child with the best possible framework by having them enact beforehand the appropriate body formations. On the other hand, we included in the play a two-plus-one configuration with one parent posing a still face in order to test for the infant's possible recourse to the other parent.

The LTP with Still Face

Out of a considerable number of possibilities, we selected the following sequence of configurations: I: three together; II: two plus one; III: two plus one with a still face; IV: reconciliation in a three together. Let us follow Odile's trajectory in this situation.

I. In the first three together, we ask the infant: Are you able to share your attention and your affects with both your parents? At the same time—and this is important—we want her to experience a new situation, that is, a three together in the LTP setting. We will know that she is able to do it if:

1. She alternates her episodes of gaze contact between her parents by distributing them more or less equally. This behavior would globally testify to triangular coordination of attention.

2. She shifts her gaze at times between her parents sufficiently rapidly to show that her orientations are coordinated rather than merely juxtaposed. This behavior would testify more strictly to triangular coordination of attention.

3. She transfers expressive signals (smile, distress, perplexity) between her parents. This behavior would testify to triangular coordination of affect and prefigure the triangular strategies at nine months.

In Odile's family, we got these three confirmations. Interestingly in regard to her coordination of affect, the infant displayed a rich, multimodal expressive pattern, looking up at a parent, cooing, smiling, opening her mouth wide, and closing the episode with a "bubbling" noise. Whereas at the beginning of the part she addressed this signal at a single parent, by the end of the three together she was transferring it between her parents.

Odile had thus experienced a three together for the first time in this particular setting and had progressed toward a more integrated triangular interaction during this very first part.

II. After two minutes, we ask the parents to adopt a two-plus-one configuration, in this case with mother as the active parent. The question addressed to the infant is: Now that you have experienced that both your parents are present and that you have coordinated your attention and affects with them, are you able to play with one of them and leave the other one aside, while also keeping the other one in your peripheral field?

We will know that she can do it if she plays mainly with the active parent, but in the meantime displaying her awareness of the third party, for instance, by glancing at him or her. Note that the third-party parent has received a special instruction in case the infant orients to him or her: to greet her discreetly and then redirect her attention toward the active parent by turning himself or herself in the latter's direction.

Odile's responses were remarkable (see photos 5.4 and 5.5). As expected, the infant mostly interacted with the active parent. But, to our surprise, she kept orienting briefly but frequently toward the third party, not only looking at him but also continuing to transfer her affect signals to him. In fact, she acted as if she had acquired a liking for this experience in the three together and wanted to prolong it. However, she was quick in perceiving that her father did not respond as enthusiastically as previously and she cut her signals short, reorienting toward her mother. By the end of the two plus one, she was merely checking on the third party.

III. We proceed by confronting the infant with a dilemma: a violation of her expectancy. We ask the previously active parent to present himself or herself to the infant as a partner, by leaning toward her, facing her, and gazing at her, but with a still face and without touching her (Tronick, Als, Adamson, and Wise, 1978). We know, as reported in Chapter 4, that infants at three months actively work at reestablishing a normal interaction. This is the first question we address to her. But in addition, we ask her: Given your previous experience of the three together and of the two plus one, will you recourse to your third-party parent to help reestablish the normal course of action, to help you understand the situation, or to help you regulate your discomfort?

The infant would demonstrate these intentions by signaling negative affects of distress, perplexity, or anger to the third-party parent or by trying to engage him or her in a normal interaction, perhaps ignoring the still-faced parent.

Odile's responses confirmed our hypotheses on the first issue: The infant displayed a classical reaction to the still face, in that she repeatedly oriented toward the still-face parent, actively trying to reanimate her. Then she began distracting herself by looking at her hands and circling her gaze around the head of the still-faced parent. Yet she gave us a negative response to the second question, in that she did not orient toward the third-party parent but once fleetingly. Note that this was consistent with her previous situation in part II, when she had experienced his unavailability.

IV. The last question we address to the infant in this three-together reconciliation phase is: Will you recourse to your previous third-party parent to help in reconciling with the previous still-faced parent?

The infant would demonstrate this ability by reestablishing contact first with the previous third-party parent; then, once better regulated, she would reengage with the previous still-faced parent.

Odile's response to this question was positive. After a long episode of sulkiness with both parents, the infant turned to father and reconciled with

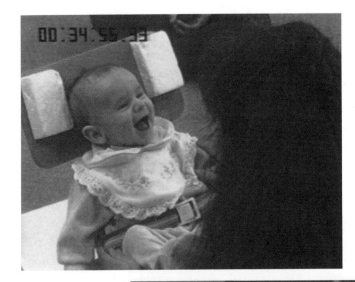

5.4: Three-month-old vocalizing and smiling at mother

5.5: She transfers these affect signals to the third-party father

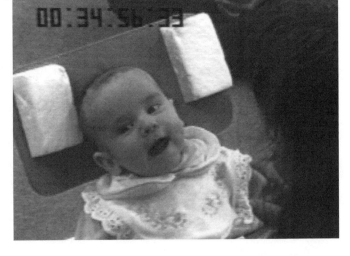

Photos 5.4 and 5.5

him, before turning to mother and reconciling with her too, taking up again the sharing of attention and affects with both of them—needless to say, to the relief of the parents.

These observations confirm our hypotheses; so do the data of the other infants in the sample and their reactions at five months, when we saw them again.

All three-month-old infants displayed strict and/or broad indicators of coordination of attention and affect in at least one or more configurations.

However, they differed in the trajectory they followed across the configurations. Not all infants excelled like Odile at alternating gaze and affect signals between father and mother in the first three together. Another infant might have focused almost exclusively on one parent. But then, contrary to Odile, she might have displayed triangular coordinations during the two plus one with still face. Still another infant might have focused exclusively on the previous third party in the reconciliation part.

However, independent of the individual trajectories at three months, all infants progressed at five months. They showed more coordination of attention and deliberate avoidance of the still-faced parent in favor of the third party; they also showed more rapid shifts, sometimes with three or more alternations, and more prefigurations of affect sharing, signaling, and social referencing.

The results on the sample of twenty families observed in the regular LTP confirmed the above findings on coordination of attention. All infants distributed their gaze differently in the two plus ones versus the three together and all infants shifted their gaze rapidly between their parents at times (Fivaz-Depeursinge and Frascarolo, 1999).

We did not take up the developmental changes that are bound to occur at the so-called object stage, around four to eight months, when the infant becomes attracted to objects. The possibility of an evolution of triangular interactions with persons in parallel and in coordination with the evolution of triadic interactions with objects is clearly one that needs consideration. Our informal observations in the LTP at six months uncovered definite instances of triangular strategies coordinated with play with objects (Donzé, 1998).

In summary, the findings suggest that the three-month-old infant develops triangular coordinations by sharing her attention and affects with both her parents. These processes prefigure the referential strategies that we observe at nine months. Many issues then require examination, particularly the exact status of these early triangular strategies. For the time being, we suggest the term *direct*, in contrast with *referential*, to mean that early triangular strategies are conducted through action rather than through the referential processes that characterize intersubjectivity at nine months.

CONCLUSIONS

Assuming our results will be replicated on larger samples, we propose the following hypotheses about triangulation, beginning with social triangulation at three months.

Just as the parents work hard in order to establish a clear frame for dialogue play at the social stage, they work hard in order to create a clear frame for trilogue play. They put into play their entire repertoire of intuitive parenting behaviors in the service of teaching the infant the conversation-like rules of triangular interaction, as if it were just as natural to aim for threesome as for twosome communion. The infant's responses indicate that she discriminates the four configurations. Her patterns of gaze orientations and her expressive addresses strongly suggest that the social infant actually establishes triangular connections in her perception and actions. She experiences moments of threesome social communion through direct interactions that prefigure the moments of threesome intersubjective communion by means of referential communication.

Clinically, the continuity between social and intersubjective triangulation is striking. It is unavoidable to assume that the sophisticated triangulation strategies of the intersubjective infant result from a practice of triangles from the beginning.

By nine months, the parents have adjusted their triangulation strategies to also refer to the infant's inner experience with respect to their family relationship. The infant refers to her experiences with one parent in addressing the other one, using the same strategies she recruits in referring to objects. Yet the degree of differentiation of the strategies still depends on the manners of triangulation she has been given to practice with her parents, so her experience of threesome intersubjective communion varies from the most positive and growth-enhancing to the most restricted, negative, and confusing.

REFERENCES

Bakeman, R., and Adamson, L. B. (1984). Coordinating attention to people and objects in mother–infant and peer–infant interaction. *Child Development, 55,* 1278–1289.

Cronen, V. E., Kenneth, M. J., and Lannamann, J. W. (1982). Paradoxes, double binds, and reflexive loops: An alternative theoretical perspective. *Family Process, 21,* 91–112.

Donzé, F. (1998). *Etude exploratoire des comportements triadiques du bébé de 3–5 mois.* DEA en Psychologie, Université de Genève.

Fivaz-Depeursinge, E. (1998). Infant's triangulation strategies: A new issue in development. *The Signal, 6*(2).

Fivaz-Depeursinge, E., Corboz-Warnery, A., and Frascarolo, F. (1998). The triadic alliance between father, mother and infant, its relations to the infant's handling of triangular relationships. Paper presented at the International Society for the Study of Behavioral Development Conference, Berne, July.

Fivaz-Depeursinge, E., and Darwish, J. (1998). *Regulating Triangular Expressive Signals in the LTP.* Research report no. 60. Centre d'Etude de la Famille.

Fivaz-Depeursinge, E., and Frascarolo, F. (1999). Three month-old infants share their attention and affects with both parents during triadic play. Paper presented at the Society for Research in Child Development, Albuquerque, April.

Gottman, J. M. (1994). *What Predicts Divorce? The Relationship Between Marital Processes and Marital Outcomes.* Hillsdale, NJ: Lawrence Erlbaum.

Kasari, C., Sigman, M., Mundy, P., and Yirmya, N. (1990). Affective sharing in the context of joint attention. Interactions of normal, autistic, and mentally retarded children. *Journal of Autism and Developmental Disorders, 20*(1), 87–100.

Krause, R. (1982). A social psychological approach to the study of stuttering. In C. Fraser and K. R. Scherer (eds.), *Advances in the Social Psychology of Language* (pp. 77–122). Cambridge: Cambridge University Press.

Meltzoff, A. N., and Moore, M. K. (1995). A theory of the role of imitation in the emergence of self. In P. Rochat (ed.), *The Self in Infancy: Theory and Research* (pp. 73–93). Amsterdam: Elsevier.

Scherer, K. (1992). Vocal affect expression as symptom, symbol, and appeal. In H. Papousek, U. Jürgens, and M. Papousek (eds.), *Non-Verbal Vocal Communication. Comparative and Developmental Approaches* (pp. 43–60). Cambridge: Cambridge University Press.

Sluzki, C., and Ransom, D. (1976). *Double Bind: The Foundation of the Communicational Approach to the Family.* New York: Grune & Stratton.

Stern, D. N. (1985). *The Interpersonal World of the Infant.* New York: Basic Books.

Stern, D. N. (1994). One way to build a clinically relevant baby. *Infant Mental Health Journal, 15*(1), 9–25.

Thompson, R. A. (1994). Emotion regulation: A theme in search of definition. In N. A. Fox (ed.), *The Development of Emotion Regulation. Biological and Behavioral Considerations.* Monographs of the Society for Research in Child Development. Serial No. 240, vol. 59, nos. 2–3 (pp. 25–52). Chicago: University of Chicago Press.

Trevarthen, C. (1984). Emotions in infancy: Regulators of contact and relationships with persons. In K. R. Scherer and P. Ekman (eds.), *Approaches to Emotion* (pp. 129–157). Hillsdale, NJ: Lawrence Erlbaum.

Tronick, E. (1981). Infant communicative intent: The infant's reference to social interaction. In Stark (ed.), *Language Behavior in Infancy and Early Childhood.* North Holland: Elsevier.

Tronick, E., Als, H., Adamson, L., Wise, S., and Brazelton, T. B. (1978). The infant's response to entrapment between contradictory messages in face-to-face interaction. *Journal of the American Academy of Child Psychiatry, 17*, 1–13.

Watzlawick, P., Beavin, J., and Jackson, D. D. (1967). *Pragmatics of Human Communication.* New York: Norton.

CHAPTER 6

The Reading of the Working Alliance Leading to Framing Interventions

Solving the LTP task has two indissociable faces. One is internal and relates to the family alliance, which is what we have explored to this point. The other face is external. It relates to the family's working alliance with the observer/consultant team (see Figure 1.1 in Chapter 1). There are major reasons for paying attention to family–team interactions. On the one hand, they tell us the articulations between a family's internal and external exchanges. Surely there is a close parallel between these two faces, in that the family's external exchanges are strongly tinged by their internal exchanges. Thus, the good-enough family alliances usually go hand in hand with the functional working alliances, whereas the collusive or problematic family alliances usually go with the difficult working alliances. On the other hand, the type of working alliance guides us in conducting the framing of the family in the most facilitative way. For us, working with volunteer or clinical families basically arises from the same perspective. Yet practically the definition of the relationship differs: Volunteer families are not asking for intervention, whereas clinical families expect it.

We start with how to assess the observer–family working alliance. Then we describe the framing interactions that ensue from this assessment with

123

volunteer families and ask whether this framing is effective. We examine the specifics of assessment and framing with clinical families in the context of systems consultation in Chapter 7.

ASSESSING THE WORKING ALLIANCE

The data we are drawing on here are those of the second session of the longitudinal sample (see Appendix A for results of the types of working alliances). Remember that the families had come for the first LTP session four weeks before, when the babies were about eight weeks old. It gave them a chance to get acquainted with the facilitator and to familiarize themselves with the studio and LTP procedure. Therefore, we were already observing fairly enduring patterns in this second session. On the teams' side, the first session gave us a chance to prepare for this second one, working with the facilitators on eventual difficulties they had encountered with the family and anticipating problems that might impede the family's best implementation of the procedure. (The facilitators were two clinician–researchers in training and they were supervised by the second author.) Thus, we observed the team's best performance under the conditions.

On practical grounds, how can we trace the interaction between the team, represented by the facilitator, and the family so as to assess their working alliance? If this assessment is also going to guide our framing of the family, it is important that it begins as early as possible in the session. In that sense, the informal exchanges during the sometimes long preliminaries—heating up a bottle, feeding or diapering the baby—are of great significance. This is a time for getting to know each other and for chat, most often focusing on baby matters. For the supervisor behind the mirror, observing the extent to which the facilitator's behavior is transformed by these interactions is valuable information on the influence of the family on its environment as well as on the "errors" the facilitator might be led to commit—and have to repair. On the other hand, a family might arrive with a baby who was not only fed and diapered but who is on the verge of going to sleep if play is not urgently undertaken. In any case, for research purposes, we cannot rely systematically on these informal conversations and it is desirable to have a more standardized situation to analyze.

The Preparation Sequence:
A Window on the Working Alliance

In scrutinizing the video-recordings, we have discovered a small piece of interaction that is invaluable in revealing the facilitator–family interaction, which is called the preparation. It begins when the group moves to the LTP setting, negotiates the task, and then separates. By force of circumstances, it is relatively standardized. It obviously is a key moment in the session, because the way the task is going to be negotiated will influence the course of the LTP. Somewhat like transitions between configurations in the LTP, it reveals the key processes that preside over the working alliance. Then, during the LTP itself, the brief signals that the family will address the team through the glass window (recall, it allows a dim view) or the comments that will refer to the team or the situation are also essential. These will not only confirm, nuance, or perhaps infirm the first assessment but will throw light on the interlacing between the family's external and internal workings. Finally, it is during the feedback session that we can both put into practice and test the hypotheses about the working alliance made during the preparation and the LTP itself.

There is no doubt that as clinicians we get an intuitive view of what is essentially going on during these microsequences so that we can assess whether the group is working together and helping each other. Yet only microanalysis will fully uncover the wealth of information that they contain. As a matter of fact, it is possible to apply the different microanalytic readings that we have developed to assess the family alliance in relation to the working alliance. Note that from this perspective the sequence starts with a transition. Then it proceeds with the establishment of a quadratic formation (during the instruction) and terminates with another transition (separation). Thus, we conducted a microanalysis of the preparation sequence as well as of the affective events between the family and the team during the LTP. Finally, we conducted a functional/clinical reading of the feedback session.

What would the preparation scene look like in functional working alliances such as in Mike's family? As the small talk comes to en end, we see the facilitator announce the impending change by looking up in the direction of the setting; the parents ratify by following the line of her gaze as they briefly reengage in the informal talk. The group then stands up in concert and moves in close formation to the setting. The setting is fine-tuned: Together the parents check the angle of inclination of the baby's seat and settle the child in it, encouraging him with enthusiastic comments on the seat and on the belt. The mother sits down and is immediately in interaction with Mike, greeting, smiling, and talking; yet this does not prevent her from also acknowledging the facilitator. Actually, we see her pleasurably glancing at the facilitator, showing her delight in communicating with Mike. In the meantime, the father has checked the positions of their seats and sits down. The transition ends when the parents are all set to play, their lower bodies facing Mike.

Now comes the establishment of the formation for listening to the instruction. The parents remain at a distance from Mike and open up the formation between their upper bodies to include the facilitator, who is standing closeby. The baby is alert and smiles successively at the three adults. As the facilitator delivers the instruction, we see the parents microenact their roles in the successive parts: As part one is spelled out, mother, who has been designated to play first, slightly leans forward; then she withdraws as part two is spelled out, and so on. Watching the sequence in slow motion, a rapid alternation of gaze of each partner to the other can be clearly distinguished, somewhat like establishing a network of mutual attention.

The transition to the separation closes the sequence. As the facilitator terminates—no questions asked—Mike intently looks at her with interest; she addresses him briefly as everyone orients toward him. The exchange terminates with a tender and admiring laugh shared by all the adults watching Mike's animation. We know that this affective event is typical of transitions. She takes leave. As she walks out, the parents and Mike briefly look at her and then pause.

During the LTP itself, mother addresses a joyful expression to the observers in the middle of a particularly intense episode, visibly sharing her pride and pleasure with them too. Then, when the parents have to give the pacifier to Mike, we hear them playfully refer to their "cheating." Again, this incident speaks for the continuing cooperation with the observers; it also shows the parents' sense of when to give precedence to their child's needs over strictly following the observers' rules.

There is no doubt that this group is working smoothly together and helping each other. It shows in each of the steps—moving in concert to the setting, agreeing on the task, and separating on a playful and enjoyable note. The facilitator's attitude is supportive and adjusted. The family flexibly adjusts; keeping in close touch with each other does not prevent them from including the facilitator and keenly tuning in to the instruction. Importantly, Mike is not overlooked. Finally, we get additional cues of the family's continuing relationship with the team during the LTP itself.

The working alliance in Nancy's family is functional too, in that the preparation proceeds as smoothly as in Mike's family. The parents are attentive, the facilitator is at ease, and Nancy vocalizes invitingly, carrying along the three adults. But what draws the attention is the contrast between the interactive styles of each of the parents. It is mother who orchestrates the network, skillfully juggling between the facilitator, father, and Nancy, whereas father is shy and reserved. However, there is a definite complicity between them. During the LTP, we observe that father's concern with implementing the LTP rules includes a touch of worry. However, he assumes the necessary authority to firmly guide the family through the procedure in a productive way.

Let us contrast the above sequences with what we observe in difficult working alliances. In Frankie's family, the parents ask several questions about the research during the preparation, intent to show their interest but interrupting the delivery of the instruction and causing confusion. From the inception of the play, we note the parents' manifest desire to follow the rules. However, there are definite obstacles. During the LTP itself, the parents disagree with each other about these rules, just as they interfere in each other's interaction with Frankie. For instance, mother is designated to play first, she turns the table, and father disapproves. She keeps it turned. Just as she succeeds in attracting Frankie's attention, father interrupts, asking whether she signaled to the researchers that she was beginning. Or, he makes an intensely disgusted face when mother plays a game with Frankie that he does not appreciate. Then, at the moment of the two-plus-one to three-together transition, they engage in a rather long contest about what comes next.

In Tania's family, father comes in, holding Tania and singing in a forceful, joyful tone. Mother follows with the luggage and a forced engaging smile. Prepared from the previous session, the facilitator asks them to sit down for a while. Father declines, arguing Tania will cry. Mother, sitting obediently, prompts him to sit anyway. The tension between them is perceptible. Father ends up sitting down, still holding Tania. The tension recedes somewhat during the conversation that follows.

As soon as the facilitator sets out to lead the family toward the LTP setting, the tension again rises. The facilitator begins with demonstrating anew how to change the infant's seat inclination (it was much too straight the last time). Mother suggests to father seating Tania in order to try the inclination. Father whispers: "She is going to cry." Mother sits down and repeats her request to father while the facilitator suggests that he should hold Tania on his lap during the instruction. Finally, the facilitator has to deliver the instruction with mother sitting and father walking around with Tania, so the facilitator cannot see if father is listening to her. In contrast, mother appears keen on showing her interest, listening and nodding intently. As the facilitator announces she is leaving, father hardly assents and mother turns to him.

Tania's family tries to collaborate with the researchers, but there is no doubt that it is difficult for them. The group is split into two dyads that cut across the functional boundaries called for by the task: mother and the facilitator, father and Tania. At no point during this preparative step is everyone in interaction with each other. Because the instruction is delivered in this split formation, each of the operations is likely to be compromised, as illustrated by the discord about the infant's seat. Finally, the separation itself is a false one since the facilitator has to return to ask father to replace his seat in its marks, thus further disturbing the initiation of the LTP.

To be sure, no shared positive affect arises that could reinforce togetherness. On the contrary, everyone probably feels lonely. The facilitator takes one step at a time, trying to help the parents overcome their anxiety, slowing down the pace in order to facilitate their understanding and decisions. Her peaceful and organized attitude appears to help the family calm down, but it does not prevent her from becoming caught between the parents. On the other hand, without the family's courage to face a situation that is clearly threatening to them, she would not be in a position to do her job. Unable to move along together, the parents' main difficulty is in appropriating the setting on behalf of Tania, who, interestingly, never objects. The infant is indeed a hostage in this situation—a hostage who up to this point has been hidden in father's arms, away from the observers' view.

In spite of the willingness on both sides to cope, at critical moments the confusing actions of the family engender actions of the facilitator that further disturb the family. The facilitator is at risk for being drawn into a coalition with mother against father. Yet perhaps most remarkable is that the family nevertheless sets out to dutifully overcome their fear of crying and go through the LTP procedure. The importance of this motivation cannot be overemphasized. It testifies to the impressive drive of parents during their child's infancy.

During the LTP itself, at two occasions when the situation is particularly out of hand, we observe father glancing at the window in our direction yet he does not explicitly request to stop. Indeed, at no point do the parents appear to question the necessity to go on. When this situation becomes sufficiently clear, the team decides that the facilitator should enter and propose to terminate. The parents are relieved and so is Tania.

Working Together and Helping Each Other

The first step for the group in working together is moving to the LTP setting. In difficult working alliances, the group may move separately, thus announcing problems in coordinating, whereas moving together marks the readiness of the group to cooperate. It reflects the group adopting a common pace and formation.

At the moment of giving the LTP instruction, it is necessary for the group to establish a clear consensus on what is the task and what precisely is expected of everyone involved. Finally, the moment of separation closes the deal. Loaded with suspense about how things will eventually work out, it is marked with a shared expression of affect, such as a laugh. When it is not, a key signal in reinforcing the working alliance is missing.

Contrary to the belief that giving research instructions is a cold and rigid operation, the facilitator has to calibrate her interactions to help the family give their best performance under the present conditions. This position requires delicately balancing precision as a facilitator with "joining" (Minuchin, Rosman, and Baker, 1978)—that is, establishing contact with the family as a clinician. Families have different styles of pacing, of appropriating space, and of dealing with stress; also, their current conditions vary. Appropriately pacing the preparation, addressing the family as a group while giving attention to each partner, and adjusting to the family's style influence the family's understanding and interpretation of what is expected of them on stage.

The timing of leaving the family is critical. Anxious parents often ask questions at this time. This preparation also involves several major tasks in rapid succession for the family. Maintaining a positive interaction with the facilitator as well as within the family may not be as easy as it appears while appropriating the LTP setting, tuning in to the instruction, and separating from the facilitator.

Following the lead of a guide may not pose a problem, or it may be difficult for some parents. It may trigger overt resistance or extreme submissiveness. Some parents take the time to familiarize themselves with a new space and help their child in turn; in contrast, others may not manipulate the table or may remain immobile in their seats. Still others may overrule the instruction of not moving their seats; being off camera will then provoke an intervention by the facilitator, which may in turn disrupt their actions. Other families might not take the time to adequately adjust the baby's seat and help their child adapt to it, possibly setting off a lasting disturbance.

Since the facilitator and the family form a group in close interaction during the instruction, the family, seated for trilogue play, arranges the space to include the facilitator, establishing a secondary and quadratic formation. Rather than conciliating the two, they may give more priority to including the facilitator (perhaps by widely opening the formation) or excluding her (by not adjusting the formation).

Within this formation, they attend to the instruction and memorize it. This process may be quite visible, for example, Mike's parents microenact their roles as they are spelled out. Another father summarizes the instruction for himself and his wife as follows: "You play, I play, we play, we talk!" Perhaps one or both partners may not pay attention, which may later interfere with the course of the LTP.

Often, one parent attends more to the baby and the other one attends more to the facilitator. In fact, this style may last during the entire LTP, with one parent taking on the responsibility of the setting and of conducting the parts and the other one assuming the caretaking role. This situation is evident in Nancy's family and it does not pose a problem. However, the division in roles may reach extremes that impair cooperation. Separating from the facilitator is a critical moment often filled with anxious questions. Awareness of being on stage may be evident, such as looking at the cameras and preening.

During the LTP we may further explore the articulations between the family's external and internal workings. As noted in Mike's family, the signals mainly serve to share affects in particularly high moments. Or, they are metacommunications between the parents that also address the team in indicating the parents' awareness of transgressing what they believe are the LTP rules (e.g., giving a pacifier is "cheating"). Or, they simply serve as coordinations (e.g., "We can call Mrs. X to come in!").

Conversely, in the difficult working alliances the parents' signals to the team may take on another meaning: basically calling upon the team to form a coalition with one of the parents against the other one. This situation is particularly evident in Frankie's family, when father interrupts mother after she begins to play with Frankie, asking her whether she has signaled to the team that she has actually begun. This strategy may be more subtle. In Bob's family, father self-consciously sets up the scene as the makings of a movie and mother goes along. We perceive that this front serves to hide the parents' inability to authentically engage with each other and with their child, but it also speaks for their uniting precisely through pleasing the team and conforming to what they imagine as the team's expectations in their case. In another family, father finally dares to propose that they take their sobbing baby out of the seat and mother reluctantly agrees, in spite of their concern of transgressing the LTP rules. Mother then keeps repeating that the baby is off camera until they hurriedly put her back into the seat. The mediation of their decisions by their representation of the authority figure is evident. Still in another family, at the time of transitions the parents call upon the team. Mother or father checks in the team's direction for confirmation but fails to check on the other parent. The point is that in cases of unnegotiable parental conflict, problematic triangulation not only captures the child inside the family but tends to colonize the environment outside the family.

It may not come as a surprise that there are narrow parallels between patterns in the working alliances and family alliances. It is of prime interest to uncover the similitudes in the form of these patterns in spite of the differences in content. Indeed, seeing family patterns from two different perspectives gives us the added advantage of the "double description" that G. Bateson prescribed: Just as binocular vision affords us depth perception, this double description enhances understanding of family process (Bateson, 1979).

FRAMING THE VOLUNTEER FAMILY

Similar to other clinical research paradigms for observing families, the LTP challenges the family in constructing new interactions together. We consider the LTP frame of observation as a context of transformation in itself. Yet we know as therapists that these experiments require expert and customized handling if they are to be growth-enhancing for the families and meaningful for clinical research.

Merely going through the procedure is not sufficient framing in itself, at least not for the majority of families. Reviewing the video-recordings with the family and providing feedback is also desirable. First, the experience calls for some kind of appropriation—if only because it is videotaped for the benefit of others. Interestingly, this also provides the family with a double description of their interactions: Watching the video-recordings from the perspective of the audience is different from and complementary to experiencing it as subjects. Second, the experience profits from elaboration. In reviewing the interactions, the issues the parents might raise are discussed, key points are examined by asking about the parents' subjective experience, and the baby's competence as well as parental intuitive behaviors are emphasized. Third, this time window provides the parents with the opportunity to share their pride, pleasures, and concerns about their baby and their own parenting. Perhaps this informal talk fulfills for them the function that was shared in earlier times with the women in the extended families (Stern, 1995). Finally, the feedback session is the time to put into practice and test the hypotheses on the working alliance formulated during the preparation sequence and the LTP.

Thus, the *standard framing format* for a session is informal chat, LTP procedure, and feedback session, including review of the videotapes. We use this format for all volunteer families.

THE FEEDBACK SESSION

There is a prerequisite to providing feedback: Do the parents consider the data recorded as valid? Do these data truly reflect their daily manners, their ways of being? Interestingly, volunteer parents usually say they do. Only a few say that they have been a little more shy than at home. A few others feel restricted by having their baby in the baby seat rather than on their laps or on the floor. Nevertheless, they have no problem understanding the rationale for it.

Once this validity has been established and qualified, we proceed to review each configuration of the LTP, focusing on the infant's recording and asking for the parents' subjective experience and their interpretation of their baby's behavior. Another important aspect is to point out the competence of their baby, such as imitating her parents, taking turns, and regulating her states and affects. Likewise, the parents' intuitive parenting behaviors can be underscored, so as to build up their confidence in these skills.

Obviously a key issue in each of the four configurations is: Did the active parent feel that he/she was his/her baby's partner? Did he/she feel that the other parent was present? Did the parents feel they were together when they were both direct partners of their baby? Did they play together, versus alternatively or separately? Did the parents feel everyone was included, in their roles, focusing on the game and staying in touch? Parents generally know right away what we mean by these questions. Then, coming to a transition, they also know pretty much what were the cues for change, which of them cued it, and if the other parent ratified the decision. Other issues include: Did he/she feel that the change was at the right time? How synchronized were the parents? How did they decide to terminate the play?

It is fairly easy to cover these issues with volunteer families, but there are important differences in the depth, wealth, and scope that are reached between functional and difficult working alliances. With the former, the elaboration is usually more detailed and the exchanges are richer and more differentiated. For instance, Mike's parents know exactly when they are miscoordinated: They readily laugh upon seeing the situation on tape. They can detect the faintest sign of disregulation of their baby and associate it with stories about him. Throughout this first year, they let us share with them their admiration for their child's growth. Their observations were insightful and subtle. The mother discussed at length her ups and downs in weaning a baby who definitely did not like a bottle. She was careful in including the father in these exchanges.

In Nancy's family, the discussions were also nourished and prolonged, the mother being very perceptive of the interaction and willing to discuss any event at length. However, in spite of her repeated attempts, the facilitator failed in including the father. He preferred to listen and take care of Nancy. As a result, we got to know much more about the mother–baby dyad than the others in the family. However, we felt this was more a matter of style than dysfunction. As a matter of fact, the family found themselves late in the first year in a crisis. In spite of the father's withdrawn attitude, the parents were able to raise the issue together with us and then talk it over in a separate consultation. Again, this situation speaks for the openness of their functional working alliance.

Surely there were also working alliances that were at the boundary between the functional and the difficult. Indeed, this is more of a continuum than a discrete categorization. In particular, in two families with stressed family alliances, the working alliance at three months was "lukewarm." Both these families were intent on cooperating, yet in one of them the relationship with the facilitator was somewhat tense and provocative; in the other one, it was extremely submissive. Interestingly, the former one evolved satisfactorily, in that this relationship became more open and play-ful. In contrast, the working alliance with the submissive relationship turned out badly. In spite of the team's preparation before sessions, the parents' de-fensiveness increased. Taking time before the LTP or afterward to provide the parents with opportunities to open up only exposed the vacuum that separated them from us. Their exclusive interest seemed to be in getting tapes of their baby. The parents got more and more distant from each other. It seemed that the only link between them was their child, with the mother focused on her and the father adopting a laissez-faire attitude. Therefore, what appeared at three months to be a potentially functional working al-liance, with resources and no evident problems, evolved into a difficult one. The facilitator triggered a minicrisis at the nine-month session. Drawn out by the emptiness of the lengthy conversation, she asked whether, like many other families at that stage, they had marital problems. The mother immedi-ately opened up and confirmed. But the father did not follow up and the in-cident was soon closed and covered up.

As stated earlier, the depth and scope of the issues we reached with most of the difficult working family alliances were restricted. Indeed, a majority of them tended to deny that anything was wrong, even in the face of the most unhappy play. Therefore, the feedback period was abbreviated or the discussion was devoted mostly to practical baby matters. For instance, in Frankie's family the discussions remained superficial. Certainly the parents were intent on watching the videos with us. However, they watched them in a daze. They answered our questions, but as far as they were concerned, they were exclusively interested in Frankie, especially his beauty. Appar-ently utterly blind to his unhappiness, they laughed at what they called his temper. They also laughed at seeing themselves contesting or interfering with each other.

The discussions with Bob's parents were just as limiting. They were con-tent when Bob did not cry during the LTP. This family was clearly dis-tressed: Bob was colicky and did not sleep at night. They attributed the problems to their child's health and temperament and never once did they question their own behavior. This fatalism gave us no entry into sharing their pain. It was not until the last session, at twelve months, that Bob's mother admitted that these first months had been really difficult.

In Tania's family, the feedback sessions were chaotic. Everyone was drained. The discussions were continually interrupted not only by Tania's crying but also by parental disputes over details. Actually, these disputes could reach intensities that were stunning. Tania's mother admitted things were difficult with Tania's persistent crying; weaning and feeding her were also calamities, but her mother felt that this was the price to pay if you wanted to have a family. Tania's father would contradict her in a contemptuous way that failed to open up a constructive conflict. It was not until much later that the parents finally asked for help with specific child problems.

In two of the seven families with difficult working alliances, the relationship seemed more dynamic and less defensive. In one of them, the parents were overly open; in the other one, the relationship was distinctly conflictual. In the open one, namely that of Yann, it was the father who, having heard of this research, asked to enter the study. He was a particularly anxious and motivated person. His wife cooperated. They looked at the video-recordings and pretty perceptively commented about their own interactions, exclaiming: "How could we do that again?" They overwhelmed the facilitator with asking many questions about themselves as well as about their baby.

In the family with the conflictual relationship, that of Claire, the young mother clearly disliked the facilitator's ways. She paused before answering the facilitator's questions, opening up her eyes as if to convey they were incomprehensible. She contested the setting, the number of sessions, the instructions, and so on. The father played the go-between, helping to smooth things out. Yet this mother submitted without delay to the facilitator's instructions, only to put forward her claims when it was too late. It took her several months before she could act on her vindications, for example, changing the hour of the session to fit her baby's or her own schedule. Although the conflict persisted throughout the first year, the exchanges became less tense and somewhat more playful and rich. Interestingly, these two families improved their family alliance over the first year, which leads us to question whether the framing we provide for volunteer families is efficient.

In this respect, it should be emphasized that efficient framing is not only desirable on ethical grounds. To understand the dynamics of growth is *the* core issue in clinical research. It is precisely where the goals of the family and the team meet, and thus where their working alliance resides.

IS FRAMING EFFICIENT?
STABILITY AND CHANGE IN FAMILY ALLIANCES

In view of the discrepencies between the patterns observed and the parents' readiness to collaborate, whether the experience has any growth-enhancing potential for problematic families may be questioned. The answer awaits empirical testing. We need to compare families seen longitudinally in this format with families seen only at the inception of the study and at follow-up. In the meantime, we can examine the data on the results of the evolution of family alliances over the first year.

We report in Chapter 3 that nine families out of twelve maintained the same type of alliance during our observation, two improved, and one declined (see Appendix A). What is the meaning of these results with respect to framing?

We have to underscore that during the first year families undergo normative crises. We know that the marital relationship is put under strain and that marital satisfaction as evaluated by the spouses themselves tends to decline (Belsky and Isabella, 1985; Belsky, Lang, and Rovine, 1985; Pape Cowan and Cowan, 1992). At the same time, not only does the infant's arrival deeply change the parents' way of life but her very development calls upon the parents' adaptive resources to adjust (Stern, 1995). In addition, family relationships are reequilibrated (Boszormenyi-Nagy and Sparks, 1973; Bürgin and von Klitzing, 1995; Lebovici, 1988, 1992; Pape Cowan and Cowan, 1992; Stern, 1995) and the economic well-being of the family is a concern. It is remarkable that a family with a cooperative alliance not only establishes but roughly maintains a healthy level of adaptation. This situation requires substantial support from the social environment. It may be assumed that the four families in our sample with a stable type A or B alliance found at least part of this support in the research setting we offered them.

The data on Ann's family, the one with a B family alliance who stepped down to a C alliance (covert subtype), is especially interesting with respect to framing issues. We have seen previously that the working alliance with this particularly submissive family evolved as difficult over the course of the year. Many possibilities were blocked from being fully implemented in the interaction. For instance, the mother was visibly sensitive to her daughter's signals, yet she restrained from responding for fear of breaking what she (falsely) imagined were our rules. A case in point was the process of triangular affect sharing at nine months. When Ann was playing with father, oriented to mother to also share her pleasure with mother, tension was observed in mother for fear of not keeping strictly to what she construed as an appropriate third-party attitude. Instead, she pressed her lips and flickered her gaze at father two or three times in a row, in a display that was clearly perplexing for the baby—to the extent that when mother reengaged normally in the three-together configuration, Ann was so utterly surprised that it took her quite a long time before she got over it.

The sensitivity of Ann's father to his baby's signals was remarkable and his ways of responding were subtle and original. Yet, in line with the characteristics of B alliances, he stopped short of continuing and sustaining the fine games he was initiating. These characteristics also marked the coordination between the parents: There were many instances of beginning role coordinations, of dancing to the same tune, of playfully sharing affects, yet they were quickly aborted. Ann displayed age-appropriate and differentiated behaviors, yet she was also likely to interrupt for various reasons: regurgitating, hiccuping, being distracted (these behaviors may be indicators of stress in infants). Unfortunately, these trends became more marked as time went by, so by the nine-month session, the family's interactions coincided with the covert and collusive type of family alliance. It was the interaction in the three-together configuration that made the difference in the assessment: The parents managed to get it over with so quickly that no three-together game was possible.

This process may well be illustrative of the classical trajectory of a family with ordinary potentialities and vulnerabilities who does not hold out in the face of the first-year normative crises. Moreover, we learned at the four-year follow-up that they had also been confronted during that first year with a crisis in opposition with their origin families. The framing they were getting from their environment and from our research setting was clearly insufficient in protecting them against this stress.

The three families who started out with a collusive family alliance did not change. On the one hand, they at least kept up the same level of coordination in the face of the normative crises of the first year. They did not exclude each other, as in disordered alliances. On the other hand, the parents did not give up their detouring triangulation of the child. In fact, the actual process of triangulation may be a potent stabilizer. However, it may be at the expense of putting a child at an increased risk for psychopathology, since her growth is partly colonized in the service of this stability. Thus, the final toll at the very least indicates that the framing provided by the research setting is insufficient for the families to change.

Out of the four families with initially disordered alliances, two improved, namely those of Claire and Yann. There is no way to tell on the basis of such a small sample whether this effect is specific to this type of family alliance. But it is worthwhile examining in more detail the difference between the families with disordered alliances who changed and the ones who did not. The most striking feature they shared at the family level is exclusion and negativity of affect, but they were different with respect to the parents' relationship.

In the two families who did not change, namely Tania's and Anthony's, the parents excluded each other in addition to excluding their child, and their negativity was addressed at each other and verging on contempt. We know from J. Gottman's work that contempt, the psychological equivalent to physical violence, is one of the red flags in marital relationships (Gottman, 1994). Consultation with each other, if it existed, was hostile. In Claire's and Yann's families, the parents excluded their child but not each other. They were not contemptuous of each other. Their negativity applied more to the difficulty of the situation. They consulted each other, although this was not effective. These differences also corresponded with differences in their working alliances with the team. As already noted, these two families had a more dynamic and open interaction with the team than the other two families, which were extremely defensive.

In summary, whereas the framing as designed in this study may be growth-enhancing or protective for families with cooperative and stressed alliances, it was effective in improving family alliances for only a small portion of those with D alliances. It should be stressed that our previous experience with framing families within the LTP setting had been mostly with clinical families. Prior to this study, we had not been working with volunteer families on a longitudinal basis. The research contract with the families was fairly strict and we did not feel authorized, even with distressed families, to intervene beyond the standard framing format, unless the families themselves articulated a request. Then we would see them in regular therapeutic consultations outside the setting. It is a very delicate situation to lead a volunteer family to make their latent demands explicit. It may be desirable to design another type of contract at the inception of such a study.

REFERENCES

Bateson, G. (1979). *Mind and Nature.* Toronto: Bantam Books.

Belsky, J., and Isabella, R. (1985). Marital and parent–child relationships in family of origin and marital change following the birth of a baby: A retrospective analysis. *Child Development, 56,* 342–349.

Belsky, J., Lang, M. E., and Rovine, M. (1985). Stability and change in marriage across the transition to parenthood. A second study. *Journal of Marriage and the Family, 47,* 855–865.

Boszormenyi-Nagy, I., and Sparks, G. (1973). *Invisible Loyalties.* New York: Harper and Row.

Bürgin, D., and von Klitzing, K. (1995). Prenatal representations and postnatal interactions of a threesome (mother, father and baby). In J. Bitzer and M. Stauber (eds.), *Psychosomatic Obstetrics and Gynaecology* (pp. 185–192). Bologna: Monduzzi.

Gottman, J. (1994). *Why Marriages Succeed or Fail.* New York: Simon & Schuster.

Lebovici, S. (1988). Fantasmatic interaction and intergenerational transmission. *Infant Mental Health Journal, 9,* 10–19.

Lebovici, S. (1992). A propos de la transmission intergénérationnelle: de la filiation à l'affiliation. *Presidential address, 5th World Congress of the World Association of Infant Psychiatry,* Chicago, 9–13 Sept. 1992.

Minuchin, S., Rosman, B., and Baker, L. (1978). *Psychosomatic Families.* Cambridge, MA: Harvard University Press.

Pape Cowan, P., and Cowan, P. (1992). *When Partners Become Parents.* New York: Basic Books.

Reiss, D. (1981). *The Family's Construction of Reality.* Cambridge, MA: Harvard University Press.

Stern, D. N. (1995). *The Motherhood Constellation.* New York: Basic Books.

CHAPTER 7

Systems Consultations with Therapists and Clinical Families

A SYSTEMS CONSULTATION

A pediatrician trained in family therapy called our center asking for a systems consultation with the family of a four-month-old infant. We invited him not to inform us beforehand of the particular problem of concern but to come prepared to formulate his request to us, keeping in mind that he was doing so in the presence of the family. Familiar with our procedure, he played by the rules and met us at our center with the family.

Having greeted the family and talked with them in order to get acquainted and explain the procedure, we asked the parents to feed the baby. The bond between the parents and Kathie was visible. The feeding began calmly enough, with both parties collaborating. Yet Kathie got more and more fussy. She was impatient with the process, putting her hands to her mouth in between spoons; the more she fussed, the more insistent she grew in getting the food quickly. The mother valiantly faced the situation, calm and smiling. When it was the father's turn to feed the baby, he sped up the rhythm but to no avail. This spiraling process seemed as if it would never end. Behind the window, the supervisor noted the paradoxical process. She was also surprised to see the pediatrician and the parent–observer sit at far ends, absorbed in their thoughts; the consultant sat far away too, observing

142 THE PRIMARY TRIANGLE

without a word. However, as the baby's crying intensified, the supervisor observed waves of auto-contact gestures between the adults, indicating the rise in tension. Otherwise, no one said a word or budged. The theme emerging was that everyone suffers in silence and puts up a brave front.

During the LTP preparation, the parents moved separately to the setting. They listened attentively to the instructions, but it was civility rather than complicity that presided over these exchanges. Distance was indeed a recurrent theme.

The parents dutifully set out to play. Mother began, from a distance too; she succeeded in engaging Kathie for a few bouts of uninspired play. It was father who unilaterally conducted the transition. He played banal physical games, lacking in inspiration. As third parties, the parents followed the dyadic play attentively yet without much emotional resonance. Distance prevented them from tuning in with each other. But it was in the three-together configuration that the issue became blatant. The parents acted as if they had physically divided their baby's body into two vertical halves, each one playing with the half on their own side, careful not to interfere with each other. Kathie withdrew, focusing on the belt. She began to fuss, sparing the parents the stress of a direct interaction.

The consultant had asked beforehand for permission to play with Kathie. Observing this play from behind the one-way mirror, the parents were to decide when to return. During that time, Kathie showed an age-appropriate sensitivity to the stranger by refusing to engage at close range. The parents came in as soon as she fussed.

At the end of this observation, the consultant team concluded that the baby was well developed for her age and that her ties with her parents were strong. The problem seemed to be the parents working together with her. A key issue was their difficulty in getting close to coordinate their roles and consequently their failure in sharing a game or tuning in affectively, which is typical in covert collusive alliances.

The consultant briefly met with the pediatrician and the family to hear their request. We learned that everything appeared normal except for Kathie's tension. Almost every afternoon she began to cry at the nursery and continued at home into the night. Having acknowledged that there was no somatic basis for the crying, the parents had accepted the pediatrician's proposition to consult with us: What was Kathie telling them with her crying? This straightforward formulation talked to the positive working alliance between the pediatrician and the family and thus authorized us to approach the issue pretty directly.

The feedback session was animated. Kathie was not late in starting to cry. Her mother held her and walked her and finally the baby went to sleep on her lap. When the consultant commented on this, the mother complained that her baby was too heavy. The pediatrician advised her and the father to put Kathie down in her crib together. It worked in spite of the parents' fear of waking her up. Note that these apparently banal issues are important in building up the parents' confidence in the therapist's prescriptions.

In showing the tapes, the consultant verified that the parents recognized themselves and their baby in the recorded interactions. However, they preferred playing with toys. The consultant noted the robustness of the child, her age-appropriate development, as well as the parents' bonds with her. Having also identified instances of their intuitive parenting behaviors, she asked them how they experienced their playing in each configuration. Their comments were sparse but clear enough: They had each played on their own.

Finally, the consultant came to the formal conclusion: "We felt that there was a definite tension somewhere between the parents and Kathie and between the family and the outer world. Perhaps the origin families, we didn't know. This finding was not uncommon, especially at this stage in family life. This family's way of protecting each other and especially their baby by keeping the tension and the pain inside was unusual. This situation required a lot of energy and self-sacrifice. At some points, the pressure became too much. Then Kathie would cry."

As the consultant was explaining the findings, Kathie let out a high-pitched squeal, abruptly waking up in her crib. Mother urgently picked her up. Father was truly amazed. How could Kathie understand this? The pediatrician replied that babies seemed to have radar in detecting emotions. Father admitted that there was pressure between him, his wife, and their origin families. Nothing more was said. The consultant presented two alternatives: working together on these issues in therapy or waiting until the family possibly grew out of them, as suggested by mother. The pediatrician proposed a meeting to discuss this question with them and the consultant closed the session by asking them to sign the authorizations for the tapes—that is, for clinical use, research, or didactic purposes as well. We did not separate without having stated our availability for another consultation if they wished.

We heard later from the pediatrician that Kathie had stopped crying soon after the consultation. He had worked with the parents for a few weeks on family issues, then the mother decided to get individual treatment for herself. (For other similar examples, see Fivaz-Depeursinge, Corboz-Warnery, and Frenk, 1995.)

THE FORMAT OF THE SYSTEMS CONSULTATION

The concept of systems consultation was put forward by L. Wynne and co-authors to refer to a punctual session, possibly repeatable, in which a therapist asks a consultant for assistance in order to identify or clarify a situation and consider the different options for intervention (Wynne, McDaniel, and Weber, 1986). This first illustration of a systems consultation shows that we modify the standard framing format used with volunteer families in two ways to accommodate therapists bringing clinical families: broadening the scope of observation to systematically include feeding, diapering, and infant–stranger interaction; and opening up two time windows for the therapist and the family—to formulate their request and to receive our formal answer to this request.

Broadening the scope of observation is always desirable. It is ineluctable in one-shot consultations. Seeing the family in different caretaking contexts not only helps clarify functional domains and problematic ones but also the extent of these difficulties. Feeding is a cooperative situation between parent and infant in which we are particularly interested to see how reciprocal control is negotiated between them. We allow the feeding to go on in its usual fashion and participate just enough for the family to feel at ease with us and the video-recording. We are particularly careful that all who are present get into the infant's rhythm; this is one way to show the parents that we and the therapist are on their side. Diapering is often the occasion for spontaneous dialogue exchanges between parent and infant, thanks to the face-to-face formation it implies. But it also involves reciprocal control. Dialogue and trilogue are different in that the family is working without a safety net—that is, without an intermediary object. Finally, it is indispensable to also observe a potentially problematic infant interacting with an experienced adult who provides the best possible framing of the infant under the conditions. It allows us to verify the infant's developmental integrity and to gauge her reactions to strangers. Thanks to the one-way mirror, the parents are also able to observe how their child regulates her affects when they separate.

Integrating the therapist is obviously the essence of the systems consultation. Doing the observation in his or her absence might breach the therapeutic alliance with the family. Problematic triangulation between the consultant, the therapist, and the family is an important issue. In addition, families are sensitive to their therapist accepting a one-down position with respect to the consultant team, which generally works in favor of the therapeutic alliance. It is also one of the reasons for the consulting team to request not to be informed of the family's problem. It is often reassuring for the family to know that we are blind to the clinical data. Furthermore, it allows us to naively approach the parents on a more equal basis. Also, bias must be avoided as much as possible. It is so much more fascinating and easy to observe interactions with a fresh mind and then open up the first window for the therapist and family request only after the observation and the assessment take on a dramatic and somewhat playful quality that is motivating.

This moment is a highlight. The therapist's request contains two essential pieces of information: First, it reflects his/her preoccupation for the optimal development of the infant in the context of the family's crisis; second, it indicates the parents' degree of acceptance of the problem in such a way that it guides the consultant in the formulation of her response. For the therapist, it is a guarantee that we will do our best to adjust to his/her perspective in working with the family. For us, it is a guarantee that the therapist has negotiated the consultation with the family.

The second time window at the end of the feedback discussion concludes the consultation with a formal answer to the therapist's and family's request. Certainly it is prepared by the operations inherent in the standard framing format. Validating all behaviors of the family is necessary to ensure that they will be open to our intervention. This process is easy when the interactions are functional and thus productive, but problematic interactions are unproductive. It is in this respect that therapists have developed specific strategies to reframe symptomatic behaviors as creative (Haley, 1963). Systems consultants turn to interventions that are specifically therapeutic rather than ordinary framing ones. The way we reframed Kathie's parents' difficulties in coordinating as coparents as a brave, loving strategy to spare each other is one such example.

Therapists are consumers of metaphors, because metaphors are the links between implicit, nonverbal communication and explicit, verbal communication. They help to convey what we subconsciously perceive in a form that is communicable but that conserves some of the wealth of intuitive knowledge. Thus, when we work in systems consultations we prepare ourselves to let metaphors emerge in our minds from the very beginning of the observation. It is indeed the main task of the supervisor, while the consultant does her job in framing and lending herself to being transformed by the therapist–family exchanges.

However, as we are about to expose, sometimes families are not amenable to this type of language. They are caught up in a position where they cannot even profit from the LTP framing context and metaphors. Under these conditions, the possibility of deterioration instead of growth is significant. At this point, we recourse to direct intervention.

DIRECT INTERVENTION

We came upon direct intervention through intuition and necessity. When we worked with clinical families on a long-term basis, using videos mainly for clinical purposes, we found ourselves in situations that required intervention.

One of the turning points was in the early 1980s, with Christina's family. Having been part of the research and therapeutic protocol on dyads with their first child, the parents asked to continue with their second child. The mother had a psychotic breakdown and was hospitalized with Christina. We were video-taping a feeding in her hospital room. No contact was discernible between this mother and her four-month-old baby. Both were looking far away. The affective climate was loaded with tension and despair. After a while, the consultant felt this negative experience seemed to be amplified by the video-recording. She saw the need to intervene in some way. She sat near the mother and held her by the shoulders, slightly rocking her; although the mother immediately solicited her attention for her own sake, the consultant insisted on focusing on the baby. The mother came to follow her line of vision and look at her baby too. After a while, Christina oriented to her mother and a shy social exchange took place between them. This change struck us as spontaneous, yet it happened under the consultant's influence.

In microanalyzing this triangular interaction (Fivaz-Depeursinge, Guillemin, Cornut-Zimmer, & Martin, 1984), we found that it was indeed under the actions of the consultant, namely her holding, rocking, and attention refocusing, that the mother spontaneously modified her interaction with Christina. She actually changed her holding by lifting her arm, creating a new context that facilitated gaze contact. It became a choice for the baby to look at her or away, rather than an obligation to look away because of inappropriate holding. Interestingly, the effect was undone as soon as the consultant stood away, yet the mother and the baby had at least experienced another type of interaction for a while.

THE CONDUCT OF DIRECT INTERVENTION

The following case illustrates how direct intervention can be practiced within the LTP setting. The family was brought by a family therapist. She saw them twice and asked for a systems consultation as a part of her assessment.

Susan was a pretty nine-month-old baby. Her parents were in their early twenties. On entering the lab, they joked about the baby's seat (a torture chair). This was visibly a stressful situation for them; they approached it bravely, keeping up a front through provocation. It indicated that the working alliance was going to be first on our agenda. During the feeding, they relaxed a bit and even agreed to sit their daughter in the LTP seat rather than on their lap, because she was always on the move. It worked. The parents collaborated and Susan ate all right. During a long chat, we learned in particular that the father, a mechanic, suffered from being separated from his daughter when he was at work. He really had a soft spot for her. The mother enjoyed taking care of her daughter and working part-time as a cashier. After a diaper change, the therapist moved behind the one-way mirror and the consultant described the procedure. The preparation proceeded smoothly, but the consultant had to deliver the instruction with the parents standing and Susan crawling all over the place. However, they listened attentively.

When the consultant left the room, disorganization was obvious. The play started all of a sudden, without a pause or an acknowledgment between the parents. Certainly the parents were affectionate, but their playfulness was provocative, sometimes verging on belligerent; it would frequently exceed Susan's tolerance. During the three-together play, the parents' intention seemed to be to teach her a turn-taking game with objects. But many of their interventions were ill-timed, even arbitrary, with countless interferences between them. The mother orchestrated the play, the father oscillating between going along, interfering, and withdrawing. It culminated when the mother invented a new game: She would take the lighter that Susan had more or less forcibly taken out of her father's pocket, light it, and exclaim how beautiful it was; then, putting her finger in the flame, she would show how it hurt. She even recruited the father to burn his finger too. He voiced his refusal and did it. Then, giving it to Susan, who immediately brought it to her mouth, the mother would let out a loud sound of disgust. Susan kept switching from delight to awe.

When the father withdrew, we saw him lose his joyful composure. His face suddenly sobered, self-consciousness came through, and he then turned toward the team's window, sometimes even mouthing an "Okay?" Yet he did not voice this concern to go by the rules to his wife. As a matter of fact, the transitions between the configurations were blurred. The transition to the last part seemed to take forever and the three-together part took more than ten minutes because the father's implicit announcements were ignored by the mother. Then, instead of making his proposition explicit, the father would reengage, not without having glanced in the direction of the team. It was not until Susan was sobbing that the parents sat back, watched her, laughed, and eventually called for the consultant.

The metaphor that had first emerged in the consultant's mind, namely playing with fire, turned out to be literally the case. The observers experienced confusion, oscillating throughout the play between identification with these young parents' awkward but affectionate actions and awe at witnessing the contradictions in their signals that could only be perplexing for the baby. This confusion indicated the high-risk situation of this infant. Susan was obviously a bright infant with age-appropriate cognitive abilities and we worried about her not having opportunities to establish appropriate intersubjective communion in the midst of this chaos. Her unfailing participation was perhaps the most alarming aspect, for it first had to be in the service of the parents' relationship. Also, the father's passive appeals to the team were obvious cues to the family's difficulty in managing on their own and to their dependence on authority figures. All of these features were characteristic of collusive alliances. The necessity to help the family regulate their affective exchanges and draw external and internal limits was clear.

When the parents eventually called for the consultant, the team had decided to do a direct intervention. She entered the room and sat by them, thanking them for their hard work, then explaining she was uncertain whether they had also done the last configuration, namely the parents together and the baby as the third party. They understood that they had not succeeded in doing it. She asked them whether they would like to try again. The parents refused on the grounds that Susan would not sit in the seat.

Note that by that time Susan had calmed down and was actually sitting quietly there.

The consultant then asked the parents to show how they would have done the configuration. After various clarifications about what she really meant, they finally sat facing each other, with the baby's seat in the middle position. This was what they thought their baby would not accept, commented the consultant. They confirmed: Yes she would want to crawl, like at home. However, they reflected, this positioning was implemented during meals, but then they would be with her as soon as she requested it. After further discussion, the father suddenly exclaimed: "But this is what is happening now . . . but then you are there!" The consultant agreed. "Suppose I am not there," she said as she sat further away. The mother exclaimed at her husband's address: "We can do as we do at home. Tell me what you did today!" The sequence that followed was revealing too. The parents were sitting vis-à-vis and their baby watched them calmly. Thus, they could draw limits between themselves and their baby when someone was there to help them structure the situation. But they were at a loss trying to connect under the observer's eye, however benevolent. They systematically avoided gaze contact beyond glances. They chose to orient toward Susan or the window so that they were not looking at each other at the same time.

We believed the parents could be helped to structure the situation, but that much framing would be needed to achieve a direct relationship between them; that is, a relationship unmediated by Susan and existing in the face of authority figures, perhaps first in the families of origin. The subsequent play between Susan and the consultant showed that under favorable conditions she could regulate her affective state fairly well and accomplish a turn-taking game.

We asked the therapist to return and formulate her request to us. We learned that the parents sought help because Susan cried every hour during the night ever since she was born. The crying diminished when they called the therapist. The therapist wanted us to confirm the parents' and her own opinion about Susan's age-appropriate development. Also, the therapist wanted help in her work. How could she get the parents to believe in their own competence so that they would finally give themselves the right to make mistakes? How could she convince them to take time off for themselves and to give Susan time as well? The therapist's alliance with the family was fragile. Her first priority was to reinforce it by underscoring the positive sides of the parents' chaotic but intense framing of their child. After a pause, we convened to review the videotapes and discuss their questions.

The first agenda was to repair the parents' sense of incompetence. They kept stating this situation had not been easy for them and for Susan. The consultant took much time in validating their feelings. She perceived how hard they had tried and she understood their stress. She linked this experience with their extreme sensitivity, repeatedly pointing out its manifestations with respect to their baby's signals; their appropriately reading her was extremely important, but it could also be a disadvantage in that they exhausted themselves in responding. So did Susan. Thereafter, the father spontaneously pointed out the difficulty he had in setting limits: He could not resist his daughter's appeals, but he knew that sooner or later he would have to. The therapist and the consultant agreed that this issue was important and required work in the therapy sessions. Finally, the consultant pointed out the positive difference it had made when she was with the family in the room versus when they were alone. This was the consultant's suggestion for helping the therapist to help the parents: Be there and stay there.

The therapy was relatively brief but nevertheless beneficial in some respects. The therapist told us that she had followed up on the limit-setting issue both with respect to the baby, whose sleeping improved, and to the families of origin. There were conflictual issues between the mother and her in-laws and the father learned to protect her in a more effective way.

This example shows the advantages of direct intervention when metaphors are not an open communication channel. Direct intervention remains implicit, yet it modifies the context in which the family interacts in ways that facilitate the partners' engagement. Not only does it bring a welcome change in the parents' subjective experience but in the infant's as well. It constitutes a probe into the resilience of the family patterns. Suppose the change leads to a new state that remains stable after the direct framing influence has been removed. Key indications of effective therapeutic resources for stabilizing the new patterns should be noted (for a discussion of where to enter the therapeutic system, see Stern, 1995; Stern-Bruschweiler and Stern, 1989).

Direct intervention requires sensitivity and experience, since intrusion is a real possibility. We have found it especially useful with the psychiatric population of extremely distressed families with whom we work. On the one hand, it is urgent to help these parents in interacting with their babies, because an infant's development will not wait. On the other hand, many of these patients have had a long experience of institutional care and of talking therapies, often ineffective in these situations. Perhaps these patients' experience of treatment has been longer and more extensive than that of their therapists. For instance, Christina's mother, a bright and sensitive borderline patient, had a knack for attracting therapists in her "nets" by means of the exact words that would strike their most sensitive chords; and then it would be a game for her to neutralize the therapist. The network of therapists she had succeeded in attracting around the family grew larger as time went by. This poses the problem of how to deal with the group of professionals around a family whose difficulties require multifocal therapy (Grasset, Fivaz-Depeursinge, and Rougemont, 1989).

THE PROFESSIONAL NETWORK AROUND THE FAMILY

Just before the discharge of the mother and her six-month-old baby from the hospital the therapists wanted us to help them plan the outpatient treatment. We would find out early in the consultation that the father accused the hospital team of causing the family's problem by keeping the mother and baby at the hospital. He opposed continuing the treatment with the outpatient team.

During the feeding (Figure 7.1a), Marie ate all right. We observed that the mother held her like a much younger baby, yet Marie did not seem to mind. The father affirmed that Marie preferred him and the mother said nothing. Interestingly, the consultant appeared not to find her place. She alternated between sitting by the father and by the mother.

After a conflictual preparation, the father predicted that Marie would only accept sitting on his lap, and the LTP play lasted hardly more than one minute. The parents were frozen. Microanalysis would uncover three main patterns that presumably corresponded to the parents' attempts to implement the first three configurations (Figure 7.1b). None were adjusted for trilogue play. Marie wriggled her arms and legs in a disorganized way, moaning, looking away most of the time except for glancing at her father or holding out her arms to him. Finally, she burst out in tears and he took her out: "She doesn't want to play, I told you," he said to the team.

Identifying with Marie, observers could feel only confused and negative, for the parents' signals were chaotic and contradictory, their actions were fragmented, and they interfered with each other. On the other end, crying

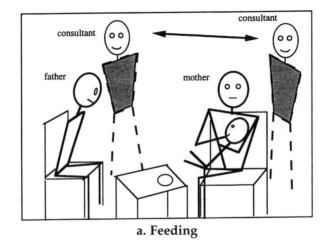

a. Feeding

PARENTS' SCREEN INFANT'S SCREEN

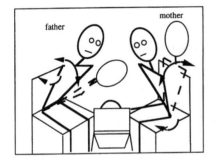

b. LTP-first trial

FIGURE 7.1 (a) Feeding; (b) LTP first trial

brought immediate relief. Identifying with the parents, we could sense extreme stress, confusion, and resentment. Their baby's crying might have hurt their sense of competence, yet it also relieved them during their difficulty in coordinating. At this point, our assessment was altogether negative. Marie clearly did not behave in an age-appropriate way. The interaction was entirely disadjusted. We did not have much insight on their strengths. We decided that the consultant would try to structure a play with them.

The pictograms in Figure 7.1c show the steps of the LTP with direct intervention. The consultant joined the family; she created a vocal envelope in supporting and encouraging the parents to engage with their baby, while

PARENTS' SCREEN   INFANT'S SCREEN

Part 1: mother-infant / father

Part 2: father-infant / mother

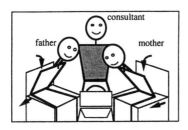

Part 3: father-mother-infant

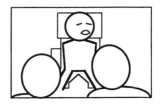

End of Part 3: without consultant

FIGURE 7.1   (c) LTP under direct intervention

placing herself in a position to set boundaries between them. This task necessitated a proper blend of empathy and firmness. Practically, it amounted to taking charge of structuring the interaction by setting up the configurations and carrying out the transitions.

In the first part, the consultant set up a space for the mother–baby dyad. She oriented the baby seat vis-à-vis the mother, then walked to the father and held him by the shoulders in order to prevent him from interfering. The result was positive. Marie focused her attention on her mother, who engaged with her. The father relaxed.

In the second part, the consultant adopted the same type of action. She created a space for the father–baby dyad and supported the mother by preventing her from withdrawing. Marie engaged with her father and the mother followed attentively.

The three-together part was more difficult. The consultant placed the baby seat in the middle and stood between the parents, with her hands on their shoulders. Yet the parents did not succeed in sustaining a game together. They nevertheless cooperated in a complementary position, in that the father allowed the mother to engage more intensely with Marie. She sang and "danced" Marie's hands under his melting eye. However, as soon as the consultant withdrew, the interaction deconstructed, the parents excluding each other, interfering with each other, and Marie crying. The consultant gave up on the last configuration.

The microanalysis of this version of the LTP under direct intervention in comparison with the first spontaneous one evidenced differences in the triangular frameworks. They respectively corresponded to C and D frameworks.

The professionals involved with this family assisted with the session behind the one-way mirror. They questioned establishing a therapeutic contract at the time of the transition between hospital and outpatient treatments. Therefore, our formal comment included them too. The message was that it was difficult for the family to accept help because they were extremely proud. Yet when they did, Marie was able to behave in a much more age-appropriate way and the parents could more fully show their parenting abilities. Help was therefore needed, even though it might have to be provided in a somewhat forceful way.

After this consultation, the parents accepted the outpatient treatment; it lasted for several years, with ups and downs, and helped Marie to grow up with less of a load on her shoulders. This was especially important since we later learned that several of her ascendants, including her mother, had suffered schizophrenia.

This example shows that systems consultations integrating the LTP framing format are useful for therapeutic as well as research purposes. There are in fact as many ways to use the LTP situation in this perspective as there are clinically significant triangles: the "motherhood constellation" triangle (Stern, 1995), namely the mother–infant–grandmother one, or the corresponding "fatherhood" one, or for that matter any transgenerational triangle with which there is a desire to work. Another case is a parent–infant dyad with their therapist. Having experimented with this situation, we can attest to the benefit of getting to sense from the inside the position of an interactive partner with respect to a problematic relationship.

A triangle that we found particularly relevant is the one constituted by a couple of parents/spouses with their therapist. The therapist finds himself/herself, not unlike the child, in a position to be triangulated by the typically collusive alliance of the couple with an unnegotiable conflict. Let us briefly turn to this transposition of the LTP model.

A SYSTEMS CONSULTATION FOR
THE THERAPIST AND THE COUPLE

We transposed the LTP to the therapist–couple interaction by designing the Lausanne triadic discussion task. It was thought out as an exercise in resolving differences and in adopting an empathic stance. Following the researchers' instructions, the therapist guided each spouse in turn in imagining his or her spouse's actions and emotions during the hour preceding their next therapy session. Then say the husband responded in confirming or contesting his wife's conjectures, so the wife had the opportunity to discover new aspects of her partner's intersubjective experience. In this procedure family therapists will recognize features of the method of "circular questioning" designed by the Milan group (Selvini-Palazzoli, Boscolo, Cecchin, and Prata, 1982; Seywert, 1990).

Formally, as in the LTP, the therapist and couple systematically moved between the four two-plus-one and three-together configurations. During the first two parts, the spouses took turns speaking about each other (two plus ones), whereas during the last part the therapist joined the spouses in discussing what this task might have contributed to their therapeutic work (three-together format). This discussion was integrated in a systems consultation that took place twice: once after the third therapy session and once just before the last one. It essentially served the purpose of assessing the therapeutic alliance between the therapist and couple. The analysis focused primarily on the nonverbal, affective aspect of their relationship: the processes of inclusion/exclusion, role organization, and tuning in affectively, or evaluating the ways they conducted transitions and repaired miscoordinations.

We do not report the details of this study here. But it is interesting to note the results of the structural reading of these observations. They indicated that the four-functions scheme was meaningful in assessing the basic affective component of the therapeutic alliance. Once it was adjusted for adult interactions, the model of formations was readily applicable to the functions of participation and organization at the body and gaze levels (de Roten, Darwish, Stern, Fivaz-Depeursinge, and Corboz-Warnery, in press–a; de Roten, Fivaz-Depeursinge, Corboz-Warnery, Ciola, and Stern, 1994; de Roten, Fivaz-Depeursinge, Stern, Corboz-Warnery, and Darwish, in press–b; Fivaz-Depeursinge, de Roten, Corboz-Warnery, Métraux, and Ciola, 1994). It was obviously where focal attention entered the scene that nonverbal interactions were revealed as insufficient in accounting for this function, although much can be read from the backchannels of the speaker and listeners. Then affective contact as displayed by facial expressions was extremely rich. By resorting to the microanalysis of affective events during mutual smiles, whether during the two-plus-one or three-together configurations or during transitions between them, we could reliably discriminate between triads with potentially positive versus problematic therapeutic alliances (Darwish, Fivaz-Depeursinge, Stern, de Roten, and Corboz-Warnery, in preparation; Stern, Fivaz-Depeursinge, de Roten, Corboz-Warnery, and Darwish, 1996). The same procedure applied to mutual smiles between therapist and patient in brief psychodynamic psychotherapy proved to be discriminative (Currat, 1997; Gilliéron, 1990).

Let us briefly describe a systems consultation with a therapist and a couple to show again that it is possible to combine the goals of research and therapy in a meaningful and productive way. A couple in their thirties asked for therapy because of communication problems that caused violent disputes between them. They had two young children and had had several individual treatments. Yet the couple relationship had not improved; on the contrary, it had deteriorated. They stated this was their last chance before separation. During the first two sessions, the partners collaborated. But the therapist had the impression she would soon become the driving force behind the treatment, with the couple merely submitting. This was the theme she had in mind when she asked for a systems consultation.

The three partners accepted the task with grace. As the consultant delivered the instructions, the therapist made a humorous comment on the research setting and the three laughed together. This apparently trivial event allowed them to experience their complicity. During the Lausanne triadic discussion, the spouses scrupulously followed the instructions, careful not to interfere with each other and restrained in their comments. They avoided gaze contact with each other, focusing on the therapist. Both partners were at a loss trying to imagine the other's experience ("I have never asked myself what he might feel") and had trouble confronting each other. There was no projection in the future, as if time had come to a standstill. The therapist established links between their statements and underscored their disagreements with humor, which helped to relax the tension. Afterward, she asked the consultant for his comments about the interactions, after acknowledging the cooperation from the couple, but also stating her fear that they might settle into a state of dependence on her that would prevent change.

After a pause for reflection, the consultant reminded them that he was basing his comments uniquely on his observations, since he did not know about their clinical situation. Nevertheless, he offered his intuition, which was that under the tranquil and harmonious aspect of the trio's understanding, there were waves of tension and pain. He suggested that this situation perhaps required that they grant themselves pauses. These respites might give them the impression that they were losing time, but they might help them prepare to face the storm together and overcome it. The couple and therapist listened attentively but kept their comments for their next session together.

The therapist reported later that this consultation was useful for their therapeutic work. They began working together: The therapist accepted her fears of the couple's dependence on her; the couple began approaching issues that were more painful. The themes of trust/distrust, closeness/distance, and the therapeutic relationship in analogy with the couple relationship, as well as their relationships with their families of origin, became the red threads of the sessions. of course, this evolution might have taken place without the systems consultation. But the very confrontation of an outsider brought a mobilization of resources and accelerated the process.

In conclusion, we illustrate in this chapter how we conduct systems consultations with therapists and clinical families, sometimes by means of direct interventions into the family's interactive patterns and within the LTP setting. In systems consultations, the feedback extends to the relationship between the family and the therapist or the network. Finally, far from being reserved for the primary triangle, the Lausanne family model applies to many other clinically relevant triads. The transposition to the therapist–couple triangle marks the path to how this model can serve in many other clinically relevant situations.

REFERENCES

Currat, T. (1997). Inférer la relation à partir des interactions affectives. Doctoral thesis in medicine, Lausanne.

Darwish, J., Fivaz-Depeursinge, E., Stern, D., de Roten, Y., and Corboz-Warnery, A. (in preparation). Mutual smiles between therapist and couple help to bind together, share miseries, repair and confront.

de Roten, Y., Fivaz-Depeursinge, E., Corboz-Warnery, A., Ciola, A., and Stern, D. J. (1994). Attentionnalité et communication à trois: analyse séquentielle des formations visuelles de triades en thérapie. *Revue suisse de psychologie, 53* (2), 104–118.

de Roten, Y., Darwish, J., Stern, D. J., Fivaz-Depeursinge, E., and Corboz-Warnery, A. (in press–a). Nonverbal communication and alliance in therapy: The body formation coding system. *Clinical Psychology.*

de Roten, Y., Fivaz-Depeursinge, E., Stern, D. J., Corboz-Warnery, A., and Darwish, J. (in press–b). From affective engagement to therapeutic alliance. *Psychotherapy research.*

Fivaz-Depeursinge, E., Corboz-Warnery, A., and Frenk, N. (1995). L'approche systémique. In M. Robin, I. Casati, and D. Candilis-Huisman (eds.), *La construction des liens familiaux pendant la première enfance. Approches francophones* (pp. 247–268). Paris: Presses Universitaires de France.

Fivaz-Depeursinge, E., de Roten, Y., Corboz-Warnery, A., Métraux, J. C., and Ciola, A. (1994). Identifying a mutual attending frame: A pilot study of gaze interactions between therapist and couple. *Psychotherapy Research, 4*(2), 107–120.

Fivaz-Depeursinge, E., Guillemin, J., Cornut-Zimmer, B., and Martin, D. (1984). Objectivation d'une hiérarchie d'encadrement par la microanalyse d'échanges entre une observatrice, une mère et son nourisson. *Psychologie Médicale, 16,* 2481–2486.

Gilliéron, E. (1990). *Les psychothérapies brèves.* Paris: PUF.

Grasset, F., Fivaz-Depeursinge, E., and Rougemont, T. (1989). Thérapie familiale de longue durée et processus de développement. *Thérapie Familiale, 10,* 147–162.

Haley, J. (1963). *Strategies of psychotherapy.* New York: Grune & Stratton.

Selvini-Palazzoli, M., Boscolo, L., Cecchin, G., and Prata, G. (1982). Hypothétisation, circularité, neutralité. *Thérapie Familiale, 3* (3), 117–132.

Seywert, F. (1990). *L'évaluation systémique de la famille.* Paris: Presses Universitaires de France.

Stern, D. J., Fivaz-Depeursinge, E., de Roten, Y., Corboz-Warnery, A., and Darwish, J. (1996). Transitions and the sharing of interactional affective events. *Swiss Journal of Psychology, 55*(4), 204–212.

Stern, D. N. (1995). *The Motherhood Constellation.* New York: Basic Books.

Stern-Bruschweiler, N., and Stern, D. N. (1989). A model for conceptualizing the role of the mother's representational world in various mother–infant therapies. *Infant Mental Health Journal, 10*(3), 142–156.

Wynne, L., McDaniel, S., and Weber, T. (1986). *Systems Consultation: A New Perspective for Family Therapy.* New York: Guilford Press.

CHAPTER 8

Bridging Infant Development and Family Process

The main goal when we began this study was to identify a family-level property, the family alliance. The avenues to this goal were studying the specific developmental trajectory of the primary triangle; observing the practicing family; revisiting the clinical notions of triangulation from a normative perspective; revisiting the infant's socioemotional development in the context of the primary triangle; and exploring micro- as well as macro-family patterns.

MULTIPLE READINGS

Looking back, we are convinced that *the* avenue to the description of family patterns is multiple readings. It is in parallel that we have developed on the one hand a clinical sense of triangular interactions, looking for our own echoes to the family's affective communication; and, on the other hand, we have elaborated the micro-readings of episodes we felt were significant. The constant back-and-forth examination is productive, generating new ideas while securing daily realities. This procedure is supported by G. Bateson (1979).

In the perspective of systems theory, the chapters shed light on one of the five aspects of the developmental system:

1. A system has a function, defined by the task it sets out to realize; reaching playful relatedness is described by the functional/clinical reading (Chapter 2).

2. In order to implement this function, the system constructs a structure, arranging its elements in an appropriate way; the structural reading features this aspect by means of the triangular framework (Chapter 3).

3. In order to sustain this structure in the face of the inevitable variations coming from its internal or external environment, the system regulates itself; the process reading features the system's dynamics by means of the type of miscoordination and repair actions taken by the partners (Chapter 4).

4. The system is able to change by making its structure more complex and differentiating its regulatory processes in response to changes in the environment; the pertinent infant changes are described by the developmental reading (Chapter 5).

5. Finally, the system sustains a permeable boundary between itself and the environment; the reading of the interactions between the observers and the family describes this boundary (Chapter 6).[1]

None of these readings attempt to precisely tap the content of the interaction. Indeed, at the beginning of an LTP session, no one would bet on precisely what is going to happen, because no two days are alike, no two families are alike, and no two stories are alike. But we can capture the forms: the type of story, the type of framework, the way miscoordinations of any kind are repaired, the strategies of triangulation, the openness and differentiation of the observer–family exchanges. Forms are the key to relationships: "A relationship consists of the forms that people build when they are together" (Gottman, 1982, p. 951).

TRIANGULAR FRAMEWORKS

"Systems love hierarchies" (Simon, cited in Sameroff and Emde, 1989). This comment captures the core of the triangular framework. Chapter 3 reveals the incredible capacity of a group to frame its own interactions. Envision again the complexity of a triangular framework. Here the partners have four functions to fulfill: Include everyone, keep to roles, share a focus, and keep affectively tuned in. They are interacting at four different physical levels: lower bodies; upper bodies; heads and gazes; facial, vocal, and gestural expressions. Then they construct formations for each function: participation, organization, focal attention, and affective contact formations. Given one type of formation is added at each level, there are ten formations. Three people have to manage these operations together. Moreover, two of them, namely the parents, conjointly guide the third one, namely the infant, who is at present only partly enacting her own contribution. But she will get better at it, providing the parents work in the zone of her proximal development. This is the story of the triangular framework and it is stunning. However, we know that this is only a rough approximation of what the partners actually do with their nonverbal interactions.[2]

We are reminded that this construct is an elaboration and an empirical application of Scheflen's notions on communication as a hierarchy (Scheflen, 1973), and above all, of Kendon's descriptions of F-formations (Kendon, 1977). Both these authors clearly envisioned this complexity and order, as pioneers do.

The results available at the time of this writing, most of which have been described in more detail in Chapters 3 and 6, indicate first that the model of the triangular framework indeed fits the observations of the actual formations. For instance, the interactions categorized in D frameworks—that is, in disordered alliances—primarily exhibit disadjustment in participation formations, whereas the interactions categorized in C frameworks—that is, in collusive alliances—primarily exhibit disadjustment in organization formations, and so on (see Chapter 3). Second, the degrees of adjustment in each configuration correlate with each other, showing that the instrument is coherent and that each configuration assesses the family alliance in the same way (Carneiro, 1998).

Third, the family alliance is fairly stable over the first year, yet amenable to change under particular circumstances (see Chapter 4). In cooperative and stressed alliances, we interpret this stability as indicating that the family had sufficient internal and external resources to face the enormous challenges of the transition to parenthood. In contrast, in collusive alliances, the stability presumably indicates rigidity, as if detouring coalitions were a cohesive factor of family patterns—yet at the cost of diverting the child's development, whereas it appears that a subtype of the disordered alliances might be more prone to change. We have reported two improvements of family alliances initially categorized in the disordered family alliances where exclusion involved the infant but not the parents.

Fourth, the type of family alliance as measured by the triangular framework at nine months is related to the child's socioaffective development at four years as assessed clinically. In particular, the parents in several problematic family alliances reported clinical-level symptoms, whereas the child in the good-enough alliance was never so identified. There is then a connection between the early family-level functioning and the child's individual development. Whereas these results do not account for causal relationships between these variables, plausibility speaks for an influence of family-level variables on child development (Fivaz-Depeursinge, Frascarolo, and Corboz-Warnery, 1996).[3]

Assuming they will be replicated, these results support the importance of hierarchic structuring to ensure the stability emphasized by systems theory (Sameroff and Emde, 1989). On practical grounds, they mean that the family alliance offers the prospect of an early assessment of the family's resources and vulnerabilities. Likewise, intervention methods are opened that would directly target the primary derailment in the triangular framework: inclusion/exclusion, role organization, focal attention, or affective contact.

There are several prospects for the validation of this model in the near future. On the one hand, a new longitudinal study is in progress at our center, with the goal of replicating the above results. On the other hand, a network called *Trilogie* has been constituted by teams who have started longitudinal studies on the primary triangle in the nineties and have included the LTP procedure in their protocol. Of particular interest is the diversity of perspectives they represent: from psychodynamics, with two studies on triangular representations (D. Bürgin and K. von Klitzing in Basel, S. Lebovici and M. Lamour in Paris), to human ethology (J. Gottman and A. Shapiro in Seattle) and family systems (M. Hedenbro in Stockholm, ourselves in Lausanne). Not only will these studies be instrumental in testing the model on large and representative samples but they will relate the measures of family alliances to outcome measures, such as the child's socioaffective development, her relationships with peers, her attachment patterns, the parents' marital relationship, and the family's functioning.[4]

REVISITING TRIANGULATION FROM A DEVELOPMENTAL PERSPECTIVE

Revisiting the infant development in the context of the primary triangle has led to exploring the family system and examining the relationship between the infant and her parents. There are many issues we might want to consider in this perspective, particularly how the father and mother coordinate their intuitive parenting behaviors as a coparenting party and how they work together in the infant's zone of proximal development. But the clinical importance of triangular process and its novelty in an early development perspective led us to highlight this issue.

Because the current definitions of triangulation were partial from a normative point of view, focusing mainly on exclusion or derailments, we have proposed a new, more exhaustive definition. It is designed to understand triangular process in the LTP, but it may be extended to other relationships.

Prior to summarizing this definition, let us stress that triangular process requires not only affective but also cognitive operations. In fact, we might debate at length whether cognitive operations dominate over affective ones. For instance, does an infant's quizzical look in a puzzling situation signal a difficult-to-understand parent or an emotion (Papousek, personal communication, March 1997)? Our position is that emotions are necessarily involved, whether they are in the foreground or in the background. This point has been eloquently stated by A. Damasio in his book entitled *Descartes' Error* (Damasio, 1994). Likewise, several developmentalists consider that the interactional regulation of affect is paramount in the first year of development (Emde, 1985; Stern, 1994; Trevarthen, 1984). Thus, our definition of triangular process comes to closely parallel current definitions of individual emotional regulation: "the processes or strategies that are used to manage emotional arousal so that successful interpersonal functioning is possible" (Calkins, 1994, p. 59).

Triangulation is essentially a process. Its function is to establish and maintain threesome relatedness in affectively loaded situations. The criteria selected to assess this process are as follows.

First, the infant and her parents effectively differentiate all four triangles that make up their three-party relationship when active versus third-party roles are considered. Note that this criterion corresponds to the conception of a system as founders of this theory conceived it (Bertalanffy, 1956; Piaget, 1967).

Second, the infant and her parents activate triangular strategies; these strategies testify to the coordination of their attention and affects with their two other partners and they are stage-appropriate. They are direct at the social stage and referential at the intersubjective stage so as to promote the growth of threesome relatedness.[5]

Third, the differentiation of the four triangles holds in three key emotional contexts: harmony, conflict, and uncertainty. The latter trigger triangulation strategies on the infant's part in the LTP over the first year. This perspective is in line with the current conceptualizations that stress the function of emotions in establishing, maintaining, or disrupting the relation between the organism and the environment (Campos, Campos, and Barrett, 1989; Emde, 1985). It is also in line with the emphasis on emotional management in the clinical notions of triangulation (Bowen, 1972). However, whereas clinical theory generally highlights conflict, the definition we propose also specifies positive affect conditions (Easterbrooks and Emde, 1987; Gottman, 1994; McHale, Kuersten, and Lauretti, 1996).

Given these criteria, four alliance-specific processes of triangulation between the two parties have emerged: differentiated, restricted, detouring, and paradoxical-undifferentiated. They are largely influenced by the parents' styles of triangulation, but the infant is an active party in this process. These processes cover the range from the most clear differentiation of triangles to confusion, from the most effective and stage-appropriate to the most ineffective and stage-inappropriate strategies.

What is the evidence for these hypotheses? At the intersubjective stage, the results presented in Chapter 5 are compelling, even if still exploratory. The criteria are fulfilled in differentiated and restricted triangulation. In detouring and paradoxical forms, the distortions of meaning and the restriction of the emotional repertoire of the infant compel clinicians and developmental psychopathologists to closely scrutinize the infant's contribution to conflict detouring and paradoxical strategies. These findings draw attention to the necessity to further study this crucial developmental issue from an experimental as well as from a clinical perspective.

At the social stage, the LTP with a still-face episode addresses even more directly than the regular LTP the three conditions that we know trigger triangulation strategies on the part of the infant: in the first two configurations, harmony; during the still face, uncertainty; and during the recovery from the still face, conflict. The pilot study shows that the situation does a good job at revealing the infant's triangular competence at that stage. The findings in both versions of the three-month-old's coordination of attention and affect are already sufficiently clear to challenge the current theories on the dyad-to-triad developmental sequence. A new study to test these hypotheses on a larger sample in the LTP with still face is now in progress.

The LTP in its two versions is a complex situation in which an infant's trajectory and strategies not only depend on herself but also on her parents' reactions to the situation. Obviously, the elucidation of the early infant's triangular strategies will also require different, more controlled situations. Tremblay-Leveau's (1997) extension of the "exclusion paradigm"[6] is pertinent (see also D'Entremont, Hains, and Muir, 1997).[7]

In conclusion, it is puzzling to realize that the three-month-old infant has not been asked explicitly by researchers whether she is able to coordinate her attention with two people and share an affect with them. Merely observing her interacting with her two parents rather than one parent opens up a whole new world. We can no longer consider that the infant awaits referential communication to handle the triangles with her parents. That there exists an early triangular competence is not surprising. Think of the parents' triangulation strategies with their infant early on. Think of how many times an infant might go through the four triangles with her father and mother. Admittedly, we do not yet know precisely how much time an infant spends in each of them, but we now know that a family is able to achieve triangulation when given the opportunity for practicing it. Moreover, a number of experimental studies as well as transcultural ones (Tronick, Morelli, and Ivey, 1992) strongly suggest the possibility of early triangular or polyadic competence, even if the findings were not analyzed in the first place from this perspective (for a review, see Tremblay-Leveau, 1997). Finally, we know that those involved in observational research on the primary triangle contemplate this possibility.[8] Perhaps the most convincing argument is that interactions involving a person as the third party and then also as the referent are bound to be more "mind-stretching" than are those involving an object. When parents respond appropriately, threesome "consciousness-expanding" states are created for all parties involved (Tronick, 1998).

Certainly, triangular interactions do not in any way lessen the importance of the dyadic interactions that make up a father–mother–infant triangle. But they are bound to change our outlook on the social competence of a young infant, the origins of triangulation, and the importance of the parents' joint responses early in life for the development of family intersubjectivity.

CLINICAL TRIANGULATIONS IN THE LIGHT OF NORMATIVE PROCESS

Discovering the infant's ability to deal with triangular relationships from the onset creates a new context for understanding the clinical notions of triangulation. We see in Chapter 4 the incredible subtleties of the dynamics of miscoordination and repair, particularly during transitions. Again, A. Kendon shows the way in discovering how the family minutely conducts a transition with the necessary preannouncements, announcements, and ratifications that mark the steps between two configurations (Kendon, 1977). We find that those families who fail in this minute handling have problematic alliances. Thus, the chapter constitutes still another pathway to characterizing the family alliance and, for that matter, other alliances such as between a therapist and a couple or between a physician and a patient. Chapter 4 also reveals a pertinent entry into the interfaces between different aspects of development.

In a revisitation of triangular process, the Interfaces study group examined the parallels between observable interactions and other levels of inquiry, such as the intrapsychic and the intergenerational. This diverse group was assembled in Lausanne by the first author and Daniel Stern, each of whom worked at a different level of description and inquiry. It consisted of Dieter Bürgin, John Byng-Hall, Martine Lamour, Serge Lebovici, Daniel Stern, and the two authors. Xerxes's parents agreed to take part in it in two capacities: as members of the research team and as subjects who allowed multiple interviewing by several people. As described in Chapter 4, after going through the LTP procedure they were interviewed on the transition from two plus one to three together. Daniel Stern used the "microanalytic interview" technique, designed to study how representations influence behavior. This technique inquires about the "state of the representation and its articulations with behavior at the instant that the behavior is performed" (Stern, 1995, p. 48). In a modified version of this technique, Stern reviewed with both parents the transition and asked them to go "inside themselves" in a shifting dialogue between their behavioral interactions and their represented life. Then Serge Lebovici, Dieter Bürgin, and John Byng-Hall successively reexamined the very same sequence with them in order to understand respectively the psychodynamic, cultural, and family script underpinnings of these interactions. The interviews were repeated concerning the same transition at one year. Finally, the second author did a follow-up interview on these issues at four years.

The results of the multiple perspective analyses dramatically showed that central psychological themes such as "triadification" (as we used to label behavioral triangulation at that time) are manifest at whatever level of examination in describing a family's exchanges: interactive behaviors, autobiographical narratives, fantasies, memories, scripts, and practices.[9] These multiple perspectives in turn led us to suggest, in analogy with the interactional level, that shared individual representations generate a collective tri-angular imaginary representation—that is, a subjective experience simultaneously shared by the three parties. Take, for instance, an episode of harmony in the form of positive affect sharing in the threesome. This interaction is represented in the bottom of Figure 8.1.

We may presume that each of the partners has an individual triangular representation of this episode in tune with the interactional triangle (middle of Figure 8.1). This sharing has an amplifying effect that affords a special intensity to the collective imaginary communion: "We are together as a threesome" (upper part of Figure 8.1). This is a powerful way to feed a family's sense and memory of "belonging," in line with D. Reiss's theory on the function of interactions for the group: Family practices and rituals realign the representations of the individuals on the group interaction, thus affording the latter with a "memorial" function (Reiss, 1981). We saw indeed that the manner of conducting the transition in Xerxes's family was ritualized, as it was in many other families (Fivaz-Depeursinge, Stern, Corboz-Warnery and Bürgin, 1998).

There is no reason to assume that the same parallels would not be found between individual and collective representations in dyads or in larger groups. For that matter, there is no reason to assume that interfaces similar to the ones we found between interactive and imaginary processes might not be at work at other systems levels.[10]

Besides, obvious correspondences exist between the early patterns of transitions as coordinated practices and the later practices and rituals in families. Family therapists have recognized the "power of daily rituals" in shaping family relationships: "Daily rituals powerfully tell us who we are to each other, sometimes without our even realizing it" (Imber-Black and Roberts, 1992, p. 167). Therefore, therapists use them in their interventions (Van der Hart, 1983). In our view, other therapeutic practices such as family sculpting and games also draw their power from modifying and strengthening the collective representations that emerge from practicing them together.[11] This situation is also true for postmodern therapies involving conarratives and conversations.[12]

THE PRACTICING FAMILY IN A CONTEXT OF CHANGE

We set out to study the practicing family in contrast with the family as represented in its members' minds. Several key aspects were involved: observ-

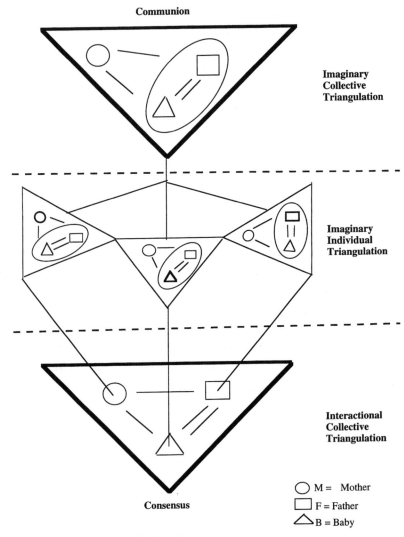

FIGURE 8.1   Collective triangulation

ing a family in action, facilitating development, and addressing both normative and clinical issues.

In our view, the LTP situation is the foremost gain of the study, insofar as it enables observation of the triangular interactions for research as well as for clinical purposes. We have seen for the first time the primary triangle in a three together and surprisingly it was done just as well as in a two together. Not only did the parents have no problem in guiding their infant in "dancing" in a triangle but the infant placed in this situation revealed unexpected competencies.

Likewise, the other configurations reveal new facts. The dyad's interaction is unmistakenly influenced by the third party and the third party's behavior is influenced by the dyad. We already knew that a parent interacted differently with his/her infant in the presence of the coparent than in his/her absence (Pedersen, Anderson, and Cain, 1980). But thanks to the systematic permutation between the three two plus ones, conducted in a truly interactional setting, we also got to systematically observe the partners for the first time in third-party positions, such as a mother sitting at close range to the father–baby dyad yet confined to a watching stance. She resonates with the dyad, works at regulating her own affects when the action intensifies, and sometimes does not resist interfering, or excluding herself, for whatever motives she has at that time. Fathers are perhaps more used to the third-party position, but they also resonate, check themselves, interfere, and exclude themselves. Most importantly, we now have suggestive indications that the infant also coordinates her behavior in the third-party position with that of her parents.

Is the LTP situation ecologically valid? The interviews with the families as well as the richness and variety of the observation data speak for validity. Yet it is necessary to test this assumption. A study by M. Hedenbro and colleagues (1998) in Stockholm is investigating this question by comparing spontaneous trilogue play with the LTP.

Extensions of the LTP

Because the paradigm aims at observing the trajectory of the primary triangle, the situation should accommodate the long cycles that characterize a family's developmental course. Therefore, one of the first priorities in the longitudinal studies is to extend the scope of this assessment to include the other developmental stages of early family life.

Fortunately, the LTP situation is easy to adapt to other developmentally prominent socioaffective issues. At the moral/verbal stage, what is outstanding is that the toddler enters the culture and begins to learn and interiorize its moral values. The parents repeatedly, patiently, and playfully negotiate the "do's" and "don't's" of daily life. Thus, we ask the family to sit around a table and to play together with toys in the four configurations of

the LTP. By its very nature, the situation confronts the family with limit setting (be it only because the toddler can by now walk away from the table) so
that playful negotiation comes to the fore. All sorts of complex or "moral"
emotions arise such as pride and mastery, empathy steps up to a new level,
and shame and guilt may be present in this circumstance, particularly in
problematic interactions.[13]

At the narrative stage, when the child begins to co-construct her autobi-
ography with her parents, we ask the parents to help their child tell a story
around a theme (the parents leave for a weekend and the child stays with
other people) while following the succession of the four configurations.[14] For
example, the father starts the story with the child and the mother watches.
Then the mother proceeds and the father watches, and so on. Needless to
say, oedipal triangulation themes flourish in these narratives. Also, the patterns that characterize these families' interactions during the first year can
be easily recognized.

Covering the prenatal stage in order to explore the premises of triangular
interactions is also important. Our colleagues in Basel, D. Bürgin and K. von
Klitzing, have already paved the way by investigating the parents' triangular representations during pregnancy.[15] Our own goal is to also tap the interactive aspect of the parents' relationship to their fetus and future child.
Therefore, we ask the parents to role-play their first encounter as a threesome with their newborn as they anticipate it, again in the four LTP configurations. This session takes place at the end of the second trimester, when
the parents have had the opportunity to physically interact with the fetus by
means of echography, haptonomy, and sensing its movements. Preliminary
results show definite correspondences between the ways the parents construct their formations to include (or exclude) their child and each other in
both prenatal and postnatal situations.[16]

It is also simple to envision how the LTP format could be adapted to later
developmental stages, up to adulthood. Actually, the format we designed
for therapist–couple groups can be applied to any developmentally salient
issue in a family (see Chapter 7).

Surely nowadays single-parent households constitute a substantial portion of our population, which the growing size of research in these domains
confirms.[17] In our clinical practice, we have resorted to two procedures, depending on the family's situation. If a significant third party is available,
such as a grandmother, a friend, a secondary caretaker, or even a therapist,
then we use the LTP procedure. The methods of analysis are strictly the

same, but obviously the interpretation of the results has to take into account the different context. If a significant third party is not available, then we use dialogue play observations. Note that the Lausanne family model with each of its readings is applicable all the same. But the operationalization of the criteria is considerably more simple. And for that matter, this is also the case when it is applied to individual rather than group therapy.

Another pressing issue is to streamline the model in order to apply it in real time and to less standardized situations, such as to free trilogue play, or to other triangles in which the infant participates, such as infant, mother, and day care worker. Preliminary work in this direction is promising (Maury and Lamour, 1994; Pierrehumbert and Fivaz-Depeursinge, 1994).

A PARADIGM ADDRESSING BOTH
NORMATIVE AND CLINICAL POPULATIONS

Another important gain has come from the concurrent observation of clinical and volunteer families. It is our good fortune that the small volunteer and clinical samples of families with whom we have worked partially overlap: The interactions of some of the volunteer families revealed problematic by clinical standards and the interactions of a few clinical families fortunately were good enough. As a result, it may be assumed that the categories of alliances pretty much cover the range encountered in the two populations.

However, we have serious doubts about the repartition of the different types of alliances. In the longitudinal sample, the good-enough alliances represent not quite half the sample. It is our impression that the problematic alliances are overrepresented, presumably due to the bias in the selection of volunteer families discussed in Chapter 6. Yet if this presumption were confirmed, then the criteria of adjustment versus disadjustment adopted in this study would come under question. At the time of this writing, this important issue is being put to test in the four-site study of the Trilogie network.[18]

Whatever the results, it remains that we now have an instrument that allows us to study the practicing family. In the long run, it will contribute to fill the gap between relationship disturbances in the mother–infant dyad and in the family (Sameroff and Emde, 1989). Besides, the main point is so obvious that it hardly needs elaboration: It is of primary importance to develop models of triangular relationships that apply to both normative and psychopathological process, if only to avoid the misfortunes of clinical theories that have originated in psychopathology and have been generalized without consideration for the world (fortunately wide) outside of the clinical domain.

OBSERVATION AS A CONTEXT OF TRANSFORMATION

In Chapters 6 and 7, we expose the preventive/therapeutic perspective inherent in developmental systems research. This point has been elegantly stated by A. Sameroff: "The act of knowing is already changing what one is trying to know" (Sameroff and Emde, 1989, p. 226). Crucial to our understanding of human development are the articulations between the different system levels—that is, the articulations between the working alliances and the family alliances and, within the family alliances, what may also be called the coparenting alliance with respect to the infant's development. Typical of interventions with families, we as researchers/consultants are faced with the task of framing a framing/developmental system, as represented in Figure 8.2.

The effect of direct intervention in the LTP setting with clinical families and their therapists is readily visible and could be systematically assessed in the classical designs of outcome research.[19] We also tried to assess the preventive effects of the framing inherent in the observation paradigm by examining the evolution of the family alliances over the first year. The fact that it was stable in most cases by no means signifies in our view that the research intervention has no beneficial framing influence. However, it should be tested by comparing groups of families with and without the research intervention.

In parallel with this issue is the necessity to investigate another articulation between the nuclear family and its environment, namely the origin families. We follow in the steps of transgenerational debts and merits, family scripts, and rituals and practices.[20] In a new study, the pregnant parents, separately and together, enact their relationships with their origin families as they see them in the past and as they transform with the birth of their child.

Another influence that should be clarified is the cultural representations construed by the families regarding our expectations as researchers/consultants toward them. Their responses to our instructions may be viewed as their manner of understanding what in our view is "right" or "wrong"— what they imagine as they decode the implicit connotations of our base in a

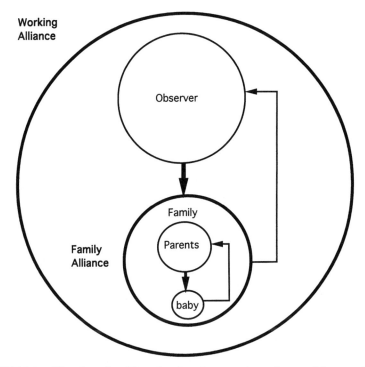

Working Alliance

Family Alliance

FIGURE 8.2   **The framing/developing interactions in working and family alliances**

university psychiatric department and as a research unit with a family systems label.[21]

Still another important line of research is the issue of genders. It might be argued that this study is guilty of ignoring the role of gender differences in the LTP. We are reminded that family process theories have stressed the hierarchy of the parental party over the child and neglected the hierarchy and the traditional power inequalities between men and women.[22] At this time, no gender difference has emerged in our findings, presumably due to the small sample sizes. It is nevertheless our hypothesis that important differences will emerge between mothers and fathers with respect to the styles of regulation of conflict. We have in mind studies showing that males as husbands and fathers are more vulnerable to stress and conflict with their partners than are females as wives and mothers (Gottman, 1994).[23] Also, it has been suggested that the wife is the "relationship architect" in the couple

(Wamboldt and Reiss, 1989). She may have the same role in the coparenting party with respect to the child, if only for her special biological function.

Finally, we have not considered the role of the infant when she suffers an illness or another physical limitation. This is obviously an important factor in a family system. The infant may influence the system in many ways (Anthony, 1984).[24]

THE PRIMARY TRIANGLE AS A WHOLE: GAINS AND LOSSES

What did we gain, or lose, in considering the family as a whole? First, we reached a point where we could see the dance between the three partners as a wholesome phenomenon in which what counted were not the moves taken by each of them but the net result of their joint actions (Scheflen, 1975). We learned to sense the merging of individual and dyadic behaviors into triangular combinations that could not be predicted from the onset. For example, one of the most illustrative figures is a mother who is overshooting her stimulations of the baby. The baby has to fight in order to cope. Then a father is undershooting them. The baby is bored. How are these two dyads going to merge into a three together? As reported, we observe two versions: merging into a more adjusted (as in stressed alliances) versus a less adjusted three together (as in collusive alliances). In other words, either mother's or father's ways eventually complement each other so that the baby is able to integrate their combination, or mother's and father's ways amplify each other, with mother even more active and father even more passive and the baby not included. Examining a posteriori the coordinations between the parents would make it possible to reasonably predict their fitting or misfitting in the three together. Particularly significant is whether they have kept to their roles as active versus third-party parents, and then how they have handled their own direct interaction in the last two plus one.

Likewise, we observe several interactions with one parent who is somewhat adjusted, the other somewhat disadjusted; again the merging would go either toward a more effective or a more ineffective three together. Therefore, it surely is a gain to see the baby in the context of the primary triangle rather than only in the dyad with the primary caretaker, as is still often the case. It draws more fully the landscape in which she is developing. In particular, it throws a complementary light on what we know about the relationship disturbances between infants and their depressive or psychotic mothers.[25]

However, we realize that we are probably also losing information on the mother–baby dyad, or on the separate father–baby and mother–father dyads. Theoretically speaking, and even if there is also some overlap between the different contexts, the family context selects dyadic behaviors that would not be recruited by a dyadic context. The converse is also true: Dyadic contexts select dyadic interactions that would not be recruited by a family context. The same holds for individual contexts. In this sense, we are both losing and gaining information on the dyads and on the individuals by placing them in a triangular context.

This important issue brings us back to R. Parke's prescription: It is necessary to observe the developmental trajectory of each family unit for its own sake (Parke, 1988). We would only be in a position to assess to which extent the family contextualized the dyads and the individuals who make it up by studying every family unit. Consequently, the comparison of dialogue and trilogue play is imperative.

This point is not only important theoretically. It has enormous implications for clinical assessment and treatment, for it forbids generalizing from the family to the dyads as well as from the dyads to the family. Therefore, it requires us to carefully assess in each case which of the family units needs to be targeted for treatment (Kaufmann, 1986). True, this principle has repeatedly been made by theoreticians in child development as well as in family process. Yet there still is a strong tendency in the corresponding clinical practices to generalize from the individual, the dyad, or the family to the other levels.

From this perspective, if we examine the types of families that convinced systems-oriented researchers that the whole constrains the parts, we find that they are now labeled "rigid" families, such as families with psychosis or incest (Singer, Wynne, and Toohey, 1978; Sroufe, 1989). Perhaps it is precisely and only such families that lack the flexibility to sustain "loose coupling" between the subsystems. Thus, predicting from the whole to the components would only pertain to very problematic families and not to the middle-range families, which function well in certain domains and less well in others, such as those described by Beavers (Beavers, 1977).

It is interesting to note that by the end of this study the family perspective had made its way in clinical researchers' minds. The publication in 1997 of a New Directions volume on family-level variables supports this fact (McHale and Cowan, 1996). This volume's main focus is the influence of the coparenting relationship (in contrast with the marital one) on the child's development. By coparenting, the authors mean "the manner in which mothers and fathers support and/or undermine one another's parenting efforts" (Gable, Belsky, and Crnic, 1995, p. 609). Observed in the context of the triad, the coparenting relationship is considered a family-level variable. Although some might object that observing a dyad without taking into account the contribution of the third partner falls short of tapping a triadic variable, the results show that this type of method "adds uniquely to understanding individual differences in children's adaptation" (Cowan and McHale, 1996, p. 95). Moreover, many of the concepts used by the authors either to build their hypotheses or to interpret their results borrow from the clinical field of family process. Thus, the volume is a major contribution to bridging child development with family process.[26]

Finally, it may well be that the time has come for viewing attachment in a broader family systems perspective. As P. Cowan recently remarked, at this point we know that a child's attachment to mother or father is not significantly correlated. But we do not know whether these two attachment relationships affect each other or combine to affect the child's development (Cowan, 1997).[27]

FAMILY ALLIANCES: AN INTEGRATION

We are back at our starting point: The primary goal of this study was to identify the emergent property of the family alliance. We think that we have succeeded in taking the leap to the triangle, in that the family alliance is truly a group-level variable rather than an addition of dyads or individuals. Thus, we assume it taps the emergent property that, according to systems theory, contextualizes the interactions of the system's elements as long as these interactions last. It differentiates between types of functioning that closely correspond to key notions in family process theory.

What is a family alliance? Emerging from the interactions between father, mother, and infant, the family alliance characterizes their degree of coordination in playing trilogue. In this common endeavor, the parents conjointly guide the infant; the infant in turn drives the parents in guiding her as she develops. There are four types of family alliances, from the most coordinated to the least. They go hand in hand with the working alliances between the family and the observers.

The first approach in characterizing the alliances is functional/clinical and is based on intuition and experience. The microanalytic readings consolidate the typology. Each chapter addresses a different question: (1) Are the family members working together and helping each other? (2) Does the triangular framework that they co-construct facilitate playful relatedness or does it prevent it? (3) Do they effectively repair miscoordinations? (4) How do the infant and the parents handle the four triangles in emotionally charged situations so as to preserve threesome relatedness? The answers distinguish the four types of family alliances in that they all point to a specific quality at the level of the family designated by the terms *cooperative, stressed, collusive,* and *disordered.* It is important to note that they concern everyone involved, including the infant. The answers to these questions are also linked to the type of working alliance, functional or difficult, established between the observer and the family.

Whereas the cooperative and stressed family alliances are "good enough," the collusive and the disordered ones are problematic: In the former, not only do the parents work together but the infant works with the parents as well, whether in a confrontative or cooperative way; this constitutes a favorable, protective context for a child's adaptation. In the latter, it is as if the parents were working against the child or against each other, however unwillingly; this constitutes a restricted, inappropriate context that puts the child at risk for her socioemotional adaptation.

In the cooperative alliances, the story line is continuous and well contoured; the play is lively, leading to many moments of playful mutual enjoyment. Positive affect markedly prevails over negative affect. The triangular framework that underlies this play is coordinated from bottom to top; the miscoordinations are effectively repaired. The triangulation strategies cover the four triangles in a differentiated way that enhances the infant's development in dealing with three-partner relationships, first socially, then intersubjectively. The threesome relatedness between the parents and their child is enriched in proportion. Thus, cooperation radiates from their interactions and characterizes the interactions with the researchers as well. Most distinctive is the manner in which the partners deal with the four configurations of their triangular interaction as a system of permutations, which is represented in Figure 8.3 as the Toblerone model.

In the stressed alliances, the conditions are less optimal, due to various factors: differences in style between the parents, their fear of the experts' authority, and the parents' sense of provocation in having to submit to the pro-

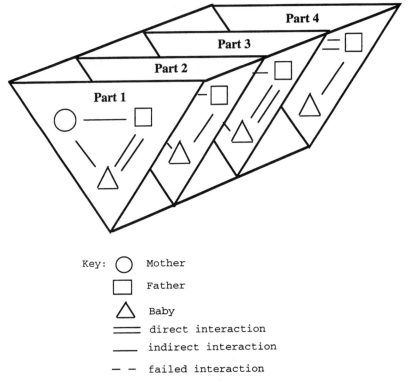

Key: ○ Mother

□ Father

△ Baby

= direct interaction

— indirect interaction

— — failed interaction

FIGURE 8.3 Cooperative Alliance
The configurations are identical and they are connected to each other in spite of the two-plus-one or three-together contents changing with each part. This allows the partners to keep a triangular thread throughout the play. The global structure is intact.

cedure. In spite of differences in content, the results of the readings are similar in form. The stories are somewhat fragmented or irregular. Positive affect still prevails but to a lesser degree than in the cooperative alliances. The triangular framework is insufficiently coordinated with respect to focal attention or affective contact. However, the solidity of participation, the clarity of roles, and the strength of the parents' solidarity constitute a resource that allows for an infant's ordinary adaptation. Repair is sufficient to maintain these resources working throughout the play; triangulation strategies, though somewhat restricted, allow the infant to experience threesome relatedness in the four triangles at the intersubjective level as well as at the social level. Finally, the interaction with the researchers is also functional even if somewhat limited. These characteristics are illustrated in Figure 8.4.

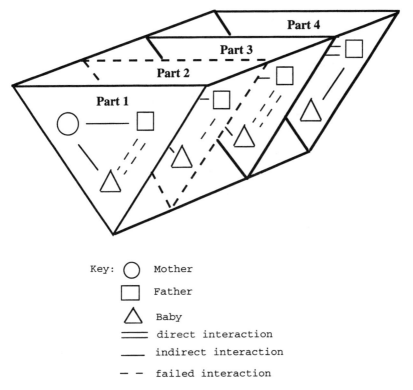

Key: ○ Mother

□ Father

△ Baby

══ direct interaction

── indirect interaction

− − failed interaction

FIGURE 8.4   Stressed Alliance

The configurations are intact except for incidents that disturb the continuity of the play line: Either one or the other configuration is fragmented and irregular (triangle in dotted lines), or an insufficient coordination at times prevents the sharing of a joint focus or the preservation of affective contact (dashed lines). Nonetheless, the global structure is conserved and the thread is maintained across the four configurations of the play.

Where collusion is the emergent property, the primary triangle radically diverges from growth-enhancing conditions (Figure 8.5). A detouring coalition by the parents onto their infant is observed. The infant learns in turn to handle tension by detouring conflict onto herself. The collusion is less obvious when the parents avoid competition at all costs. Yet, in spite of these differences in content, the results of the readings are similar in form. The story line is notably fragmented, as if the theme has switched from working toward playful mutual enjoyment to overt or covert competition. Negative affect prevails, even when the parents keep up a conventional front. The triangular framework is insufficiently coordinated down to the organization

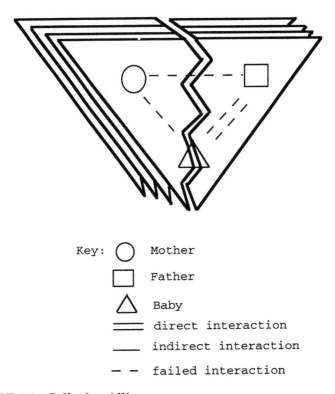

Key: ◯ Mother

□ Father

△ Baby

━━ direct interaction

── indirect interaction

− − failed interaction

FIGURE 8.5   Collusive Alliance

The configurations are split in their middle and flattened out. Whereas the interferences between the parents split the father–mother–infant triangle in the middle, the infant is "divided" into two parts and led into assuming a go-between position between her parents. Moreover, the pattern is repeated in spite of the changes of roles between parts, giving the impression of flattening out in time.

of roles. However, participation constitutes a resource that keeps the parents and the infant together. Repair is notably ineffective in reinstating roles. The deviant triangulation strategies invariably lead the infant in a go-between or scapegoat position. The interaction with the researchers is defensive, marked by overt or covert attempts at establishing detouring coalitions.

Finally, it is where disorder is dominant that the primary triangle is most at risk (figure 8.6). Not only is collusion observed between the parents to detour their conflict onto the child but exclusion is also evident. Exclusion of the infant affords the interaction an ambiguity that is perplexing for the observer as well as for the partners. It contrasts with the multiple signals that some of the parents address to the researchers. These signals reflect a loose boundary between the family and the team and mark an attempt at establishing detouring coalitions with them. The story line is utterly disconnected and a goal is no longer detectable. Negative affect prevails. The triangular framework is insufficiently coordinated from the bottom up. The resource on which the family relies is the parents' motivation to cooperate with the researchers, however ambivalently, reflecting the motivation to work for their child's well-being.

In the rigid disordered alliances—those that remain stable over the first year—exclusion not only involves the infant but the parents as well. Likewise, the parents openly send negative signals to each other, such as disgust or contempt. In the chaotic disordered alliances—those that improve over the first year—exclusion involves only the infant and the negativity of the parents is expressed with respect to the situation in which they are engaged. But in both rigid and chaotic alliances, repair regularly amplifies disorder and triangulation strategies are so limited and paradoxical that they prevent the infant from experiencing the four triangles in a clear manner and from reaching threesome relatedness in emotionally charged situations. Rather, the infant withdraws, albeit to take on the role of parent at times. Finally, the interaction with the researchers is in tune with the family alliance: chaotic but relatively open versus rigidly defensive. Figure 8.6 shows that the Toblerone has almost disappeared.

In summary, good-enough family alliances master the complex system of triangular relations; as there is a shift toward the problematic alliances, complexity is lost and replaced by complication, repetition, and loss of depth in the time dimension. Yet already in early childhood another family unit might well have become pertinent. Whereas the family starts off as a triangle, sooner or later it usually develops into a quadrangle. Let us stress that in our view there is no reason to consider the triangle as more fundamental than the quadrangle or than larger family units. We thought out the paradigm to apply to these units too. For instance, it is possible to envision the systematic permutations between the four triangles that make up a quadrangle and adapt the operational definitions of the different readings. We already know of a fascinating study of a four-way family conflict. It shows how the family establishes conventions in order to regulate the conflict and to make its way between different routines (Hardway and Duncan, submitted for publication).

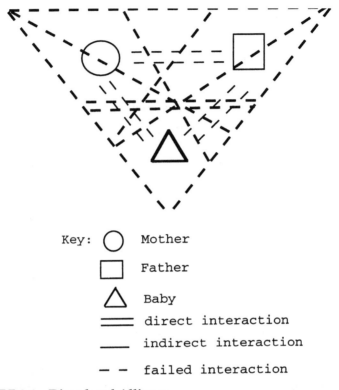

Key: ◯   Mother

        ☐   Father

        △   Baby

        ═══   direct interaction

        ───   indirect interaction

        ─ ─   failed interaction

FIGURE 8.6   Disordered Alliance
The global structure is hardly perceptible (dotted lines). Triangles of different shapes are juxtaposed, more or less overlapping each other. The parts of the play are no longer distinct. There is no depth or continuity between the structures. The three partners are entangled. It is no small paradox that they are both linked to and isolated from each other.

CONCLUSIONS

To be at the boundary between family process and infant development, between clinical practice and research, may be hazardous at times. However, the constant back and forth between these perspectives is creative. Thanks to pioneers such as L. Sander, J. Bowlby, and E. Wertheim, who resolutely integrated infant development and the system approach, our journey to the primary triangle has been illuminating. At this point, it is too late to disentangle our debts to either field or method. Perhaps it is more important to acknowledge the contributions of the numerous authors who have guided us. We hope the references to their writings and studies in which we found inspiration convey our fondness for their work. We hope that continuing in their steps will help bridge infant development and family process.

NOTES

1. For accounts of developmental systems theories, see Butterworth, 1995; Fivaz, 1996; Fogel, 1992; Fogel and Thelen, 1987; Gunnar and Thelen, 1989; Mounoud, 1992; Sameroff, 1993; Sander, 1977; Thelen, 1989; Thelen and Smith, 1994; Wertheim, 1987. For applications to couple and family therapy, see Anderson, Goolishian, and Winderman, 1986; Cosnier, 1994; Elkaïm, 1985; Hoffman, 1981, 1990; Salem, 1996; Welter-Enderlin and Hildebrand, 1996.

2. The criteria described in Chapter 3 for this model's operationalization were further elaborated for macrogestalt coding by means of an instrument called GETCEF (Grille d'Evaluation des interactions Triadigues du Centre d'Etude de la Famille). A manual is available along with tapes for training at the Center for Family Studies (Fivaz-Depeursinge, Cornut-Zimmer, Borcard-Sacco, and Corboz-Warnery, 1997). At the time of this writing, it allows for reliably coding participation, organization, and focal attention formations. The coding of expressive formations is still microanalytic. This is the reason for collapsing the disadjustments of focal attention and expressive formations in the B framework.

3. Curiously, when we examined the scores provided by the parents on the Child Behavior Check List (Achenbach and Edelbrock, 1983), a paper-and-pencil measure, we did not find significant group differences. We note that links between parental perception of child adjustment and observational measures of family processes do not inevitably emerge in studies that use both self-reports and observations; for related findings and discussions of this topic, see McHale, Kuersten, and Lauretti, 1996; Sigafoos, Reiss, Rich, and Douglas 1985).

4. Particularly interesting with respect to understanding the family alliance are the first results of the Seattle group on physiological patterns of the three members of the family during the different configurations of the LTP (see Shapiro, 1998).

5. It is interesting to note that for C. Trevarthen there exists a form of "primary intersubjectivity" from the beginning of life. Contrary to other developmental theorists, he posits that all emotions exist in rudimentary form in the newborn; the intersubjectivity that appears at nine months, which he calls "secondary intersubjectivity," is only more effective and clear than "primary intersubjectivity," notably allowing for new coordinations between person and object interactions (Trevarthen, 1993). He stresses that this position has found support in the recent findings on early imitation, particularly that newborns imitate emotional expressions (Field, Woodson, Greenberg, and Cohen, 1982; Maratos, 1982). Indeed, as noted in Chapter 5, imitation of people is a "discovery procedure" for understanding and identifying people, just as manipulation is the means to explore objects (Meltzoff and Moore, 1997).

6. Tremblay-Leveau confronts the infant with two experimenters; having successively established contact with the infant, the experimenters then turn to each other, thus "excluding" the infant. Preliminary results indicate that the young infant coordinates her attention between the two adults and follows the direction of their gaze to each other (Tremblay-Leveau, 1998).

7. D'Entremont and colleagues introduce a puppet as the third party in their interaction with an infant. The experimenter turns her head intermittently to talk to the puppet. A majority of the three- to six-month-old infants' first eye turns are in the direction of the adult head turn, showing the ability of the infant to coordinate her attention with the adult (D'Entremont, Hains, and Muir, 1997).

8. See Bürgin & von Klitzing, 1995; Byng-Hall, 1995; Fivaz-Depeursinge, Stern, Corboz-Warnery, and Bürgin, 1998; Fivaz-Depeursinge, Stern, Bürgin, Byng-Hall, Corboz-Warnery, Lamour, and Lebovici, 1994; Stern, 1995.

9. For detailed results and comments, see Byng-Hall, 1995; Emde, 1994; Fivaz-Depeursinge, Stern, Corboz-Warnery, and Bürgin, 1998; Fivaz-Depeursinge, Stern, Bürgin, Byng-Hall, Corboz-Warnery, Lamour, and Lebovici, 1994; Stern, 1995; Stern and Fivaz-Depeursinge, 1997. For studies in the same vein, see also Fivaz-Depeursinge, Maury, Bydlowski, and Stern, 1995; Hervé, Andreu, and Maury, 1998; Maury and Lamour, 1994.

10. In this perspective, several other research groups are investigating the parallels between interactions in the mother–infant dyad and in adult individual psychotherapy (see Beebe and Lachman, 1994; Lachmann and Beebe, 1996; Stern, Sander, Nahum, Harrison, Lyons-Ruth, Morgan, et al., in press; Tronick, 1998); or parallels between the family at early stages and at later stages in couple or family therapy (Welter-Enderlin, 1996; Welter-Enderlin and Hildebrand, 1996); or parallels between infant and adult psychiatry (Gauthier, 1992, 1995).

11. See especially Caillé, 1991; Onnis, 1989; Rey, 1994.

12. See Andersen, 1991; Anderson and Goolishian, 1988; Salem, 1996; Sluzki, 1991; Tomm, 1988; White and Epston, 1990.

13. For an account of the moral stage, see Emde, Biringen, Clyman, and Oppenheim, 1991; Emde and Buchsbaum, 1990; and for moral emotions in problematic families, see Zahn-Waxler and Kochansky, 1990.

14. The theme is inspired by the McArthur Story–Stem Battery (Bretherton, Oppenheim, Buchsbaum, and Emde, 1990). The co-construction of narratives between child and parent(s) has been promising in studying the child's emotion organization and regulation (Favez, in press; Oppenheim, Nir, and Warren, 1997).

15. Comparing prenatal triangular representations with their enactments in the LTP postnatally reveals a strong connection between these two faces of triangulation (Bürgin, 1998; Bürgin and von Klitzing, 1995; Hedenbro, 1998).

16. Predicting from the prenatal stage has lately come to the foreground. For instance, see Borgeat, David, Saucier, and Dumont, 1994; Bydolvski, 1997; Fava-Vizzielo, Antonioli, Cocci, and Inveernizzi, 1993; Lebovici, 1988, 1992; Zeanah and Barton, 1989.

17. See especially Barnard, 1997; Hervé, Andreu, and Maury 1998; Lyons-Ruth, Easterbrooks, and Davidson, 1997; Osofsky and Eberhart-Wright, 1992.

18. In particular, the Basle study compares a sample of families with risk factors due to parental psychopathology and/or sociocultural risk to a normative sample. The Seattle prospective study compares families with high versus low marital satisfaction at the newlywed stage. Finally, the Stockholm study investigates a representative sample of the Swedish population.

19. For other forms of early intervention, see Ansermet, 1994; Ben Aaron and Harel, 1997; Cramer, 1980; Cramer, Robert-Tissot, Stern, Rusconi-Serpa, Besson, Palacio-Espasa, et al., 1990; Hedenbro, 1997; McDonough, 1993; Robert-Tissot, Cramer, Stern, Rusconi-Serpa, Bachmann, Palacio-Espasa, et al., 1996; for a discussion, see Stern, 1995.

20. See especially Boszormenyi-Nagy & Sparks, 1973; Byng-Hall, 1986; Wertheim, 1973.

21. For a discussion of cultural representations in mental health, see Duruz, 1994; Duruz and Lob, 1997.

22. See Ball, Cowan, and Pape-Cowan, 1995; Levy, Wamboldt, and Fiese, 1997.

23. See also Frascarolo, 1994, 1997; Gottman, 1994; Zaouche-Gaudron and LeCamus, 1996.

24. To pick a few studies that have examined these influences: when she starts to walk (Campos, Kermoian, and Zumbahlen, 1992), when she cries excessively (Papousek and von Hofacker, 1995) or is ill (Parmelee, 1989) or is depressive (Guedeney, 1997); when she reacts to her parents' psychopathological state (Murray, Stanley, Hooper, King, and Fiori-Eowley, 1996) or is at risk for any reason (Field, 1980). In all these situations, it would be interesting to observe the effect of these conditions on triangular relationships.

25. For instance, see Anthony, 1976; Field, 1986; Hart, Field, Stern, and Jones, 1997; Kumar, 1994; Kumar and Robson, 1984; Masson, Fivaz-Depeursinge, and Ciola, 1977; Murray, 1992; Murray and Cooper, 1996; Rosenblum, Mazet, and Bénony, 1997.

26. So were two landmark volumes on developmental systems (Gunnar and Thelen, 1989; Thelen and Smith, 1994). See especially Sameroff's discussion of two studies of family process in the light of systems theory, namely the study of Patterson and Bank on families with conduct disorders, and the study of Belsky, Rovine, and Fish on the developing family system that we summarized in the introduction (Sameroff, 1993). Likewise, see the detailed discussion about family systems and developmental psychopathology by Wagner and Reiss (1995).

27. In response to Cowan's comment, IJendoorn and de Wolff combine the findings of meta-analytic studies they conducted to draw a data-based model of the attachement network in the family (IJzendoorn and de Wolff, 1997). This point of view meets with J. Byng-Hall's plea for a family system's view of attachment (Byng-Hall, 1986), as well as other authors who try to capture a wider perspective, for instance Byng-Hall, 1986, 1990; Fonagy, Steele, Steele, Moran, and Higitt, 1991; Grossman, Grossman, and Schwan, 1986; Main and Weston, 1981.

REFERENCES

Achenbach, T. M., and Edelbrock, C. (1983). *A Manual for the Child Behavior Checklist and Revised Child Behavior Profile.* Burlington: Queen City Printers.

Andersen, T. (ed.) (1991). *The Reflecting Team: Dialogues and Dialogues About the Dialogues.* New York: Norton.

Anderson, H., and Goolishian, H. A. (1988). Human systems as linguistic systems: Preliminary and evolving ideas about the implication for clinical theory. *Family Process, 27,* 371–393.

Anderson, H., Goolishian, H., and Winderman, L. (1986). Problem determined systems: Towards transformation in family therapy. *Journal of Strategic and Systemic Therapies, 5,* 1–14.

Ansermet, F. (1994). Psychanalyse et pédopsychiatrie de liaison en pédiatrie. *Neuropsychiatrie de l'Enfance, 42*(4–5), 173–179.

Anthony, E. J. (1976). How children cope in families with a psychotic parent. In E. N. Rexford, L. W. Sander, and T. Shapiro (eds.), *Infant Psychiatry. A New Synthesis* (pp. 239–250). New Haven: Yale University Press.

Anthony, J. (1984). The influence babies bring to bear on their upbringing. In J. Call, E. Galenson, and R. Tyson (eds.), *Frontiers of Infant Psychiatry* (pp. 259–266). New York: Basic Books.

Ball, F., Cowan, P., and Pape-Cowan, C. (1995). Who's got the power? Gender differences in partners' perceptions of influence during marital problem-solving discussions. *Family Process, 34,* 303–321.

Barnard, K. (1997). Influencing parent–child interactions for children at risk. In M. Guralnick (ed.), *The Effectiveness of Early Intervention* (pp. 249–268). Baltimore: Brookes Publishing Co.

Bateson, G. (1979). *Mind and Nature.* Toronto: Bantam Books.

Beavers, W. R. (1977). *Psychotherapy and Growth: A Family Systems Perspective.* New York: Bruner/Mazel.

Beebe, B., and Lachman, F. (1994). Representation and internalization in infancy: Three principles of salience. *Psychoanalytic Psychology, 11*(2), 127–165.

Ben-Aaron, M., and Harel, J. (1997). The child's active role in the move from two to two plus one, as seen in the mother–child and father–child psychotherapy—a dynamic approach to treatment of relational disturbances in childhood. *Twenty-first Annual Conference of the Israeli Association of Psychotherapy,* Tiberias, Israel.

Bertalanffy, L. V. (1956). General system theory. *General Systems Yearbook, 1,* 1–10.

Borgeat, F., David, H., Saucier, J., and Dumont, M. (1994). Perceptual defense and vulnerability to postpartum depression. *Acta Psychiatr. Scand., 90,* 455–458.

Boszormenyi-Nagy, I., and Sparks, G. (1973). *Invisible Loyalties.* New York: Harper and Row.

Bowen, M. (1972). Toward the differentiation of self in one's own family. In J. L. Framo (ed.), *Family Interaction: A Dialogue Between Family Researchers and Family Therapists* (pp. 11–173). New York: Springer Verlag.

Bretherton, I., Oppenheim, D., Buchsbaum, H., and Emde, R. (1990). MacArthur Story–Stem Battery (Unpublished manual).

Bürgin, D. (1998). *Triangulierung. Der Übergang sur Elternshaft.* Stuttgart: Schattauer.

Bürgin, D., and von Klitzing, K. (1995). Prenatal representations and postnatal interactions of a threesome (mother, father and baby). In J. Bitzer and M. Stauber (eds.), *Psychosomatic Obstetrics and Gynaecology* (pp. 185–192). Bologna: Monduzzi.

Butterworth, G. (1995). The self as an object of consciousness in infancy. In P. Rochat (ed.), *The Self in Infancy: Theory and Research* (pp. 35–51). Amsterdam: Elsevier.

Bydlowski, M. (1997). *La Dette de Vie. Itinéraire psychanalytigue de la maternité.* Paris: Presses Universitaires de France.

Byng-Hall, J. (1986). Family scripts: A concept which can bridge child psychotherapy and family therapy thinking. *Journal of Child Psychotherapy, 12*(2), 3–13.

Byng-Hall, J. (1990). Attachment theory and family therapy: A clinical view. *Infant Mental Health Journal, 11*(3), 228–236.

Byng-Hall, J. (1995). *Rewriting Family Scripts. Improvisation and Systems Change.* New York: The Guilford Press.

Caillé, P. (1991). *Un et un font trois.* Paris: ESF.

Calkins, S. (1994). Origins and outcomes of individual differences in emotion regulation. In N. Fox (ed.), *The Development of Emotion Regulation: Biological and Behavioral Considerations* (pp. 53–74). Chicago: University of Chicago Press.

Campos, J., Campos, R., and Barrett, K. (1989). Emergent themes in the study of emotional development and emotion regulation. *Developmental Psychology, 25,* 394–402.

Campos, J., Kermoian, R., and Zumbahlen, M. (1992). Socioemotional transformations in the family system following infant crawling onset. In R. Fabes and N. Eisenberg (eds.), *Emotion and Its Regulation in Early Development* (pp. 25–40). San Francisco: Jossey-Bass.

Carneiro, C. (1998). *Articulation des registres conjugal et parental: le couple devant l'enfant.* Travail de DEA, Université de Genève.

Cosnier, J. (1994). *Psychologie des émotions et des sentiments.* Paris: Retz-Nathan.

Cowan, P. (1997). Beyond meta-analysis: A plea for a family systems view of attachment. *Child Development, 68*(4), 601–603.

Cowan, P., and McHale, J. (1996). Coparenting in a family context: Emerging achievements, current dilemmas, and future directions. In J. McHale and P. Cowan (eds.), *Understanding How Family-Level Dynamics Affect Children's Development: Studies of Two-Parent Families* (pp. 93–106). San Francisco: Jossey-Bass.

Cramer, B. (1980). Thérapies brèves avec parents et enfants. *Psychologie Médicale, 12*(3), 589–594.

Cramer, B., Robert-Tissot, C., Stern, D., Rusconi-Serpa, S. D. M., Besson, G., Palacio-Espasa, F., Bachmann, J., Knauer, D., Berney, C., and d'Arcis, U. (1990). Outcome evaluation in brief mother–infant psychotherapy: A preliminary report. *Infant Mental Health Journal, 11*(3), 278–300.

Damasio, A. (1994). *Descartes' Error.* New York: Avon Books.

D'Entremont, B., Hains, S., and Muir, D. (1997). A demonstration of gaze following in 3- to 6-month-olds. *Infant Behavior and Development, 20*(4), 569–572.

Duruz, N. (1994). *Psychothérapie ou psychothérapies?* Neuchâtel: Delachaux et Niestlé.

Duruz, N., and Lob, R. (1997). II. Psychothérapeutes: Analyse de trois présupposés. *Psychothérapies, 17*(2), 67–77.

Easterbrooks, M. N., and Emde, R. N. (1987). Marital and parent–child relationships: The role of affect in the family system. In R. A. Hinde and J. Stevenson-Hinde (eds.), *Relationships Within Families* (pp. 83–103). Oxford: Oxford University Press.

Elkaïm, M. (1985). From general laws to singularities. *Family Process, 24*(2), 151–164.

Emde, R. N. (1985). An adaptive view of infant emotions: Functions for self and knowing. *Social Science Information, 24*(2), 337–341.

Emde, R. N. (1994). Commentary: Triadification experiences and a bold new direction for infant mental health. *Infant Mental Health Journal, 15*(1), 90–95.

Emde, R., Biringen, Z., Clyman, R. B., and Oppenheim, D. (1991). The moral self in infancy: Affective core and procedural knowledge. *Developmental Review, 11*, 251–270.

Emde, R. N., and Buchsbaum, H. K. (1990). "Didn't you hear my mommy?" Autonomy with connectedness in moral self emergence. In D. Cicchetti and M. Beeghly (eds.), *The Self in Transition: Infancy to Childhood* (pp. 35–60). Chicago: University of Chicago.

Fava-Vizzielo, G., Antonioli, M., Cocci, V., and Inveernizzi, R. (1993). From pregnancy to motherhood: The structure of representative and narrative change. *Infant Mental Health Journal, 14*(1), 4–16.

Favez, N. (in press). Patterns of maternal affect regulation during the co-construction of preschooler's autobiographical narratives.

Field, T. (ed.) (1980). *High-Risk Infants and Children.* New York: Academic Press.

Field, T. (1986). Models for reactive and chronic depression in infancy. In E. Tronick and T. Field (eds.), *Maternal Depression and Infant Disturbance* (pp. 47–60). San Francisco: Jossey-Bass.

Field, T., Woodson, R., Greenberg, R., and Cohen, D. (1982). Discrimination and imitation of facial expressions by neonates. *Science 218*, 179–181.

Fivaz, R. (1996). Ergodic theory of communication. *Systems Research, 13*(2), 127–144.

Fivaz-Depeursinge, E., Cornut-Zimmer, B., Borcard-Sacco, M., and Corboz-Warnery, A. (1997). *The GETCEF. A Grid for the Analysis of Triangular Interactions,* 2nd ed. Research Report No. 67, Center for Family Studies.

Fivaz-Depeursinge, E., Frascarolo, F., and Corboz-Warnery, A. (1996). Assessing the triadic alliance between father, mother and infant at play. In J. P. McHale and P. A. Cowan (eds.), *Understanding How Family-Level Dynamics Affect Children's Development: Studies of Two-Parent Families* (pp. 27–44). San Francisco: Jossey-Bass.

Fivaz-Depeursinge, E., Maury, M., Bydlowski, M., and Stern, D. (1995). Une consultation mère-nourrisson: Entretien clinique, microanalyse et méthodes interprétatives. In O. Bourguignon and H. Bydlowski (eds.), *La recherche clinigue en psychopathologie.* Paris: PUF.

Fivaz-Depeursinge, E., Stern, D. N., Bürgin, D., Byng-Hall, J., Corboz-Warnery, A., Lamour, M., and Lebovici, S. (1994). The dynamics of interfaces: Seven authors in search of encounters across levels of description of an event involving a mother, father, and baby. *Infant Mental Health Journal, 15*(1), 69–89.

Fivaz-Depeursinge, E., Stern, D., Corboz-Warnery, A., and Bürgin, D. (1998). Wann und wie das familiale Dreieck entsteht: Vier Perspektiven affektiver Kommunikation. In R. Welter-Enderlin and B. Hildenbrand (eds.), *Gefühle und Systeme* (pp. 119–154). Heidelberg: Carl-Auer-Systeme.

Fogel, A. (1992). Movement and communication in human infancy: The social dynamics of development. *Human Movement Science, 11,* 387–423.

Fogel, A., and Thelen, E. (1987). Development of early expressive and communicative action: Reinterpreting the evidence from a dynamic systems perspective. *Developmental Psychology, 23*(6), 747–761.

Fonagy, P., Steele, M., Steele, H., Moran, G., and Higitt, A. (1991). The capacity for understanding mental states: The reflective self in parent and child and its significance for security of attachment. *Infant Mental Health Journal 121,* 201–217.

Frascarolo, F. (1994). Engagement paternel quotidien et relations parents-enfant. Thèse de Doctorat en Psychologie, University of Geneva.

Frascarolo, F. (1997). Les incidences de l'engagement paternel quotidien sur les modalités d'interaction ludique père-enfant et mère-enfant. *Enfance, 3,* 381–387.

Gable, S., Belsky, J., and Crnic, K. (1995). Coparenting during the child's 2nd year: A descriptive account. *Journal of Marriage and the Family, 57,* 609–616.

Gauthier, Y. (1992). Child and adult psychiatry: Comparison and contrast. *Canadian Journal of Psychiatry, 37*(6), 440–449.

Gauthier, Y. (1995). Lebovici in perspective. Special issue in honor of Serge Lebovici: Creativity and the infant's competence. *Infant Mental Health Journal, 16*(1), 16–20.

Gottman, J. M. (1982). Temporal form: Toward a new language for describing relationships. *Journal of Marriage and the Family, 44,* 943–962.

Gottman, J. M. (1994). *What Predicts Divorce? The Relationship Between Marital Processes and Marital Outcomes.* Hillsdale, NJ: Lawrence Erlbaum.

Grossman, K. E., Grossman, K., and Schwan, A. (1986). Capturing the wider view of attachment: A reanalysis of Ainsworth's strange situation. In C. E. Izard and P. B. Read (eds.), *Measuring Emotions in Infants and Children* (pp. 124–171). Cambridge: Cambridge University Press.

Guedeney, A. (1997). From early withdrawal reaction to infant depression: A baby alone does exist. *Infant Mental Health Journal, 18*(4), 339–349.

Gunnar, M., and Thelen, E. (ed.) (1989). *Systems and Development.* Hillsdale, NJ: Lawrence Erlbaum.

Hardway, C., and Duncan, S. D. J. (submitted for publication). "Me First!" Structure and dynamics of a four-way family conflict.

Hart, S., Field, T., Stern, M., and Jones, N. (1997). Depressed fathers' stereotyping of infants labeled depressed. *Infant Mental Health Journal, 18*(4), 436–445.

Hedenbro, M. (1997). Interaction, the key to life: Seeing possibilities of children through videopictures. *Signal, Oct–Dec.,* 9–15.

Hedenbro, M. (1998). Transition to parenthood: From triadic representation to triadic interaction. Paper presented at the International Society for the Study of Behavioral Development.

Bern Hervé, M., Andreu, M., and Maury, M. (1998). Infant's contributions during triadic mother–infant–therapist consultations. Poster presented at International Society for the Study of Behavioral Development, Bern.

Hoffman, L. (1981). *Foundations of Family Therapy: A Conceptual Framework for Systems Change*. New York: Basic Books.

Hoffman, L. (1990). Constructing realities: An art of lenses. *Family Process, 29*(1), 1–12.

IJzendoorn, M., and de Wolff, M. (1997). In search of the absent father—meta-analyses of infant–father attachment: A rejoinder to our discussants. *Child Development, 68*(4), 604–609.

Imber-Black, E., and Roberts, J. (1992). *Rituals for our Times*. Northvale, NJ: Jason Aronson.

Kaufmann, L. (1986). The rationale for the family approach with adolescents. In S. C. Feinstein (ed.), *Adolescent Psychiatry. Developmental and Clinical Studies* (pp. 493–503). Chicago: University of Chicago Press.

Kendon, A. (1977). Spatial organization in social encounters: The F-formation system. In A. Kendon (ed.), *Studies in the Behavior of Social Interaction* (pp. 179–208). Lisse, IN: Peter DeRidder Press.

Kumar, R. (1994). Postnatal mental illness: A transcultural perspective. *Social Psychiatry Psychiatric Epidemiology, 29*, 250–264.

Kumar, R., and Robson, K. (1984). A prospective study of emotional disorders in child-bearing women. *British Journal of Psychiatry, 144*, 35–47.

Lachmann, F., and Beebe, B. (1996). Three principles of salience in the organization of the patient–analyst interaction. *Psychoanalytic Psychology, 13*(1), 1–22.

Lebovici, S. (1988). Fantasmatic interaction and intergenerational transmission. *Infant Mental Health Journal, 9*, 10–19.

Lebovici, S. (1992). A propos de la transmission intergénérationnelle: de la filiation à l'affiliation. *Presidential Address, 5th World Congress of the World Association of Infant Psychiatry*, Chicago, 9–13 Sept. 1992.

Levy, S., Wamboldt, F., and Fiese, B. (1997). Family-of-origin experiences and conflict resolution behaviors of young adult dating couples. *Family Process, 36*, 297–310.

Lyons-Ruth, K., Easterbrooks, M., and Davidson, C. (1997). Infant attachment strategies, infant mental lag, and maternal depressive symptoms: Predictors of internalizing and externalizing problems at age 7. *Developmental Psychology, 33*(4), 481–692.

Main, M., and Weston, D. (1981). The quality of the toddler's relationship to mother and to father: Related to conflict behavior and the readiness to establish new relationships. *Child Development, 52*, 932–940.

Maratos, O. (1982). Trends in development of imitation in early infancy. In T. G. Bever (ed.), *Regressions in Mental Development: Basic Phenomena and Theories* (pp. 81–101). Hillsdale, NJ: Lawrence Erlbaum.

Masson, D., Fivaz-Depeursinge, E., and Ciola, A. (1977). Expérience d'hospitalisation conjointe mère-enfant dans un Centre de Traitement Psychiatrique de Jour (Hôpital de Jour) pour adultes. *Archives Suisses de Neurologie, Neurochirurgie et Psychiatrie, 120*(1), 83–100.

Maury, M., and Lamour, M. (1994). *Etude des interactions triadiques dans le développement précoce de l'enfant* (No. 4R00081): Inserm.

McDonough, S. C. (1993). Interaction guidance: Understanding and treating early infant–caregiver relationship disorders. In C. Zeanah (ed.), *Handbook of Infant Mental Health* (pp. 414–426). New York: Guilford Press.

McHale, J., and Cowan, P. (ed.) (1996). *Understanding How Family-level Dynamics Affect Children's Development: Studies of Two-Parent Families.* San Francisco: Jossey-Bass.

McHale, J., Kuersten, R., and Lauretti, A. (1996). New directions in the study of family-Level dynamics during infancy and early childhood. In J. McHale and P. Cowan (eds.), *Understanding How Family-Level Dynamics Affect Children's Development: Studies of Two-Parent Families* (pp. 6–44). San Francisco: Jossey-Bass.

Meltzoff, A., and Moore, M. (1997). Explaining facial imitation: A theoretical model. *Early Development and Parenting, 6,* 179–192.

Mounoud, P. (1992). A man touching a woman: Unpredictable outcomes. *Human Movement Science, 11,* 489–496.

Murray, L. (1992). The impact of postnatal depression on infant development. *Journal of Child Psychology and Psychiatry, 33*(3), 543–561.

Murray, L., and Cooper, P. (1996). Impact of postpartum depression on child development. *International Review of Psychiatry, 8,* 55–63.

Murray, L., Stanley, C., Hooper, R., King, F., and Fiori-Eowley, A. (1996). The role of infant factors in postnatal depression and mother–infant interactions. *Developmental Medicine and Child Neurology 381,* 109–119.

Onnis, L. (1989). *Corps et contexte: thérapie familiale des troubles psychosomatiques.* Paris: Editions sociales françaises.

Oppenheim, D., Nir, A., and Warren, S. (1997). Emotion regulation in mother–child narrative co-construction: Associations with children's narratives and adaptation. *Developmental Psychology, 33*(2), 284–294.

Osofsky, J., and Eberhart-Wright, A. (1992). Risk and protective factors for parents and infants. In G. Suci and S. Robertson (eds.), *Human Development: Future Directions in Infant Development Research* (pp. 25–39). New York: Springer-Verlag.

Papousek, M., and von Hofacker, N. (1995). Persistent crying and parenting: Search for a butterfly in a dynamic system. *Early Development and Parenting, 4*(4), 209–224.

Parke, R. D. (1988). Families in life-span perspective: A multilevel developmental approach. In M. E. Hetherington, R. M. Lerner, and M. Perlmutter (eds.), *Child Development in Life-Span Perspective* (pp. 159–190). Hillsdale, NJ: Lawrence Erlbaum.

Parmelee, A. (1989). The child's physical health and the development of relationships. In A. Sameroff and R. Emde (eds.), *Relationship Disturbances in Early Childhood.* New York: Basic Books.

Pedersen, F., Anderson, B., and Cain, R. (1980). Parent–infant and husband–wife interactions observed at age 5 months. In F. A. Pedersen (ed.), *The Father–Infant Relationship. Observational Studies in the Family Setting* (pp. 44–70). New York: Praeger.

Piaget, J. (1967). *Biologie et connaissance*. Paris: Gallimard.

Pierrehumbert, B., and Fivaz-Depeursinge, E. (1994). From dyadic towards triadic relational prototypes. In A. Vyt, H. Bloch, and M. H. Bornstein (eds.), *Early Child Development in the French Tradition: Contributions from Current Research* (pp. 269–285). Hillsdale, NJ: Lawrence Erlbaum.

Reiss, D. (1981). *The Family's Construction of Reality*. Cambridge, MA: Harvard University Press.

Rey, Y. (1994). Le jeu de l'oie (Loi) systémique. *Résonnances, 6*, 53–56.

Robert-Tissot, C., Cramer, B., Stern, D., Rusconi-Serpa, S. D. M., Bachmann, J., Palacio-Espasa, F., Knauer, D., de Mulralt, M., Berney, C., and Mendiguren, G. (1996). Outcome evaluation in brief mother–infant psychotherapies: Report on 75 cases. *Infant Mental Health Journal, 17*(2), 97–114.

Rosenblum, O., Mazet, P., and Bénony, H. (1997). Mother and infant affective involvement states and maternal depression. *Infant Mental Health Journal, 18*(4), 350–363.

Salem, G. (1996). *L'approche thérapeutique de la famille*. Paris: Masson.

Sameroff, A. J. (1993). Commentary: General systems and the regulation of development. In M. R. Gunnar and E. Thelen (eds.), *Systems and Development*. Hillsdale, NJ: Lawrence Earlbaum.

Sameroff, A. J., and Emde, R. N. (eds.) (1989). *Relationship Disturbances in Early Childhood*. New York: Basic Books.

Sander, L. W. (1977). Regulation of exchange in the infant caretaker system: A viewpoint on the ontogeny of "structures." In N. Freedman and S. Grand (eds.), *Communicative Structures and Psychic Structures* (pp. 13–34). New York: Plenum Press.

Scheflen, A. E. (1973). *Communicational Structure: Analysis of a Psychotherapy Transaction*. Bloomington, IN: Indiana University Press.

Scheflen, A. E. (1975). Models and epistemologies in the study of interaction. In A. Kendon, R. Harris, and M. R. Key (eds.), *Organization of Behavior in Face-to-Face Interaction* (pp. 63–91). The Hague: Mouton.

Shapiro, A. (1998). The role of physiology in the dynamics of the mother–father–baby triad. *15th Biennnal International Society for the Study of Behavioral Development Meeting*, Berne.

Sigafoos, A., Reiss, D., Rich, J., and Douglas, E. (1985). Pragmatics in the measurement of family functioning: An interpretive framework for methodology. *Family Process, 24*, 189–203.

Singer, M. T., Wynne, L. C., and Toohey, M. L. (1978). Communication disorders and the families of schizophrenics. In L. C. Wynne (ed.), *The Nature of Schizophrenia. New Approaches to Research and Treatment* (pp. 499–511). New York: Wiley.

Sluzki, C. (1991). The therapeutic transformation of narratives. *Cahiers Critiques de Thérapie Familiale et de Pratiques de Réseaux*, pp. 181–201.

Sroufe, L. A. (1989). Relationships and relationship disturbances. In A. J. Sameroff and R. N. Emde (eds.), *Relationship Disturbances in Early Childhood* (pp. 97–124). New York: Basic Books.

Stern, D. N., Sander, L., Nahum, J., Harrison, A. Lyons-Ruth, K., Morgan, A., Bruschweiler-Stern, N., and Tronick, E. (in press). Mechanisms of change in psychoanalytic therapy.

Stern, D. N. (1994). One way to build a clinically relevant baby. *Infant Mental Health Journal*, 15(1), 9–25.

Stern, D. N. (1995). *The Motherhood Constellation*. New York: Basic Books.

Stern, D. N., and Fivaz-Depeursinge, E. (1997). Construction du réel et affect. *Cahiers critiques de théerapie familiale et de pratiques de réseaux*, 18(1), 77–85.

Thelen, E. (1989). Self-organization in developmental processes: Can systems approaches work? In M. Gunnar and E. Thelen (eds.), *Systems and Development. The Minnesota Symposium in Child Psychology* (pp. 77–117). Hillsdale, NJ: Lawrence Erlbaum.

Thelen, E., and Smith, L. B. (eds.) (1994). *A Dynamic Systems Approach to the Development of Cognition and Action*. Cambridge and London: MIT Press.

Tomm, K. (1988). Interventive interviewing III: Intending to ask linear, circular or reflexive questions. *Family Process, 27*, 1–16.

Tremblay-Leveau, H. (1997). *La triade: une nouvelle matrice de développement?* Rapport d'habilitation, Université de Rouen.

Tremblay-Leveau, H. (1998). Sharing attention with another on a third person in 3- and 6-month-old infants. 15th Biennnal International Society for the Study of Behavioral Development Meeting, Bern.

Trevarthen, C. (1984). Emotions in infancy: Regulators of contact and relationships with persons. In K. R. Scherer and P. Ekman (eds.), *Approaches to Emotion* (pp. 129–157). Hillsdale, NJ: Lawrence Erlbaum.

Trevarthen, C. (1993). The function of emotions in early infant communication and development. In J. Nadel and L. Camaioni (eds.), *New Perspectives in Early Communicative Development* (pp. 48–81). London: Routledge.

Tronick, E. Z. (1998). Dyadically expanded states of consciousness and the process of therapeutic change. *Infant Mental Health Journal 19*(3), 290–299.

Tronick, E. Z., Morelli, G. A., and Ivey, P. K. (1992). The Efe forager infant and toddler's pattern of social relationships: Multiple and simultaneous. *Developmental Psychology, 28*(4), 568–577.

Van der Hart, O. (1983). *Rituals in Psychotherapy: Transition and Continuity*. New York: Irvington.

Wagner, B., and Reiss, D. (1995). Family systems and developmental psychopathology: Courtship, marriage, or divorce. In D. Cicchetti and D. Cohen (eds.), *Developmental Psychopathology. Vol. I: Theory and Methods*. New York: Wiley.

Wamboldt, F. S., and Reiss, D. (1989). Defining a family heritage and a new relationship identity: Two central tasks in making of a marriage. *Family Process, 28*, 317–335.

Welter-Enderlin, R. (1996). *Deine Liebe is nicht meine Liebe*. Freiburg: Herder.

Welter-Enderlin, R., and Hildebrand, B. (1996). *Systemische Therapie als Begegnung*. Stuttgart: Kett-Cota.

Wertheim, E. S. (1973). Family unit therapy. The science and typology of family systems. *Family Process, 12*, 361–376.

Wertheim, E. S. (1987). GST and the research process as illustrated by a naturalistic study of parental adaptation to first pregnancy. *Systems Research, 4*(1), 13–21.

White, M., and Epston, D. (1990). *Narrative Means to Therapeutic Ends.* New York: Norton.

Zahn-Waxler, C., and Kochansky, G. (1990). The origins of guilt. In R. Thompson (ed.), *Nebraska Symposium on Motivation, 1988: Socioemotional Development* (pp. 183–258). Lincoln: University of Nebraska Press.

Zaouche-Gaudron, C., and LeCamus, J. (1996). Analyse des processus de subjectivation au travers de la relation père-nourrisson. *Psychiatrie de L'enfant, 391*, 251–296.

Zeanah, C. H., and Barton, M. L. (1989). Introduction: Internal representations and parent–infant relationship. *Infant Mental Health Journal, 10*(3), 135–141.

Appendix A: LTP Results

Name	SES	Age (weeks)	Family Alliance	Triangular Framework Category (score)		Repair	Triangular Process	Working Alliance
F1—Xerxes	S	13	Smooth Cooperative	A	(02)	swift	differentiated	functional
		21	Smooth Cooperative	A	(06)	swift	differentiated	functional
		37	Smooth Cooperative	A	(00)	swift	differentiated	functional
F2—Mike	M	14	Smooth Cooperative	A	(05)	swift	differentiated	functional
		30	Smooth Cooperative	A	(06)	swift	differentiated	functional
		40	Smooth Cooperative	A	(01)	swift	differentiated	functional
F3—Nancy	M	16	Stressed Cooperative	B	(07)	costly	restricted	functional
		27	Stressed Cooperative	B	(14)	costly	restricted	functional
		38	Stressed Cooperative	B	(07)	costly	restricted	functional
F4—John	M	14	Stressed Cooperative	B	(08)	costly	restricted	functional
		27	Stressed Cooperative	B	(16)	costly	restricted	functional
		36	Stressed Cooperative	B	(16)	costly	restricted	functional
F5—Ann	M	15	Stressed Cooperative	B	(15)	costly	restricted	functional
		20	Collusive (covert)	C	(23)	costly	detouring	difficult
		37	Collusive (covert)	C	(18)	costly		

(continues)

Name	SES	Age (weeks)	Family Alliance	Triangular Framework		Repair	Triangular Process	Working Alliance
				Category	(score)			
F6—Bob	S	13	Collusive (covert)	C	(17)	elusive	detouring	difficult
		24	Collusive (covert)	C	(20)		detouring	difficult
		40	Collusive (covert)	C	(23)	elusive	detouring	difficult
F7—Frankie	S	15	Collusive (covert)	C	(19)	aggravated	detouring	difficult
		29	Collusive (covert)	C	(17)		detouring	difficult
		38	Collusive (covert)	C	(20)	aggravated	detouring	difficult
F8—Lynn	M	16	Collusive (covert)	C	(21)	elusive	detouring	difficult
		28	Collusive (covert)	C	(20)		detouring	difficult
		39	Collusive (covert)	C	(17)	elusive	detouring	difficult
F9—Anthony	M	15	Disordered (rigid)	D	(25)	absurd	paradoxical	difficult closed
		20	Disordered (rigid)	D	(25)			difficult closed
		45	Disordered (rigid)	D	(33)	absurd	paradoxical	difficult closed
F10—Claire	S	15	Disordered (chaotic)	D	(33)	aggravating	undifferentiated	difficult open
		28	Collusive (covert)	C	(17)			
		37	Stressed Cooperative	B	(07)	costly	restricted	functional

F11—Yann	S			Category	(score)			
		16	Disordered (chaotic)	D	(33)	absurd	paradoxical	difficult open
		25	Disordered (chaotic)	D	(36)		detouring	difficult open
		41	Collusive (covert)	C	(22)	aggravated		
F12—Tania	M	18	Disordered (rigid)	D	(36)	absurd	paradoxical	difficult closed
		28	Disordered (rigid)	D	(25)			
		41	Disordered (rigid)	D	(25)	absurd	paradoxical	difficult closed

Triangular Framework Scores:

A = 0–6   C = 17–24

B = 7–16   D = 25–36

SES = Socioeconomic status

S = Superior; M = Middle

Appendix B:
The Lausanne
Triadic Play Instructions

In this exercise we ask you to play together as a family. You will settle the baby in the seat and follow the directions for the four separate parts of the exercise. In the first part you will choose who starts playing with the baby: For example, you as the mother try to make your baby do what he (she) usually does with you and during this time you as the father will simply be present. After a little while, when you feel ready, you can change roles: This is the second part. For example, you as the father can play with the baby and you as the mother will simply be present. You can choose the moment to pass on to the third part in which you will both play with your baby together. In the last part, you will talk a while together and it will be your baby's turn to be simply present. Throughout these four parts you can decide who should begin playing with the baby, the length of each part, and the position of the table (centered on mother, father, or between the two). You can begin as soon as you feel ready and can give us a signal when the exercise is over.

Index